Sandtray

Sandtray

Playing to Heal, Recover, and Grow

Roxanne Rae, MSW, LCSW, BCD

JASON ARONSON
Lanham • Boulder • New York • Toronto • Plymouth, UK

/

Published by Jason Aronson
A wholly owned subsidary of The Rowman & Littlefield Publishing Group, Inc.
4501 Forbes Boulevard, Suite 200, Lanham, Maryland 20706
www.rowman.com

10 Thornbury Road, Plymouth PL6 7PP, United Kingdom

British Library Cataloguing in Publication Information Available

Library of Congress Cataloging-in-Publication Data
Rae, Roxanne, 1951–
 Sandtray : playing to heal, recover, and grow / Roxanne Rae, MSW, LCSW.
  pages cm
 Includes bibliographical references and index.
 ISBN 978-0-7657-0980-6 (cloth : alk. paper)—ISBN 978-0-7657-0981-3 (electronic)
 1. Play therapy. 2. Sandplay—Therapeutic use. 3. Child psychotherapy. I. Title.
 RJ505.P6R37 2013
 618.92'891653—dc23   2013001031
 ISBN 978-1-4422-4777-2 (pbk:alk. paper)

∞™ The paper used in this publication meets t e minimum requirements of
American National Standard for Information Sciences—Permanence of Paper
for Printed Library Materials, ANSI/NISO Z39.48-1992.

Printed in the United States of America

For
my social-work mentor and friend,
Betty J. Russell, LCSW, BCD,
and
my mom and first playmate,
Barbara Stanford Curry

Contents

Preface

Imagine "Sandtray," the therapies that use sand, water, and miniatures to unleash the power of creative play. Play in a three-dimensional sand "world" may evoke both joy and self-understanding. Knowing ourselves, "a key to psychological survival," functions as a basic protection from life's difficulties and a foundation for resolving them (Holmes, 2001, p. 4). The poet and Buddhist leader Daisaku Ikeda asserts that "Creativity means to push open the heavy, groaning doorway of life itself. . . . For opening the door to your own life is in the end more difficult than opening the door to all the mysteries of the universe" (Ikeda, 2012, p. 7). The Sandtray process presented here offers a powerful method to secure not only survival but also growth for a dynamically contributive life.

Sandtray, a highly personal and inventive process often considered an extension of play or expressive arts treatments for children, also enhances the lives of adults. The stories of real people who move sand, water, and/or miniatures, and reap healing, recovery, and growth—from three-year-old Jada to eighty-three-year-old Mary—demonstrate my approach to Sandtray in this book.

Through the Sandtray process, we discover our deeply held beliefs and tap our distinctive strengths and resources. A *Creator* plays to access the implicit imaging activity of the right hemisphere of the brain that lies out of the reach of everyday consciousness. The right hemisphere serves as the recorder of traumatic events. Successful treatment of trauma needs to include a method to access this part of the mind. The many stories in this book demonstrate that Sandtray provides this means.

In the first chapter, the basic concepts of the Sandtray/Sandplay pioneer Margaret Lowenfeld and the views of this author are explored. The Sandtray apparatus and process are introduced with the story of six-year-old Eddy. Chapter 2 acquaints readers with interpersonal neurobiology and its essential concepts of linear (left brain) and implicit (right brain) functions and describes how and why this information is useful in psychotherapy. The field of interpersonal neurobiology is changing rapidly and its concepts are evolving. Yet, the field is highly instructive for psychotherapists. In the third chapter, the fundamental principles of attachment theory show how the quality of human connection influences treatment. The physical, intellectual, and emotional components of communication are identified, highlighting how Sandtray techniques facilitate integration of our implicit, nonlinear experiences.

Chapter 4 familiarizes readers with how people may form meanings and patterns of experience. A schema of "energetic modes" and "contextual fields" is offered as a framework to assist therapists as they prepare to use the Sandtray methods outlined in this volume. The fifth chapter offers therapists an exercise to increase their awareness of any tendency to judge or interpret. The linear structure of cognitive reference points, called "Sandtray aspects," is introduced. Then, self-care and multicultural concerns are addressed, preparing therapists to engage in the techniques explained in the next four chapters.

Using the terms *Creator* for the maker of the world (client), and *Witness* for the facilitator and guide (psychotherapist), I present the Sandtray *aspects* in chapters 6 through 9. These aspects pinpoint ten observable occurrences within a Sandtray process and form a foundation for session interactions. *Witnesses* can use these aspects to aid *Creators* in learning from the sand world. The novice Sandtray therapist will find information and instruction to initiate the use of these techniques, while the experienced therapist will be able to integrate this new information with ease. Chapter 10 sets forth the Sandtray aspects as they are applied to the moving sand worlds of children, while the final chapter looks at the use of these Sandtray methods with children suffering from complex trauma.

This book has been a decade in the writing, inspired by my clients, colleagues, and workshop participants. Betty Russell, LCSW, BCD, mentored me for the past forty years. Working with her, the idea for this volume twinkled in my mind and continued to mature. Betty did not allow me to wallow in my "comfort zone" without a challenge. Nor did she push me to face my fear and confusion alone. Learning with this master of balance as my social-work mentor has been my heart's treasure. Betty is known in the greater Sacramento area as a master therapist. She provides CEU workshops and has been in private practice since 1974. Prior to private work, Betty was a supervisor with the Sacramento County Department of Social Welfare and taught MSW students at the School of Social Work, California State University, Sacramento.

I remain ever grateful to Gisela Schubach De Domenico, PhD, of Vision Quest for Symbolic Reality in Oakland, California. My ability to use the Sandtray methods grew exponentially in my eleven years of study with her. Through her workshops, Gisela kept Lowenfeld's theories alive in the United States. Her systemization of Lowenfeld's Sandtray methods and her reflective/directive technique inspired the "Sandtray aspects" presented here. From Gisela I learned the implementation of Lowenfeld's "modes" and the essence of what has evolved into the "contextual fields." Most important, Gisela urged me to document, research, and write about my Sandtray work. Through Gisela's Sandtray teachings and my ongoing study, I am now able to share these effective techniques with others through this book.

Several other people aided me in my ten-year writing journey. Among them are my beloved partner, Thomas Paterson, PhD, who offered innumerable supports, including his surgical editing and call for active verbs; my generous friend Elizabeth Sherbow, PhD, LPC, who ventured through each paragraph with me and elicited my knowledge through wise inquiry; and my long-time friend Donna Parten, MSW, who edited many versions of this text and raised helpful questions.

Throughout this decade of writing, several friends and former and current colleagues read portions of this book, giving useful feedback: Jennifer Campbell, LPC; Deborah Domitrovich, MA; Rosemary Dunn-Dalton, LCSW; Janelle Gerber, MS; Jozeffa Greer, LMFT; Susan and John Hawksley; Heather Lawrence, MSW, RSW; and Judy McDowell Carlson, MS. I am grateful for the literary advice of my dear neighbor Donald Reynolds, PhD. I thank Mary Foret, PhD, for suggesting the use of the terms *Creator* and *Witness* years ago and my friend and Sandtray teacher Jackie Baritell, LMFT, for her detailed review and comments on the last five chapters of this book. For technical assistance in the preparation of this manuscript I am grateful to Dash Antel, Susan Dyssegard, Brian LeBlanc, and Gretchen Thiel.

Had I not faced and overcome the obstacles which emerged from my life in the effort to complete this work, this book would not exist. So, for teaching me the principles of "Never be defeated" and "Do your best" as a young social worker, I am indebted to the Sacramento, California, pioneer women's division members of the Soka Gakkai International-USA, a Buddhist-lay organization.

Readers who wish to view the Sandtray photographs included in this book in a color format may do so at my website: www.roxannerae.com. On the website, additional photographs are available for some vignettes. This site also includes articles I previously published, a biographical statement, and my resume.

With deep respect I offer appreciation to my clients, their families, my supervisees, and my colleagues who have allowed me to use their most intimate work to teach Sandtray. As is customary, I have altered identifying details to protect individuals' confidentiality.

Roxanne Rae MSW, LCSW, BCD
Ashland, Oregon

List of Photographs, Drawings, and Charts

Photographs below are available in color at www.roxannerae.com.

CHAPTER ONE

Sand Play Beginnings

Sand. Wet or dry. Moving, forming, creating, destroying, re-creating. Throughout the world, children are innately drawn to sand. At beaches, rivers, empty lots, backyard sand boxes, wherever children find sand, they dig in and manipulate its grains. Sand play is so common it appears to be an essentially mundane activity of little note, certainly with no place in psychotherapy and self-development. When I first encountered Sandplay therapies, for example, I was in graduate school and seeking to learn and master the most effective social work practices to help people. "Sand" did not seem to have a serious role in that mission. Even though, growing up, I knew about sand firsthand, it seemed far removed from "therapy," and far too simple. Not so. As the pianist Van Cliburn reminds us: "Within simplicity is great, enormous complexity" (Cliburn, 2008). So, it is not surprising that I have taken quite some time to unravel the multiple complexities of sand therapies.

Without noticing, I had been absorbing the properties of sand and water since childhood. My parents took our family to California's Sacramento River Delta to escape the overwhelming heat. While they water-skied with our neighbors, I created kingdoms of sand and river clay on the beach. When I attended grade school, we lived in a working-class housing tract. My mother periodically built brick planters and borders to beautify our yard by using cubic yards of beautiful golden sand for her landscaping. My brother had his collections of soldiers, vehicles, and dinosaurs. I added rocks, leaves, pods, and sticks to the sand pile. For hours we created vast topographies in the sand, and I remember feeling a bit sad when the sand pile dwindled at the end of my mother's projects.

As an adolescent in the San Francisco Bay Area during the late 1960s, I had opportunities to participate in meditation and the embodied imagery methods of Psychodrama and Gestalt Therapies. As I developed my skills, I found that each employed a form of physiological grounding and body awareness. Such approaches, along with Buddhist philosophy, emphasize the oneness of the universe with body, intellect, emotion, and spirit. After practicing these techniques, I noted a fundamental shift in my personal perspective that allowed me access to the interrelationship between my body, emotions, images, and thoughts. This experience led me to doubt the dualistic view of a fundamental mind/body separation that was presented in some of my college coursework. Later, my graduate studies in medical social work reinforced my understanding and acceptance of the interactive oneness of body, brain/mind, and spirit.

As a young social worker, I was able to view the completed sand worlds of my foster-child clients at the end of their treatment sessions. I consulted with their therapists, who used Sandtray methods. Most of these youths were suffering from abuse, neglect, and severe attachment disruptions. As I watched them improve, my curiosity about Sandtray techniques intensified. I "knew," at a deep level of my being, that making sand worlds helped these shattered young lives to resolve trauma—and to repair. I understood I had much to learn about the rich and mysterious intricacies of Sandtray therapies. Compelled by the pain of my clients, I was unaware, at the time, that this quest would also help me.

Beginning with my formal training as a Sandtray practitioner, I experienced the transformative powers of these methods. Now having had years of experience as both a *Creator* and a *Witness* in the Sandtray process, I learned how this apparatus eases creative freedom and flexibility. These qualities allow this technique to offer greater access to the unspoken, implicit beliefs that form the substratum for our conscious actions.

Since 1975, I have studied and applied expressive arts and play therapies. I am thrilled to find human play is now valued as a biologically based activity for all ages. As psychiatrist Stuart Brown explains: "The ability to play is critical not only to being happy, but also to sustaining social relationships and being a creative, innovative person" (Brown, 2010, p. 6).

I do not view Sandtray as a stand-alone method of treatment. With the exception of adults who come to me specifically requesting a Sandtray consultation, I routinely use Sandtray techniques within the context of both play and verbally based therapies. As with other treatments, a comprehensive history and assessment are made. Sandtray is not a "magic cure." As with any method of advancement one may seek, Sandtray requires a commitment of time, a willingness to be open to one's inner experience, and active participation.

Nonverbal and less verbal methods of self-exploration are meant to evoke the vague and indescribable elements of life, as well as those already accessible to us. Sandtray offers a versatile way to connect to the nonverbal qualities of our experiences and conceive of a way to bring them into our everyday lives. Early in my therapy practice, I discovered clients increasingly showed less interest in using traditional art therapy techniques once they tried Sandtray. Often they said, "I can't draw, dance, or paint." As early as four years of age many of the children believed they had inadequate artistic skills and were unwilling to try, even in a noneducational setting.

This feedback from my clients gradually led me to expand my capacity to use Sandtray methods. I often worked with severe complex trauma in young children who had no words to express their confusing and painful experiences. The more familiar I became with sand techniques, the more apparent it became to me that this less verbal modality facilitates the integration of physical, intellectual, and emotional experiences promoting a more coherent sense of self. I have consistently found that the intrinsic qualities of Sandtray exponentially increase my clients' abilities to synthesize and communicate ideas, and it does so far more effectively than words alone or other less verbal methods.

From my present perspective as an experienced psychotherapist, events which seemed inconsequential when they occurred are now illuminated as stepping stones to my current approach to this work. When I started formal Sandtray training, I was a relationally based therapist rooted in child development and object-relations theories and well-grounded in systems theory. Under the guidance of my social-work mentor Betty Russell, I sought to combine treatments that encompassed the whole of a person's life and his or her environment. This path led me to work with the psychobiologist Stanley Keleman, who focused on the reciprocal relationship between physical anatomy and development of the self. His concept of "emotional anatomy" illuminates the connection between one's *emotional feelings*, such as anger, frustration, and excitement, and *physiological sensations*, such as muscle tension, skeletal position, and motility (Keleman, 1985). In the late 1980s I began Sandtray studies with the psychotherapist Gisela Schubach De Domenico. Through study with her, I learned the treatment methods of the British child psychiatrist Dr. Margaret Lowenfeld. I was trained to teach De Domenico's approach to Sandtray based on Lowenfeld's work. Although my approach to Sandtray has evolved over the years, my current thinking and methods remain rooted in Lowenfeld's views.

This book seeks to demonstrate the effectiveness of Sandtray methods for healing, recovery, and growth. I have now practiced and taught Sandtray and other treatment methods for nearly four decades. With close study and the assistance of my mentor, I learned that the therapy sessions where I seemingly achieved fortuitous results with clients actually grew from specific efforts I myself made. This book will explore both the subtleties of this work as well as the overt techniques applied.

The Birth of Sandtray: Lowenfeld's Influence

During the late 1920s, Margaret Lowenfeld explained how children's thinking was different from the linear format of adults. She theorized that physical sensations, emotions, memories, and thoughts are interwoven in children's minds. She called this form of thought "Picture Thinking" (Lowenfeld, 1993, p. 5). After much experimenting with her patients using nonverbal play, Lowenfeld sought "to find a medium which would in itself be instantly attractive to children and which would give them and the observer a 'language,' as it were, through which communication could be established" (Lowenfeld, 1993, p. 281). The Sandtray tools and environment allowed children to express themselves in an intensely personal, visual, and kinesthetic manner. By circumventing the use of words, children did not have to conform to the consensual reality of the adult worldview. Inspired by H. G. Wells's book *Floor Games*, Lowenfeld devised a therapeutic tool that encouraged the use of many senses. This technique facilitates a more complete and focused communication that is unimpaired by the structure of language. Her psychotherapeutic method using sand, water, and miniature items of both the real world and fantasy became known as "Lowenfeld's World Technique" (Lowenfeld, 1993).

Since Lowenfeld's introduction of the sand world at her London children's clinic in 1928, practitioners worldwide have adopted the use of her tools. Sandtray techniques are employed with patients from toddlers to seniors, with couples, with families, and with groups. This *world* formation is so versatile that it has captured the attention of a wide spectrum of psychotherapists with a variety of treatment styles. Sand worlds have also spawned a scholarly literature in journals and books. The Sandtray apparatus is now applied in a number of fundamentally dissimilar physical environments and within a foundation of diverse theoretical frameworks. Lowenfeld conducted her play-based research and treatment primarily with school-aged children, but adults have found her sand techniques no less useful in self-understanding and in communicating complex concepts.

A Peek at Place and Process

A well-equipped Sandtray apparatus offers many choices to a potential sand world *Creator*. The best introduction to Sandtray is to visit a richly furnished playroom office. Photographs and words must suffice here (see figure 1.1).

More sand boxes and colors of sand offer exponentially greater choices. A wide array of miniatures at hand helps evoke physical, emotional, and intellectual modes of experiencing for participants (items in appendix A). Other than the general safety boundaries of the playroom, one rule established at the start of a Sandtray session is to keep the sand in or over the box. Another instruction is to discuss with the therapist any desires to throw sand or break items so that together both of us may problem-solve how to meet these needs safely. As an introduction to the Sandtray process, consider the following child's story drawn from my experience as a psychotherapist.

Figure 1.1. A peek at place and process

Eddy's Story: Sneak Attack

Eddy, seven years old, grew up in a stable family with a secure sense of attachment. He had been functioning well in school and social activities. He was brought to therapy during a crisis. Eddy and his younger sister had been fondled and directed in sexual contact with each other by their female babysitter, a relative. Although this teenage girl had pressured Eddy to keep their "game" a secret, he refused. His parents immediately reported the abuse to authorities and sought play therapy. Eddy presented himself as a bright and articulate boy. He had dutifully reported the abuse in a matter-of-fact manner. Initially he seemed flooded by these sexual experiences, talking about them often. He expressed embarrassment, but knew that he was not being blamed for the behavior.

By the time he arrived for treatment he had been interviewed multiple times, including on video tape. With the passing of these few weeks Eddy was no longer able to discuss the abuse incident, and seemed to want to forget about it. However, his parents reported that he demonstrated increased anxiety during the day and whimpered in his sleep. His parents were also concerned about the increased frequency of his nightmares.

The spacious playroom was equipped with an art table and materials, games, puppets and dolls, and many other play options. The far end of the room had shelves of well-organized miniatures and a nesting stack of sand trays. There were natural tan, red, black, and white sands to choose from. On an initial brief visit to orient Eddy to treatment, he played with other items and ignored the Sandtray area until the last few moments of his time. He stated he would play in the sand on his next visit.

When Eddy began his first Sandtray he was silent and placed items with deliberate concentration (see figure 1.2). He started by requesting a bin of multi-colored "army men," yet chose a tall guard tower and placed it in the sand first. He then added a cannon, gray army men, and a plastic rock formation. Next, he placed two gray soldiers in the tower and said, "They shoot the other ones" and described how these two were striving to be vigilant. I also learned these same two soldiers could "see everything" in the sand world.

Eddy placed more army figures, taking great care as to the positions they faced. He confirmed that this was a war, but that "I don't know what it's about." He was moving the objects and appeared to be acting out complex fighting scenes. At one point he informed me that some of the people "kind of know each other" and that's why it is a battle. He continued detailed play in this manner, adjusting items, adding another cannon, and additional gray army personnel.

As he created in the sand, we continued to engage intermittently in tentative discussions of the world. He began to describe some of the soldiers as "good guys," and some as "bad guys," although he used only gray figures for all of

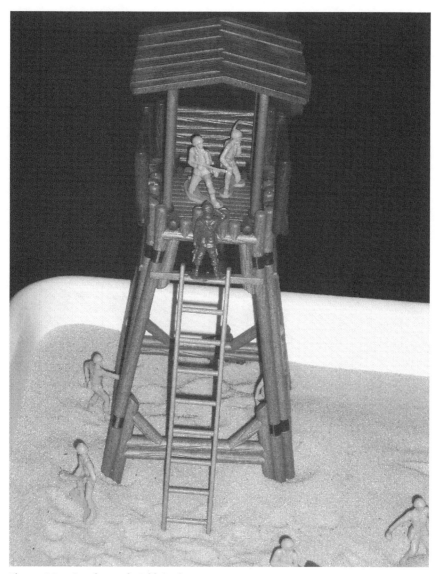

Figure 1.2.   Sneak attack: Eddy's view.

them. Shortly after his identification of two distinct factions, Eddy added an army hospital and told me it was for "both sides." He then made a shift in his stance, becoming more relaxed and active in his body movements, and subsequently more verbal.

Eddy then decided to make the "good guys" and "bad guys" different colors. However, the "bad guys" had to be all the "same kind of green." This change led to a dialogue in which he told me, "It's easier to see who the bad guys are, when they're all the same color." The two gray soldiers on guard in the tower were then approached by green "bad guys." A couple of these soldiers violated the tower's territory and were placed on the back side of the tower, between it and the sand tray wall. There is one soldier who "sneaks up on them" from the same side as the battle. Eddy says, "No one knows she's there." She is very sneaky and the soldiers in the tower do not see her until she is at the top of the ladder. Referring to the two figures in the tower, he then said, "They are looking the other way. They are in danger."

This war continued in detail with various overt and sneak attacks. Both sides suffered losses, received reinforcements, and even the "good guys" made mistakes. Then one cannon directly threatened a "good" soldier. This soldier perceived his danger. We discussed this man's perspective of his choices, and Eddy moved him to safety.

As the conflict continued, Eddy counted down to me the number of "bad guys" who were left fighting. With only four "bad guys" remaining, one of the "good guys" was "shot so hard" that he landed with his head upside down in the sand. Then, a fellow fighter perched himself on top of this fallen comrade. From there, he shot his big gun, annihilating the last of the "bad guys."

Within the context of this sand world, I could be with Eddy as he explored a variety of experiences that he could not talk about at that time. Working with images in this way quickly helped Eddy sort out who was "good" and "bad" and he began to discern how to identify the differences. He also explored the uncomfortable experiences of being "in danger" and having people near who "violate territory" and are "sneaky." Through the two soldiers in the tower he portrayed his distinct sense of separateness, or being different (as a result of this abuse). He was only able to speak about these feelings later in treatment. However, he did explore them in my presence where we could acknowledge them together, forming a foundation for communications about the abuse. The conflict between people who at the first were alike in color, and "kind of know each other," may have reflected Eddy's awareness that because the perpetrator of the abuse was a distant but previously trusted relative, a major rift was occurring throughout the extended family. Information on the depth of the family's conflict emerged sometime later in a session with his parents. Eddy's example shows only a glimpse of his initial treatment process.

Of note in this story is that Eddy came to play in the sand and created this world spontaneously. He was not prompted with "Show me what happened in the Sandtray," or "Show me what the bad lady did to you that night." Eddy was never told in any way that he needed to focus on his abuse experience. Eddy's world emerged from his life when he was given free reign to make anything he desired with the tools at hand. The techniques I will discuss in this volume focus on this creation of free and spontaneous sand worlds.

Our reading of these case stories is like viewing a frame or two of a lifelong movie. We are indebted to the Sandtray *Creators* and their parents who have been willing to share their intimate lives with us all. Learning from them, we may gain a deeper understanding of the Sandtray process, and have an opportunity to become more effective and compassionate psychotherapists.

In this chapter I have provided a brief introduction to Sandtray and my personal approach to psychotherapy. I have demonstrated the use of the Sandtray process by exploring a traumatic event in the life of a young boy. His case also illustrates how to begin to form a mutual language with a *Creator* based on the sand world. Next, I will set forth some principles from the theory of interpersonal neurobiology that form a foundation for how and why this Sandtray process is effective, once again presenting vignettes from actual clinical case studies.

CHAPTER TWO

Language and Image

Language includes the ability to communicate ideas, feelings, and thoughts through systems of behavioral, verbal, or written signals. These systems include rules about how the components may be properly combined. A healthy human infant is ready to learn verbal language at birth. The specific type of language is not predetermined and only becomes so after about one year of age. Once we learn the traits of our culture, we usually communicate verbally. Prior to acquiring language, we "think" in images based on our sensory experience, forming personal impressions of our world. The consensually agreed-upon system of symbols that is language tends to be somewhat removed from this idiosyncratic experience. Every dialect has a unique formation of cultural knowledge imbedded within it. By its very nature, language tends to be inaccurate and falls short when we want to share a deeply individual viewpoint. This is why poets, songwriters, and storytellers are celebrated for their artistic ability to create a bridge of words that overcomes this deficit.

The Sandtray therapy pioneer Margaret Lowenfeld provided an example of the challenges of verbal communication. Based on her work after the First World War with desperate Polish refugees, she struggled to articulate to others the emotional impact of her experiences. Fluent in four languages, Lowenfeld felt frustrated with her limited capacity to express the intensity and qualities of her work in helping war victims. Her inability to communicate clearly further solidified her belief that language is inadequate to express the wealth of human experience. Lowenfeld saw the Sandtray as a "cipher language" in which the child's meaning of the objects he or she arranges becomes essential to a therapist's understanding of the core of the child's life (Lowenfeld, 1993, p. 7). She grasped the value of picture or image-thinking and employed the Sandtray as an activity that functioned as a source of communication.

Image Play: An Exercise

When I am teaching, to demonstrate the imprecision of words, I ask students to think of a tree until an image comes to them. As you read this, you may want to take several moments to create your own mental picture of a tree and see what emerges from your own mind. Each individual holds his or her own picture in his or her mind. The word *tree* does not evoke the same image for all people. Given time to sit with the image, a person might link this tree image to a personal memory of a specific tree, a pine or oak, bare, leafy or flowering. Another person will make such a connection only when invited to do so. One participant may describe a weeping willow and warm memories of playing with cousins at a favorite auntie's home. Another class member may recall hours of fun in a sycamore tree-house, until the scary day her sister fell from the tree and was injured. Yet another person will have an image of the tree from which his parent routinely cut the switches to beat him.

Each participant's image of *tree* is subtlety nuanced based upon his or her own personal history and constellation of individual meanings. Every person develops differently, so no two people will have exactly the same perceptions or configuration of distinct meanings. The Sandtray technique helps bridge the inevitable gaps in personal meaning that exist between the *Creator* and the *Witness*. Sandtray also spans an individual's intrapersonal gaps between his or her "unconscious," or less actively available aspect of mind, and his or her "conscious," or readily accessible form of mind. In short, the encrypted communication that emerges from the Sandtray material provides deeper self-understanding. This communication also empowers the *Witness* to learn, to understand, and to apply the personal language of the *Creator* to expedite the client's healing and self-knowledge.

When individuals compose a Sandtray using the "World Technique" apparatus, the nonverbal, creative aspects of their lives are likely to be awakened. Sandtray increases access to our implicit mental processes and helps us experience and clarify them, discovering how they function in our everyday lives. In our more socially compatible, linear thinking minds, our names and meanings for items and events tend to align with our community's meanings. The stories of Lori and Mary below highlight how Sandtray seeks to illuminate each individual's richly significant, distinct, and broad-based experiences which spring from a personal multisensory reality. This reality encompasses images and affects in a fluid and uniquely coalesced form. To the degree that we, as therapists, limit psychotherapy to the exploration of verbal content, we engage only a fraction of the client's life and we narrow available assets.

The following vignettes illustrate how *Creators* can learn from their idiosyncratic, preverbal thinking once the concrete sand world in front of them is explored. *Creators* commonly pick objects without a precise reason or meaning in mind at the moment of choosing.

Lori's Story: Ignoring King Kong

Lori, nine years of age, demonstrates through her play the significance of the nonverbal aspect of communication. This girl had a history of severe sexual and physical abuse subsequent to early relational trauma. During one of her many Sandtrays she formed a mound of sand. In its center was a woman relaxing in a hammock amidst her garden. "Comfortable" and "pretty" items were placed predominantly in view. What lay unseen at that moment was the gorilla figure of King Kong. He was buried beneath this idyllic scene.

Both Lori and her therapist watched as this woman's safe place had been created with the ape buried beneath it. However, the woman in the tray became shocked and surprised when King Kong emerged, disrupting her world. Lori reported that the woman "feels terrified" and that she collapses into "helplessness" as King Kong destroyed her secure garden. As we explored this event, what became explicit to Lori was the recognition of how and why the calm of her daily life could be disrupted by the "King Kong waiting beneath the hill." The woman in the Sandtray pretended that King Kong did not exist. She refused to pay attention to this destroyer. So she was shocked each time he reappeared in her life. To share and acknowledge this truth, initially with few words, was the beginning of Lori's recognition of old terrors and learning to manage them.

Mary's Story: Discovering Mortality

Mary, an eighty-three-year-old professional woman, created a series of Sandtrays over two days. Early in the period she formed a beautiful nature scene using a small yellow glass blob, like a tiny stone, and hid it in the foliage. Mary commented that she did not know why she chose this item but knew that it needed to be placed there. She shared that she was compelled to add a yellow object, and this glass "felt right." During the initial exploration of her first world, this piece seemed insignificant. Over two consecutive days of sand work, this item's meaning for her gradually emerged along with its central importance.

Incorporating the Sandtray techniques discussed later in this volume, Mary's use of the piece of yellow glass transformed to show her how she, as she proceeded into her eighties, continued to deny her own mortality. Mary began to see that this denial existed and how it functioned. She identified that she had taken no practical steps to inform her family of her wishes should she die or become unable to care for herself. Later in the Sandtray process Mary began to consider practical steps she could take to address this reality in her everyday life.

These examples are words on paper, and do not carry the full, felt experiences of the Sandtray *Creator* and the *Witness*. The internal shifts which occur in every session stem from the sensory, affective, and cognitive processing between the *Creator*, the Sandtray, and the *Witness*. Sandtray techniques include cognition but are not solely based on conscious thought. An influential leader in the fields of neurobiology and attachment, Dr. Daniel Siegel, succinctly reminds us that "we must keep in mind that only a part of memory can be translated into the language-based packets of information people use to tell their life stories to others. Learning to be open to many layers of communication is a fundamental part of getting to know another person's life" (Siegel, 1999, p. 43). The manner in which I apply the Lowenfeld technique is relationally based and relies heavily on the affect-laden resonance between participants. Using these Sandtray techniques affords access to a variety of levels of communication which deepen the implicit and explicit qualities in the relationship between the *Creator* and *Witness*. The next section begins to look at nonverbal communication in society and the Sandtray process.

Communicating

We may "click" with one new acquaintance, eagerly anticipating a friendship will bloom, and with another person there is little sense of interpersonal connection. Differences in feeling tone occur no matter how open-minded or big-hearted we may be. A sense of harmony, or its lack, is present in all relationships. Once we learn to pay attention to the "flow" of feeling connected, we can determine more readily when and how human relationships easily resonate and when they falter. This information assists us in communication and therefore improves the practice of psychotherapy.

Public acknowledgment of the awkwardness of "fit" between people occurs frequently in political campaigns. Seasoned political analysts grapple to find language to describe their own perception of nonverbal disharmony or positive rapport between presidential running mates. For example, commentators noted how some campaigners lacked "good body language" or "good chemistry." In short, they sensed "bad vibes." Television increasingly brings into focus politicians' behavioral cues that signal a sense of congeniality and comfort as well. Many people inherently recognize the qualities of harmony or flow within relationships, even when they have difficulty describing them.

News analysts have acknowledged the public's increasing awareness of nonverbal qualities in relationships. Television commentators who have interviewed noteworthy people face-to-face are now themselves being interviewed. These discussions focus on the interviewer's felt sensations of connection, authenticity, rapport, and other less tangible qualities experienced during the conversation. Ease and discomfort between people is a viscerally felt sense which we physically respond to. The importance of our awareness of the "energy" of our stance has been demonstrated even with animals. For example, in Cesar Millan's television program, *The Dog Whisperer*, he teaches human "pack leaders" the concepts of unspoken communications. More and more people are beginning to form a shared language to speak to this elusive yet critical aspect of our lives, the nonverbal energetic links between us.

Our culture refers to "our heart versus our head" as two different functions of knowing. Someone locked in an intrapersonal conflict between these two kinds of knowing may discern somatic physical activation in two separate areas of the body. In the English language *to know* denotes both kinds of experiences. In Greek, the word *logos* is used to describe the linear and cognitive functions that include reason and language; the word *gnosis* depicts the intuitive, spiritual, or "heart" form of knowledge. These two modes of "knowing" can be observed in Amy's story.

Amy's Story: Frozen Tears

Amy, sixteen years old, had created many Sandtrays and we had a well-established relationship. Once, while I was witnessing the formation of her sand creation, Amy abruptly sat back and poured a small amount of water over the head of a mermaid in the upper righthand corner of the tray. Grief pierced through me. Instantly I knew this young woman was suffering (gnosis). The next second, when I thought about what had just happened, I could not make sense of my reaction (logos). My mind raced, wondering about the countertransference response that had emerged within me. With rapid self-reflection, I was able to stay attuned to Amy, becoming increasingly certain that my sadness reflected the client's state of being and not mine.

As we continued processing the Sandtray, I tentatively shared with Amy my response to her pouring of the water without offering any interpretation. Her eyes welled with tears. Amy began telling me of a long-time school friend who had just died. This friend had suffered from a chronic illness for years and the class knew he would die young. However, their group of friends had not known of the recent worsening of this boy's illness. Amy felt "frozen" and unable to grieve when she heard the news of this boy's death earlier that day.

During the verbal processing of the sand world, I learned that when Amy came to the session and then poured water, she thought of this action as an expression of her tears for her friend. The nonverbal communication through the Sandtray, and my reflection to her, created a vehicle for Amy to express her deep sense of loss. Amy's sand world served to provide her with a way to thaw her frozen state. She began to be able to organize her thoughts and feelings in a coherent fashion and release her own real tears. Amy became able to allow herself to recognize, tolerate, and share her grief.

Brain and Mind

Underlying the work described above is science that illuminates the different operations of the brain. Understanding some of these scientific concepts can help psychotherapists, particularly those of us using less verbal and nonverbal techniques. Language and image are each primarily the properties of different parts of our brains. The field of interpersonal neurobiology unites the "knowledge of how the brain gives rise to mental processes (neuroscience) with knowledge of how relationships shape mental processes (attachment research)" (Siegel and Hartzell, 2003, p. 31). This field provides us a foundation to consider how therapy works. The person-to-person connection is the forum in which all treatment occurs, even the most concrete and cognitively based approaches.

Long before our technological abilities to image the brain, people have wondered how the human brain is linked to various qualities of the mind. In dictionaries the definition of the word *brain* focuses on descriptions of anatomy and physiological function. The word *mind* is described by concepts such as will, perception, thought, imagination, memory, and emotion. Nichiren Daishonin, a thirteenth-century Buddhist monk, wrote: "When we look into our own mind at any moment, we perceive neither color nor form to verify that it exists. Yet we still cannot say it does not exist, for many differing thoughts continually occur" (Daishonin, 1999, p. 4). Psychotherapists may pursue an understanding of the brain's energetic flow within the context of genetics, interpersonal relationships, and the environment. The origin and workings of the mind itself remain a mystery.

We commonly speak of our brain as a singular entity, but functionally, we have two brains, a left side and a right side, each with essentially different ways of processing information. Language is linked to the left hemisphere (explicit functions), as are other linear aspects including cognition, facts, and planning. Image is linked to the right hemisphere (implicit functions), and is independent of language, nonlinear, and bodily based. Although I will refer to a "left" and a "right" brain, the two hemispheres are fundamentally integrated in a complex manner. Most human actions engage both sides of our brain (see figure 2.1).

Our "Two Brains"

Left Hemisphere/Explicit (language dependent)	Right Hemisphere/Implicit (independent of language)
• Linear	• Non–linear
• Cognitive	• Emotional
• Fact based	• Image based
• Thinking mind focus	• Global whole body sensation
• Focused attention required for encoding memory	• Focused attention is not required for encoding memory
• Constructs a linguistic narrative/internal sense of self	• No words/no subjective sense of self
• Develops by approximately 3 years of age	• Functioning at least from birth

Function During a Traumatic Event or Reenactment:

• Overwhelmed•Flooded•Inhibited	• Activated

Links Between Interpersonal Neurobiology and Other Views:

• Lowenfeld's Secondary System	• Lowenfeld's Protosystem
• Logos	• Gnosis

Figure 2.1. Brain and mind

Scientists identify two main forms of memory: explicit (left brain) and implicit (right brain). We often speak of memory solely as the ability to recall an event or remember where we placed our keys. Memory entails much more, because it is a complex web of genetics, brain cell activity, and environmental interaction. Memory is formed from our moment-to-moment experience as additional connections are continuously created in the brain. Through multiple mechanisms, memory unites past, present, and future. Memory informs and shapes our future because memory is the way that our brain is influenced by immediate experience. Each newly formed memory can subsequently change the next response. Throughout this constant composition of memory we are forgetting some experiences while engraving others in our minds. We tend to let go of most events with little emotional intensity. Events which are terrifying, overwhelming, and traumatic are less likely to be accessible to us, too. We tend to remember experiences containing a moderate to high level of emotional intensity.

Healing-arts practitioners are most effective when we recognize how knowingly to invite left-versus-right hemisphere functions during treatment. We also need to develop our abilities to identify which type of information is spontaneously emerging from a client. During a traumatic experience or traumatic reenactment, the left hemisphere of the brain (explicit memory) is usually inhibited or overwhelmed while the right hemisphere (implicit memory) is activated. Such highly intense emotional material will most likely be encoded in the right brain. Of significance, the information from the right hemisphere of our brain does not require processing through the left hemisphere. Therefore, traumatic experiences may not be readily available to consciousness for cognitive interventions, as these experiences are processed primarily in implicit memory.

Implicit (right brain) mental activities are the dominant source of memory until an individual begins to acquire language. It follows that the core of the self is nonverbal and ingrained within physiologically based patterns of emotional regulation. The aspects of memory encoded in the brain's right half is bursting with a wealth of multisensory images which have been part of a person's existence at least since birth. To gain greater clarity within the therapeutic relationship, therapists will serve their clients well by recognizing the distinctively different mental functions of the right and left hemispheres.

Children are generally more open to implicit mental material and they more readily engage in play than adults. A focused look at one central theme of Renee's elaborate Sandtray series will help demonstrate the value, even for adults, of accessing and clarifying implicit versus explicit memory.

Renee's Story: Revealing Implicit Beliefs

Renee came for a Sandtray consultation specifically to work on a sense of "being stuck" with a major project for her company. Now sixty years old, she had enjoyed a lengthy and successful career. This project would exponentially add to her professional advancement and she had volunteered to lead it. Renee felt confounded by her inability to satisfy the project's timeline. A psychologically sophisticated and astute woman, Renee had participated in years of useful psychotherapy incorporating art, journaling, and various forms of Sandtray. She devoted a full week to address this impasse, attending three Sandtray sessions. Renee also set aside time to write and meditate between appointments. She requested the option to leave her sand work untouched between these sessions, which we were able to do.

Day 1:

Renee initially shared fearful images of an impending birth after a recent dream. On awakening, she felt flooded with a sense of overwhelming terror and pain. The intensity of this emotion is what drove her to call for a consultation. As Renee created her Sandtray, the third item she chose was the Incan symbol of serpent, puma, and condor stacked atop one another. As she placed this item in the Sandtray, Renee stated, "They are all vying for dominance and not working in harmony." Immediately afterward she formed the sand, making a central pear-shaped area in blue, which she identified as a "womb." I noticed that the narrow end was facing directly away from her. Facing the Incan figure, next she placed a heavy Celtic woman straining to give birth. Its back was to the womb. Renee then went on to work in other areas of the tray.

Later, while exploring the Sandtray, Renee discovered that the pregnant figure she had chosen was "totally self-absorbed in her own pain and fear," so much so that the pregnant woman was unable to be aware of the many figures of support that had been placed around the tray. Renee commented that the pregnant figure had her back to the womb, stating the woman was "caught in the struggle of her current contraction," and was unable to go through with the birth (see figure 2.2).

While examining the womb area, Renee first realized its emptiness. Lingering with this experience, Renee stated softly, "That's not accurate; it is filled with much life." She proceeded to place brightly colored objects inside the womb. These included a red glass "heart of harvest" with a golden wheat grain painted in the center. Renee also added a string of pearls, which she called, "pearls of wisdom."

The womb shape, now teaming with vibrant life, had changed the feeling of the tray so significantly for Renee that toward the end of the session she replaced the initial pregnant woman with a different object. She chose another

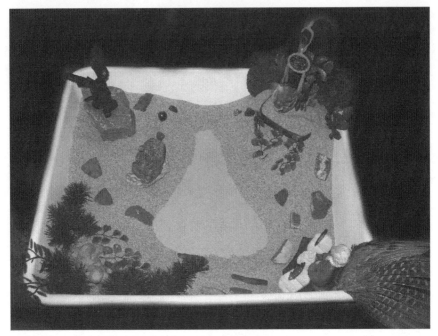

Figure 2.2. Pregnant woman with her back to the womb

pregnant woman that she said, "focused on the birth itself." This figure was initially placed on the same rock as the first woman. However, instead of facing away from the womb, it was set facing toward it.

Then Renee sat quietly, allowing some time to reflect on the changes she had made. Suddenly, she exclaimed that in the new pregnant figure she could see the baby's head poking out! She informed me that the pregnant woman must move. She found a seemingly "perfect" place for this item right near the rounded top of the womb, where it was placed next to a starfish. This was the last adjustment made in the tray during the first session. Prior to leaving, Renee circled the tray and looked at her creation from all perspectives.

Day 2:

During this second session Renee started with her previously created Sandtray. She approached the world by looking at it from all directions. We carefully reviewed how she initially formed her sand world. Then Renee quickly added new items around the birth canal and womb. They depicted "delight, joy, welcome," and other celebratory emotions. She also "increased protection for the impending birth" by placing a dragon, a tree of life, and a lotus flower nearby. Renee asked to hang the sun over the center of the tray. I had no logistical way to accommodate this request. She held the sun up, holding it over various places in the sand world. To my surprise, the sun sat sturdily on top of the Incan symbol once she placed it there. Renee reported feeling a massive sense of physical and emotional relief with the changes she made in the Sandtray during this second session.

Day 3:

Renee's third session occurred several days later. We began by reentering the experiences of her sand world and reviewing its history. We reflected on the changes she made in the previous two sessions. Renee renewed her focus on the womb area. Maintaining a synchronous emotional state with her, I quietly wondered aloud, "How did this great sense of aliveness get here?" After pondering silently, Renee began to laugh. She said that this "womb exists in the sand like a static lake with no apparent flow."

After another period of quiet observation, she blurted out, "The birth canal is closed!" Renee considered the idea of a pregnant womb with an "intact hymen" very funny. We both laughed. Her creation no longer resonated with her inner sensations. Renee shared that in its current state, the life visibly present in the womb had no way to become formed or fertilized. We observed together that this life clearly existed concretely in front of us, was fully developed, and ready for its birth. She suddenly chuckled, saying, "What is required for this birth is some kind of breakthrough!" Renee moved the sand to depict an unblocked birth canal, making additional adjustments to accommodate this new direction. For some minutes, we basked in the positive affect of this momentous event (see figure 2.3).

The intense pain and terror associated with fearful images of an impending birth, however, continued to be a nagging mystery to Renee. She had been writing and meditating about this issue throughout the week. She chose to begin to explore these feelings verbally, with this glorious "birth" in front of us.

There was a sudden and significant affective shift away from the positive feeling tone of the "birth." I experienced the change as viscerally intense, for even sitting silently, it felt gut-wrenching. As we proceeded, she shared insights from her past therapeutic work. Renee already knew (logos) that growing up she had a mother whose achievements she was not allowed to outshine. Even when she was a very young child, Renee felt a palpable threat should she attract attention away from her mother.

As we explored her early childhood and subsequent relationship with her mom, it became apparent that this mother-daughter dynamic had changed in actuality more than thirty years ago. Renee, however, had recently been functioning and behaving as if this threat was current, even in the face of overwhelming cognitive evidence to the contrary. In fact, she described multiple ways in which her mother had overtly celebrated Renee's professional endeavors.

Figure 2.3. Renee's "Birth" after the "breakthrough"

Renee felt stunned to recognize that she still had such intense pain and fearfulness within her, and that it was negatively influencing her current ability to achieve. Renee expressed her insight of this discrepancy between what she thought (logos) and what she deeply believed (gnosis). She accepted that her fear, which "did not make sense" to her now, may have made perfect sense when it was formed in her childhood.

We then made a plan that would assist her in continuing to integrate this new information into her everyday awareness. She subsequently reported major progress in her professional work and has not felt the need for further intervention on this issue.

Renee's Sandtray provides one example of old, nonverbal (implicit) learning which may direct one's current reality. For Renee, this early memory of her relationship with her mother was, in her present life, an error of belief that she still held within the nonverbal realm of her mind. Although this belief was likely accurate when formed, it did not change as her relationship with her mother evolved. She described that the evolution of their relation-ship occurred after she was an adult and therefore functioned dominantly within the verbal (explicit) realm. Implicit errors in belief such as Renee's cannot be explored, changed, or integrated solely with intellectual under-standing. Such a transformation requires a vital affect-laden experience ac-cessed through right-brain (implicit) memory. The Sandtray process provides an enlivened context using visual, kinesthetic, and readily manipulated tools to aid in the manifestation of inner transformation.

In Western societies, developmental and cultural pressures demand a shift of awareness to the verbal, linear thinking part of our brain during about the third year of life. Yet our nonverbal hemisphere continues to process information throughout our lives. By acknowledging the processes of the image-thinking, implicit mind we open ourselves to an essential source of self-knowledge. Once we begin to value our nonlinear knowing (gnosis) we may exponentially increase access to intrapersonal resources. Then we can begin to discover ways to apply our new knowledge to our external world. As illustrated by Renee's case, the use of the Sandtray techniques can provide direct access to this right brain memory and serve to integrate previously implicit material into active awareness. This integration of brain function supports one's well-being.

One way Sandtray engages preverbal mental activities is to relax the linear-thinking mind (left brain) so that the image-forming mind (right brain) has the opportunity to come forth and allow its impressions of life to become known. To introduce a new person to the use of Sandtray, I often characterize this process as an awake dream or a meditation. As described by the neurobiology researcher Jaak Panksepp: "In the dream, emotional reali-ties may stand up to be counted as the less important details and pretenses of our conscious lives fade with the onslaught of sleep. Great and small hopes for the future lie side by side within the brain along with the awful realities of the past" (Panksepp, 1998, p. 128). The Sandtray process appears to function similarly. That is, unexpected memories blend with fantasies, wishes, wor-ries, and emotions to create new images and ideas. Like dreams, the affective experiences in the Sandtray are "lived" within the *Creator's* body and mind, and can influence everyday emotional states, thoughts, and images. Sandtray teaches people to become mindful of their own processes—both internal and interactive.

In chapter 2 we have seen that some of the difficulties encountered in sharing the qualities and the intensities of human experiences are eased through the Sandtray process informed by Lowenfeld's methods. Research in neurobiology clarifies that these difficulties may stem from the differences between our right-brain image-thinking and our left-brain linear-thinking functions. The cases presented demonstrate how the holistic right brain continues to hold sway throughout our lives, even when we believe that our linear left brain is fully in control. The use of Sandtray can expand understanding of one's own implicit right-brain functions, enhancing self-awareness and clarifying one's choices. In the next chapter we build upon this scientific foundation and focus on the features of the personal relationship between the Sandtray *Witness* and the *Creator*. I will illustrate the significance of implicit life-to-life connections that influence treatment outcome.

CHAPTER THREE

Harmonic Resonance

Playing Together

A deep and wondrous joy may be created in our lives by being together, play-ing together. The web of human connection is upheld by the inconspicuous essentials of our hearts and our minds. This principle is portrayed beautifully by the poet Antoine de Saint-Exupéry: "And now here is my secret, a very simple secret: It is only with the heart that one can see rightly; what is es-sential is invisible to the eye" (De Saint-Exupéry, 1943, p. 70). Neuroscience reveals human secrets that allow us to understand better ourselves and our relationships. The neurobiological view of an attachment bond is the unspo-ken, reciprocal sharing of bio-emotional states between partners. Not hav-ing a name for this kind of interaction in my earlier teaching and writing, I described it functionally as "harmonic resonance." Scientifically this concept is often labeled as "intersubjectivity" or "affect synchrony." These terms refer to a nonconscious joining of the energetic pulse of minds, brains, and bodies in the formation of a life-to-life communication.

Mind, brain, and body: these are the biologically based, foundational elements of who we are. As the brain scientist Jill Bolte Taylor eloquently writes: "Although many of us may think of ourselves as *thinking creatures that feel*, biologically we are *feeling creatures that think*" (Taylor, 2008, p. 19). As humans, we tend to view ourselves not as the integrated whole that we are but as split: body/mind, soul/flesh, or reason/emotion. Yet every aspect of our selves is involved in our close connections with one another, including any qualities we devalue or do not acknowledge.

Deep bonds of attachment are often evident when they are dynamically captured in the arts. The popular film *Slumdog Millionaire* (2008), for example, provided the audience with intense visual cues illuminating the bond between Jamal Malil and Latika, beginning as childhood friends. In Tolkien's novel *The Lord of the Rings* (1954–1955), the profound devotion between Frodo Baggins and Sam Gamgee ultimately determined the direction of their lives. In J. K. Rowling's *Harry Potter* series (1997–2007), Harry, Ron, and Hermione remain lifelong comrades despite the myriad trials of adolescence. Each of these relationships is the product of a multitude of moment-to-moment interactions.

Rhythmical patterns, when comprised of enough heart-to-heart connection and empathy, generate security and deeply unite individuals. None of us becomes who we are without direct contact with other people. A scholar of clinical psychiatry, Jean Bolen, states that "anyone's self-esteem, accomplishment, development of talent, has to do with whether we have been listened to and valued, loved for ourselves, encouraged and supported to do what we believe we could do" (Bolen, 2008, p. 103). Our formative attachment relationships are often rich in nonverbal communications, such as knowing looks or seemingly sudden bursts of laughter. Our forming sense of self and our view of the world around us is shaped by those to whom we are closest. Life-to-life bonds may also be formed in psychotherapy as Jada's story from a short-term treatment period indicates.

Jada's Story: Rebalancing Joyful Energy

Jada was brought to my playroom just prior to her third birthday. Our sessions demonstrated the power of dynamic, overlapping, and affect-filled play. By two years of age Jada had developed no speech. Subsequently, her hearing difficulties were uncovered and treated surgically. Jada had been advancing in her weekly speech therapy.

However, when Jada returned from a multi-week visit with her grandparents exhibiting behaviors unusual for her, her parents became concerned. She acted abnormally defiant, used a growling voice when angry, and had rapidly blinking eyes. Jada required three sessions over ten days to return her to her previous congenial disposition. Though the results were dramatic, on the surface her play did not appear profound. Her Sandtrays were unremarkable to look at. She used rakes, scoops, and funnels to move and form sand. When her father asked me in amazement, "What did you do with her?" my honest reply was, "We played and processed the play and the Sandtray, as I usually do." In truth, that was just the short answer.

Of significance, my position as the family's "helper" was well-established. A trusting association had been developed. I had worked with the oldest son, an intense, sensitive, and gifted child. This foundation of a positive relationship allowed Jada the freedom to enter the playroom expecting a good experience. From the information provided by the family I had reason to suspect that Jada's grandparents had a difficult time providing consistent positive emotional regard for her. In the past they tended to compare her with her older brother, overtly favoring him and devaluing her.

Our therapy sessions were filled with a myriad of spontaneous interactions, including a joy-filled sense of playing together. I focused on her play and her Sandtrays within the context of our synchronous relationship. Both verbally and nonverbally, I reflected the flow of Jada's play, encouraging free experimentation and open expression. Our moment-to-moment contact created a reciprocal engagement of mutual respect, delight, and discovery. Many relational details strengthened our positive personal bond and were the essence of the play that helped return Jada to balance.

Long before games such as "Peekaboo" and "This Little Piggy Went to Market," the verbal and nonverbal rhythms of human connection begin. Caregiving related to feeding, elimination, temperature, and comfort can promote a basic cadence between infant and parent. Moment-to-moment contact creates interactive patterns based on multisensory experiences such as touch and pressure, balance and motion, gaze and prosody. *Prosody* refers to the emotional music of human language. Minute grains of interactions gather to form the mountain of an attachment relationship. In such moments together, instantaneous communication is flowing between people so quickly that it cannot be recorded in the conscious mind (primarily left brain). Each partner is influencing and being influenced by the other, developing an interactive regulation. Through countless re-engagements in this improvisational dance, the infant and caregiver form their own unique "togetherness," a dyad that is different from the sum of the two individuals. It is through experiencing the caregiver that the infant begins to sense his or her self. In psychotherapy, too, the qualities of the human bond may influence the ability of both the client and therapist to engage in and advance treatment.

Despite the fact that play therapy pioneer Margaret Lowenfeld became known for her research designs that sought to minimize transference, by 1937 she had become aware that the character of the therapist influenced a child's play. To emphasize the emotional sturdiness required of a Sandtray

Witness, Lowenfeld declared: "There is much that is shocking in the content of the primary [nonverbal] system both of children and ourselves" (Urwin and Hood-Williams, 1988, p. 262). Lowenfeld's view that the therapeutic bond is formed in a manner that precludes the therapist's neutrality is now supported by recent findings from interpersonal neurobiology.

In the light of interpersonal neurobiology, the client-therapist pairing may be seen as analogous to the infant-caregiver dyad. The couple is embedded in a dynamic relational space that is co-created in their moments together. During therapy a client becomes a healthier-functioning human being within the context of this vital relationship with the therapist. The British pediatrician Donald Winnicott asserts: "*Psychotherapy takes place in the overlap of two areas of playing, that of the patient and that of the therapist. Psychotherapy has to do with two people playing together*" (Winnicott, 1982, p. 38; italics in original). People routinely create and modify relationships. Without attention and effort directed toward all the layers of interactive patterns, a therapist does not necessarily create effective relationships. Lessa's story shows that when relational harmony is achieved it can be a moving experience for all involved.

Lessa's Story: Harmonious Play

During my first training demonstration of Sandtray techniques without a co-instructor, it seemed that "magic happened." A friend and colleague assisted me by creating a spontaneous Sandtray in front of the class. Lessa's sand work allowed me to fulfill the *Witness* role and illustrate a variety of ways the Sandtray material may evolve to open new meanings for the *Creator* of the world.

Lessa struggled with anxiety as she made a world that indicated how she clung to her past and feared her future. She was sincere in her efforts, and as we progressed through the Sandtray techniques, she articulated her feelings and thoughts more clearly. At the end of the demonstration, Lessa reported a powerful transformative experience where she gained a new sense of perspective that linked her past and present to her future in a way she found helpful.

Afterward, we both opened ourselves to questions and discussion on any aspect of the Sandtray process the class had observed. Before long someone challenged us, saying that she found it difficult to believe that the demonstration had not been planned or rehearsed in any way. I admitted that it had been "perfect" in that I was able to illustrate all of the basic techniques we would practice that day. It was only during this discussion that Lessa and I looked at each other with amazement. We both realized that despite studying Sandtray together, this public presentation had been the first Sandtray process we had ever done together as *Creator* and *Witness*.

✑

This experience with Lessa brought to life the principle that beneath any successful technique, the foundation of a positive relationship is required. My colleague and I had deep respect, trust, and concern for each other prior to this event. Her authentic efforts, the qualities of our heart-to-heart connection, and the appreciative attention from the class formed a secure environment. This setting allowed the class to observe the dynamic and meaningful result as it emerged. On the other hand, resonant, authentic, and empathetic nonverbal Sandtray sessions can provide the *Creator* with an experience of being seen, deeply known, and understood by a compassionate *Witness*. Such encounters can also be the foundation for a secure relationship, which may lead to further verbal exploration of emotions, thoughts, and bodily states that are unapproachable without this sense of trust.

The Relational Core

Recent research tells us that humans are born neurologically prepared with the potential to share energy with one another's brains. What psychotherapists have long referred to as empathy, compassion, intuition, and rapport are biologically based. In therapy both the therapist and the client bring their own relational dance moves to the therapeutic stage.

Therapists must be able to enter a shared affective state with the client to offer both affective resonance and containment. Sandtray therapists benefit from understanding and facilitating the process of the "'*relational unconscious*,' whereby *one unconscious mind communicates with another unconscious mind*" (Schore, 2008, p. 2; italics in original). This concept of crucial, implicit (right-brain to right-brain) communication is the underpinning for explicit, verbal language and may be the core piece of transformation in therapy. Simply put, no matter what the words are in a given conversation, both people's right hemispheres are "speaking" volumes to each other. Such interactions are not solely brain functions, but a system of two biological beings in attunement with each other.

With both Jada and my colleague, I accompanied them in their work as I held and honored each creation with an accepting heart. With Jada my focus was to invite increased spontaneity in her play and for us to delight together with each new discovery. As a co-creating *Witness*, both *Creators'* play moved me deeply. In each case, we formed a synchronous, nonconscious joining that encompassed the pulse of our minds, brains, and bodies. These rhythms of human connectedness entail what has been called "mindsight," referring to "the ability to perceive our own minds and the minds of others" (Siegel and Hartzell, 2003, p. 9). Mindsight necessitates taking in all of another person's communications, not just their words and observable behavior. Tasks of the

Sandtray and play therapist include the ability to be attentive to one's self and to the client, as the process of creating a psychobiologically attuned intersubjective field unfolds. The neurobiology and attachment theorist Allan Schore explains that while the left brain communicates through conscious behavior and language, the right-brain is centrally active and "nonverbally communicates its unconscious states to other right brains *that are tuned to receive these communications*" (Schore, 2003, p. 49; italics in original). Schore further argues that the right-brain hemisphere functions are *dominant* in developing our humanity through their significance in first establishing, and then maintaining, our awareness of ourselves and others.

Similar patterns occur in the client-therapist relationship to those observed in the infant-caregiver dyad. The overall quality of patterns such as harmony, dissonance, and re-attunement within the caregiver and baby dyad play a significant role in the infant's brain growth. These interactive patterns influence our basic human capacities, such as a sense of self, ability for stress management, and the formation of subsequent healthy relationships.

Along with skill and knowledge, every therapist brings his or her own implicit relational patterns into the therapy process. Schore explains that when a mother hears her infant cry it is registered within her right brain. He goes on to state: "Incidentally, when these stress calls are muted and come out years and years later in psychotherapy, the right hemisphere of the therapist is going to pick them up" (Schore, 2003). Therapy can bring about change in an adult because a person's early experience creates malleable patterns, not set templates. Therefore, in treatment we have the opportunity to modify these early experientially based patterns.

Human nervous systems anticipate the kinds of experiences that we have had in the past. Wonderfully, each moment is fresh and holds the potential to construct new experiences. Even when complex trauma has formed the brain's expectation of continuing trauma, the surprise inherent in both authentic human interaction and the Sandtray process can work to break these negative tendencies.

One part of the "magic" that occurred with Jada and Lessa is illuminated by the principle of heightened affective moments. This concept refers to "interactions that are organized when a person experiences a powerful state of transformation, either positive or negative" (Beebe and Lachmann, 2002, p. 189–90). Jada's play was joyful, while Lessa experienced more tension and fear of the future. In both cases change was embedded in the joint construction of intense shared feeling that impacted both the *Creator* and the *Witness*. Heightened affective moments can begin to transform dysregulated affect patterns that interfere with people's lives. Consider Lucia, a child who experienced abuse and neglect on a foundation of attachment deficits which had compromised her self-development.

Lucia's Story: Secrets

Lucia, a pretty girl with bouncing brown curls, came eagerly to my playroom. Her mouth smiled, but her eyes did not. At nearly six years of age she had lived in foster care for one and a half years prior to being brought into treatment on an urgent basis. Her family had been successfully participating with Children's Protective Services in a plan to reunite when her newborn half brother died from Sudden Infant Death Syndrome (SIDS). By the time I met Lucia, five weeks later, her mother had relapsed in her alcohol and drug treatment. As the oldest, Lucia was a parentified child and had bonded well with her new baby brother during weekly visitations. Lucia's future once again became uncertain.

When Lucia was four and a half years old she was placed in foster care after her stepsister, Susie, died while her mother was bathing all the children together. Lucia was placed in a foster home with her biological brother and infant half sister. Another stepsister was placed elsewhere and disappeared from Lucia's life. Because of pending abuse allegations regarding Susie's death, the children had no opportunity to attend a funeral service for Susie, or to grieve with the family. Eventually, the cause of Susie's death was listed as "undetermined" by the coroner, but abuse was not ruled out.

Prior to foster placement, Lucia's blended family consisted of her biological brother, two stepsisters, and an infant half sister whose biological father was Lucia's stepfather. Both mother and stepfather suffered from untreated Posttraumatic Stress Disorder (PTSD). Lucia's stepfather was a war veteran and her mother had suffered extreme sexual and physical abuse beginning in early childhood. The parents had a violent history with each other and they disciplined their children by hitting them with shoes, belts, and other items at hand. Both parents also had a history of drug and alcohol abuse. As a result of their own trauma, these parents were unable to provide their children with a stable physical or emotional environment.

Although the SIDS death of Lucia's infant brother brought Susie's earlier death to the forefront, Lucia would not directly speak of her sister's death in treatment sessions. Neither would she address her sister's death through art or play. As time passed we created a warm bond rooted in our play communications. From her I learned how to lie down perfectly still behind the couch and hold my breath as a way to survive "when your parents are fighting with knives." She openly expressed her lonely struggle to care for her younger siblings when her parents would leave the children all alone. Her presenting symptoms of anxiety, enuresis, and nightmares were addressed.

As our relationship grew and Lucia felt increasingly safe, she forgot about the rule "not to talk about Susie." Sometimes Lucia would begin to talk about Susie and then would abruptly stop herself. I observed the stiffening of her body, pressing her lips together, even placing her hands over her mouth. As soon as Lucia would realize her "slip," she would abruptly change the subject. Then she would withdraw until she could again manage the interaction between us without talking about her dead sister. It eventually became clear that she had been coached to keep events of Susie's death a secret. This "secret-keeping" was reinforced by her parents even during supervised visitations. Lucia loved her mother and did not desire to betray her. Lucia yearned to live with her again. She believed the truth would prohibit her from ever doing so. This secret was an unbearable burden for this saddened child.

Lucia built the Sandtray shown at a time when her mother had yielded again to her addiction and it seemed the family would never reunify (figure 3.1). Mother had not been visiting her. Lucia had spent previous weeks in treatment "playing baby," often becoming sillier the longer she played this role. Nine months into treatment, this Sandtray became Lucia's first direct expression of her grief for her dear sister Susie. Just prior to creating this tray, Lucia brought the only "baby picture" she had of herself. In it, she was a toddler sitting alone on a bed that filled a tiny, dingy hotel room. This is where she had cared for her

Figure 3.1. Lucia's bathtub memorial

siblings on her own. After sharing those past experiences verbally, she wanted to play baby again. This time, she did not become silly. She seemed to absorb the nurturing by becoming quiet and relaxed. Her body softened and stilled. I perceived that she was allowing a more authentic resonance to connect our lives than ever before. Lucia, shifting her play, then rushed over to the Sandtray area, quickly and silently forming this sand world shown.

First, Lucia placed the candle-filled menorah, then a large round candle. The purple bath tub was the third item placed. Lucia was focused, quiet, and gentle in a way that I had not experienced her in our nine months together as she placed at least thirty-five more candles. She asked for water to fill the tub. Once the candles were lit, we sat viewing the world in a reverent rapport. Lucia then whispered, "It makes me think of Susie." The sadness was palpable and we both had tears welling. "I thought so," I said quietly. "It is sad when we lose someone we love."

From this point on, Lucia was less anxious and more authentic in treatment. It seemed she no longer had to carry the secret inside. We both remembered the day this world was created. However, it was not until much later that we were able to talk about how sad she felt that this Sandtray was her only memorial to Susie. Eventually Lucia was able to express her feelings about her many losses: her infant brother, her home with both of her parents, her stepsister Susie, and her surviving stepsister who had also been removed. I was fortunate enough to have treated Lucia through the family's eventual reunification.

What occurred between Lucia and me on the day she created this "memorial" Sandtray evolved from many layers of co-created play. Over months, we formed a unique relational dialogue of sounds, facial expressions, and energetic shifts. We each brought our patterns of memory and action learned in the past. With the recognition that every moment is new and contains the potential to create a unique connection, we formed a fresh relationship based on mutual warmth, trust, and respect. I consciously focused on welcoming her life into the playroom. I invited and supported authentic feeling states, allowing for great freedom of expression through physical body movement, emotional expression, and intellectual paths. It was the relational space that formed the environment for Lucia's transformations as much as it was the play and Sandtray facilities. Despite having been coached against revealing the details of Susie's death, Lucia experienced psychotherapy as a safe holding environment. In such a play space she could learn to touch the reality of her experience, experiment with what she could tolerate, and find her own way to make sense of it without being pushed or pressured by anyone else's agenda.

Bodies Speak

In Western cultures our schools teach about the human body as a sum of its parts. We tend to study individual systems such as the nervous, circulatory, and pulmonary. In reality, of course, these units are neither separate nor parallel, but function interactively. Through a complex network of nerve cells, our bodies and brains are directly connected and function as one. "Input from the body forms a vital source of intuition and powerfully influences our reasoning and the way we create meaning in our lives" (Siegel, 2010, p. 43).

Western societies similarly are inclined to treat body, emotion, brain/mind, and spirit as separate though perhaps related entities. Eastern philosophy is more likely to consider each of these as an individual function of one essential entity. Our bodily senses are fundamental in creating a secure attachment and harmonious attunement with our environment. After all, it is our biological nature to assess continually our environment for level of risk. Physical, intellectual, and emotional shifts occur when working with Sandtray methods. It is not unusual for persons working in the Sandtray to have abrupt physical needs, such as needing to use the bathroom or becoming ravenously hungry, despite the fact that these biological needs were taken care of just prior to the session. Even though I share this observation during Sandtray trainings, we are often laughing at ourselves by mid-afternoon as we are looking for the chocolate to satisfy our cravings.

Treatment literature increasingly addresses the role of our physical bodies. The body psychotherapist Roz Carroll describes the significance of the attachment bond in the treatment relationship: "Engaging with the client in a way which brings feelings explicitly into the therapeutic relationship where they can be felt, responded to and acknowledged is critical to working in depth." Further, the "small details such as the timing of comments, the words used, the exchange of looks or smiles, have a significant impact on the client's sense of self" (Carroll, 2006, p. 57). Likewise, the Sandtray therapist's attention to minute relational details, including those of our own bodies, helps form a safe context for the client. This relationship allows a client's sensations, affects, and thoughts to emerge within the present session that may have been previously cut off, having been too painful, overwhelming, or intolerable.

Children are often brought to psychotherapy for social/emotional issues without much concern for serious medical problems, past or present. At times, as image-thinking is evoked through the medium of Sandtray and play, the *Creator's* body has an extended opportunity to "speak" through the combination of images formed. The following Sandtray stories illuminate how the *Creator's* body may communicate using the Sandtray process:

Joey's Story: Body Pipes

Joey was a slender boy, four years of age. His parents brought him for play therapy when the tensions of their custody conflict increased. At the intake interview they mentioned that Joey had needed surgery as a newborn and had required several subsequent surgeries. His last surgery had been more than one year ago and no further medical interventions were expected. The parents assured me that he had done well and did not seem to remember much about these events. As far as they were concerned the surgeries were inconsequential history.

On entering the playroom Joey was immediately attracted to the black sand. His play appeared focused and purposeful. With intensity he used a shovel to

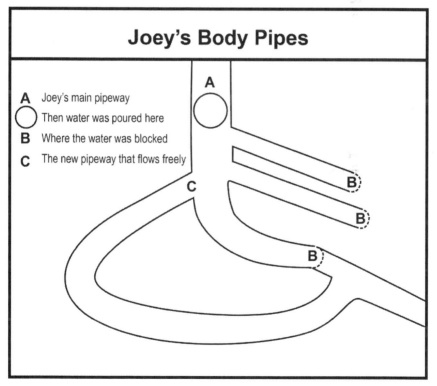

Figure 3.2. Joey's body pipes

make a "pipe way." He then made more pipe ways or channels off of the main one. Joey added a small amount of water and proceeded to describe to me areas where the water "didn't flow all the way." He then chose to add water from a squirt container and used tools to adjust the sand. Joey then formed a new pathway that made the water flow freely back to the main channel, avoiding the blockage. Joey was delighted with this change and began to smile and laugh. He seemed relieved of his tensions and began working with miniatures for the last several minutes of the session (see figure 3.2).

I later telephoned his parents to gather some details about his surgeries. They were surprised when I asked if the medical treatment was to repair urinary tract flow. They confirmed this fact. When I described Joey's play, his parents were astounded. In his subsequent play activities Joey focused on his more immediate concerns regarding the changes in his family.

Alicia's Story: Illness in the Center

Alicia, thirteen years of age, was brought to treatment to assist her with managing her response to her parents' conflict about visitation and custody. The parents lived in different states, and she was available only for short-term therapy over the summer. This adolescent's ulcerative colitis (UC) was mentioned only in the context of her parents' conflict over her medical care. Mother, a medical professional, wanted conventional medical treatment, while Father, an artist, believed that Alicia's body would heal itself and therefore had provided no medical care. A pediatric gastroenterologist performed Alicia's colonoscopy. He stated that her disease was so severe that removal of her colon was likely in her future, even with an aggressive medical approach.

When Alicia came into the playroom, she was generally compliant yet guarded. She seemed mature for her age and intellectually focused. She did not mention her UC with its pain and her difficulty in managing bowel symptoms. It soon became clear that this young woman protected herself from her parents' intense conflict primarily through denial and compartmentalization. She demonstrated little ability to integrate her experiences from each parent's home into a cohesive personal sense of wholeness. Although bright, Alicia had poor problem-solving skills and few friends. When distressed, she had the tendency to become explosive or completely withdrawn from others.

As the summer waned, Alicia prepared to return to her father. In early August she created a Sandtray with doll house furniture. She moved this furniture around frequently throughout the session. Of note, she initially put in a very tiny bathroom, with a tub, toilet, and a sink, that was of a much smaller scale than all the other furniture. Alicia initially placed these pieces in the corner as far away from her as possible, smoothing the sand first. As she added other household items, she moved this small bathroom set to the center and added the larger-scale bathroom set in the same corner. Subsequently, she moved this larger set to the center, removing the tiny one. Alicia spent much time rearranging and adding household items. Toward the end of the session she stated that she "felt finished" with the tray.

When we first looked at her Sandtray together, she had little to say. I made some concrete reflections about her creative process. We noticed together how the bathroom was in the center of this "house." We continued the Sandtray process, exploring any possible message that may be coming to her from her own inner wisdom. She began to speak of her UC for the first time. Alicia recognized that concerns about her symptoms and their social consequences were uppermost in her mind. She reported that creating this Sandtray brought her illness "to the center" of her focus, and admitted that she could not ignore her bodily "messages" any longer. I did not confront Alicia in any way. I felt connected to her with an intention to provide support and clarity for whatever was emerging. Alicia's own image-thinking process, manifested in the Sandtray, presented her reality to her in a way that she could recognize and begin to own it (see figure 3.3).

I saw Alicia intermittently over future years until she was eighteen. The parenting plan dictated that these were usually short treatment periods. Alicia

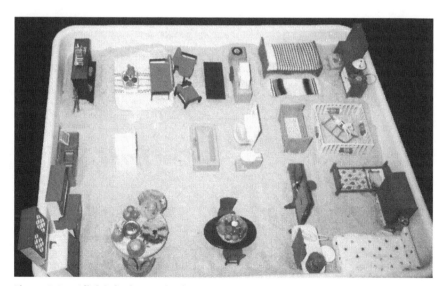

Figure 3.3. Alicia's bathroom in the center

never again had difficulty directly addressing illness issues with me after creating this tray.

The details of bodily based experiences are rarely shared by Sandtray *Creators*. This lack of sharing may be associated with an absence of linguistic clarity. Language is inadequate to communicate the vast array of possible bodily shifts and sensations. Yet a tiny change within the sand world may furnish the needed nonverbal medium of expression and the result may resonate pervasively throughout one's body, and even one's life. I can best demonstrate this by describing my own experience.

My Story: Entirely Stuck

In one of my professional trainings with Gisela Schubach De Domenico, I formed a tray about a journey, which was the only direction given. My protagonist, a pregnant woman, became entirely stuck as she focused her energy on a large layered rock that felt as if it were blocking her way. As I experienced what I created, this image evoked intense frustration and the stirrings of hopelessness for me.

As Dr. Schubach De Domenico passed by and checked in with me, she could see my increasing distress. With great respect, and only after receiving my permission, Gisela reached into the tray and moved this figure one quarter turn away from the rock, so that she was facing forward along her path. I was stunned! The rock had not been blocking her way at all. The moment the woman turned away from the rock, I felt a huge "click" in my chest. It was so strong that I had a sensation of sound. Vibrations rippled out to every part of my body. I breathed a deep sigh of relief, and continued the exercise without the tension I had previously experienced. Also, my physical disability, a back, neck, and spine injury, which was the difficulty that I had been thinking about when I placed the rock in the tray, never again held the power to trap and immobilize me. I developed a different perspective and relationship with this issue from that moment on (see figure 3.4).

In this chapter, I have offered some examples of my encounters within the Sandtray process, highlighting how Sandtray facilitates integration and healing in people as they encounter the implicit, nonlinear aspects of their experiences. Since therapy always occurs in a relationship, the *quality* of this

Figure 3.4.   Facing along the path

personal connection profoundly influences the course and outcome of treatment. By the nature of our chosen medium, Sandtray and play therapists
have the opportunity to access and utilize less verbal modes of communication that originate primarily in the right hemisphere of the brain. To increase
our effectiveness we must become acute observers of relational details. I have
shown how doing this requires close tracking not only of words and play
content but also of bodily states and energy flow, in both our own and our
clients' lives.

CHAPTER FOUR

Making Meanings

Physiological changes occur in our brains in response to experience—no matter where or how an experience takes place even when it's only inside our heads. Meanings are formed in our minds and are carried deep within our lives. One example from literature occurs when Professor Dumbledore reassures his famous student, "Of course it is happening inside your head, Harry, but why on earth should that mean it is not real?" (Rowling, 2007, p. 723). Whatever the external reality is, we ourselves assign its value, positive or negative. How is it that our meanings form and change? Certainly some judgments are inborn and serve to further human survival, while others are learned from our environment in both explicit and implicit ways. Experiences exist in multiple layers of meaning and therefore may not be in harmony with one another or accessible to our everyday consciousness. As demonstrated by Renee's example in chapter 2, engaging the Sandtray process can help an individual understand and transform disharmony between his or her own varied layers of meaning.

As a function of our human neurobiology, affective values are immediately registered in our bodies. "By the time a message reaches our cerebral cortex for higher thinking, we have already placed a 'feeling' upon how we view that stimulation" (Taylor, 2008, p. 19). Without using linear thinking, we assign significance, such as good/pleasure or bad/pain, to our experiences. As a child grows, these evaluations become more complex and are believed to evolve into the broad variety of adult human emotions.

I had an opportunity in 2007 to observe this process of quick assignment of meaning at an art gallery opening for a show entitled "What Do You See?" in Ashland, Oregon. The artist Irene Kai aimed to demonstrate how snap judgments prohibit humans from creating peace. She displayed large, poster-sized prints of her photography. By intent, these images were suggestive of sexual organs but they were actually unusual views of non-sexual parts of the human body, such as hands and fingers. I watched as some people opened the door actively engaged in conversation, stilled themselves as they glanced at the art work, then turned and left without discovering the artist's purpose. Clearly, some people were instantly repelled by the images and what they assumed them to be, never entertaining ideas about her intent.

How we see ourselves and our environment is the "clay" which we use to form meanings. As humans we process information through our senses and nervous systems to distinguish safety, risk, and danger. Professor Stephen Porges of the University of Illinois at Chicago Brain-Body Center has called this basic subconscious function "neuroception" (Porges, 2007). A person's patterns of neuroception help determine his or her essential sense of safety, allowing for some level of engagement or triggering defensive responses or even withdrawal. Some infants enter the world with compromised central and autonomic nervous systems. Others come neurologically prepared to engage, yet find poorly receptive environments as their caregivers are unable to provide the physical and interactive nurturing to optimize neurodevelopment. Such limits may result in a general decreased sense of safety that leads to lessened ability for authentic social interaction, including psychotherapy.

Drive for Meaning

A Buddhist philosopher has said that "human beings are animals that seek meaning in life" (Ikeda, 2010, p. 57). Margaret Lowenfeld believed in the existence of a human drive to make meaning of our experiences. She argued that our minds seek to group perceptions into patterns forming mental representations. Lowenfeld further stated that humans have "'a strong inner drive . . . to externalize themselves, or to re-create their experiences *in order to be able to assimilate them*'" (as cited in Urwin and Hood-Williams, 1988, p. 78; italics added by authors). The Sandtray apparatus provides an ideal environment for re-creation and assimilation. Lowenfeld also asserted that experience comes before knowledge. She based her views in part on anthropologists' discoveries of artifacts that were linked to the lives of the people who made them. Children play in a manner that is based on their internal images and promptings, even after they begin to acquire language. Adult artists have described a similar nonlinear sense of "being moved" to create their art works.

The Sandtray process encourages the expression of our meanings and groupings, many of which are not noticed by us in our everyday mindset. Sandtray is a vehicle to express various states of being that exist within us simultaneously, including those ideas that appear to be contradictory or are impossible to express verbally. In any Sandtray session some portion of the *Creator's* meanings is brought into focus as new connections and groupings are also formed. These may or may not be explored or shared verbally with the *Witness*. The story of Kaci provides a way to begin to look at layers of meaning within a Sandtray session.

Kaci's Story: Layers of Meanings

By thirty-seven years of age, Kaci was a high-level business professional, married with three children. In psychotherapy, she frequently worked with Sandtray and used art successfully to explore the impact of her childhood trauma on her ongoing depression.

One day she arrived in a happy mood, immediately approached the Sandtray, and stated that she did not bring in a specific issue to work on that day. Kaci spontaneously used water for the first time. Creating a "mixing place," she poured the water into her lower left corner. Making comments about how fun-filled and carefree she felt doing this, she proceeded to use scoops and funnels to form molded shapes from the wet sand, and place them on the dry sand areas of the tray.

After sitting silently with her creation, she got up, gathered marbles and glass blobs, and placed them on the top of each damp sand form. Kaci slowly began to speak of this place in the sand as a "city." She described various qualities of these structures and the relationships between the "buildings." She then conveyed her impressions of how she perceived these shapes as being connected to personal and business relationships in her life.

Later, after more silence, Kaci began to talk about how all of the buildings were actually separate, distinct from one another. She began to speak of how we, as humans, are essentially alone in life. She pondered aloud that despite our many seemingly close relationships, we basically are born and die alone.

Kaci moved through a variety of changes of affect and energetic shifts as she looked at her sand world from different levels of meaning. She started out quite playfully. Then she made cognitive analogies between her city's buildings and her everyday relationships. She concluded in a quiet, thoughtful manner, sharing existential ideas.

As illustrated by Kaci's story, all *Creators* hold multiple personal meanings for each item in the sand world. Every miniature is chosen for some reason. A *Creator*'s explicit purpose may or may not match any conceivable implicit one. By offering a well-rounded collection of miniatures, the *Witness* provides the *Creator* an opportunity to manifest concretely many different experiences simultaneously. During a Sandtray session the focus is on activating the *Creator*'s experiences from the past, those currently present, and those emerging in the moment.

Angel Image: An Exercise

Consider the photograph of items that have been named "angels" by Sandtray *Creators* at one time or another (see figure 4.1). Notice how unique each figure is. Observe what is evoked inside you as you review these images. They are all different sizes. Each miniature may be regarded as male or female, adult or child, playful or serious. Each "angel" has its own color and texture, facial expression, and physical position. Each figure has the potential to bring an assortment of differing characteristics to the Sandtray process. Specific feelings and functions may be depicted as well as qualities such as power and affect. As you look at the picture, imagine the properties each of these figures evokes in

Figure 4.1. Angels

your mind's eye, and consider how you might want to use them in your own Sandtray.

As in this exercise, our minds are metabolizing our experiences constantly. Some scientists believe that dreams are a mechanism of this processing function that occurs during sleep. But, again, what is the mind? After much struggle, Daniel Siegel offered this definition: "The human mind is a relational and embodied process that regulates the flow of energy and information" (Siegel, 2010, p. 92). After we are born, our brains continue to develop in our early relational environment to form each person's unique preverbal thinking patterns. Observing how a *Creator* takes in, forms, and expresses various meanings will assist the Sandtray *Witness* in facilitating the exploration of explicit and implicit life components as they appear in the sand world.

Patterns of Experience

Engaging in exercises such as the angel image above or the tree exercise in chapter 2, we can begin to notice and track our own experiential patterns. Knowing our own patterns also assists us in identifying those of a *Creator*. One way to consider patterns is with the concepts of "modes" and "fields" of experience. By acutely observing the *Creator's* more accessible and less accessible modes and fields as the sand world is created and explored, the *Witness* is better able to invite the *Creator* to expand his or her experiential window of tolerance in a manner that is congruent with the *Creator's* flow of mind.

The Sandtray contains and focuses the portion of our experiential patterns that we happen to bring forth at the time the world is formed. The sand world then becomes available to us for closer consideration. The structure presented here considers *modes*, defined as the kind of emerging energetic expression, and *fields*, defined as the context in which the modes emerge. In addition to the fact that the concepts discussed here may be observed in many facets of our daily lives, the framework of modes and fields provided here is a tool intended to guide therapists in their *Witnessing* function. Like any constructed way of viewing life, these modes and fields are neither pure nor separate from each other.

Out of necessity, these categories are described in a linear format. In reality, these modes and fields function simultaneously and are dynamically interconnected. Knowing our own patterns, and being sensitive to the patterns of the *Creator* within this schema, will enhance our ability to be helpful. With careful review and consideration, a *Witness* may discern which ways of experiencing come smoothly for the *Creator* and which ways are more difficult.

Energetic Modes

Lowenfeld's theories identify three *modes* of experiencing (Lowenfeld, 1993, pp. 271–72). They are: physical/bodily based, intellectual/thinking, and emotional/feeling. She named the underlying neutral force at the core of these modes "E." While Lowenfeld only defined "E" functionally, I conceptualize this "E" as a universal life force that is expressed through her three structures. Generally speaking, "E" simultaneously flows along all three modes, yet the balance between them fluctuates. When an increase in one type of energy is required, it becomes the focus, while the other two are decreased or cut off. Although she does not describe why this occurs, it is an observable process. For example, when someone musters physical resources, such as during a final effort to finish a difficult rock climb, then the other two modes would be inhibited. During an important exam when intellectual resources are particularly required, thinking would be the focused mode. Many of us have been engaged in an intense emotional experience only to realize at its end that we had not been attuned to the cognitive information available, or that we had physically been holding our breath.

Throughout the entire Sandtray session the *Witness* closely attends to these three modes as part of the intersubjective field as presented in chapter 3. In Jada's case, my ability to observe, meet, and reflect her energetic modes of play allowed me to support her positive affects as soon as they arose. With Joey's "pipe way," tracking his modes led me to a possible sense of meaning. The intersubjective field of the *Creator* and *Witness* holds the core indicators of the energetic modes activated in any given moment. Some clues for observing the most predominant modes can be identified:

- The *physical mode* may be strongest when *Creators* are deeply involved in using their bodies to move sand and/or objects with few words, and somatic shifts are readily observed by and/or experienced within the *Witness*.
- The *intellectual mode* may be indicated when the *Creators'* fluent use of words is presented in the sentence format of common language.
- The *emotional mode* may be distinguished by the *Creator's* use of words that are singular, brief phrases without linguistic structure, deep silence, or an intense emotional resonance within the *Witness*.

Balance and flexibility in the activation of these functions are a source of health. When harmony does not exist, some modes may be constricted or blocked while others become overused, creating tension and distress. One purpose of using Sandtray is to open or rebalance the *Creator*'s flow of "E" in order to diminish tensions. Many experiences are a blend of the above three modes such as intuitions, premonitions, and spiritual epiphanies.

Contextual Fields

The contexts or *fields* for experiences, initially called "realms" by Schubach De Domenico, include the idiosyncratic, communal, archetypal, and universal. As we create and play in the sand, we convey our experiences, both real and imagined, which can bring the discovery of new and various layers of meaning. Remember that experience precedes the formation of meaning. In Sandtray we may consider how the *Creator* approaches the fields of experiences (which modes are activated), and the relationship of one field to another. The *Witness* also attends to the fields and modes that are becoming more readily activated when the *Creator* and *Witness* explore the world together. This sharing informs the *Witness* as to the direction of reflection and inquiry about the experiences in the tray. As a therapist, my sense during a Sandtray session is one of riding the crest of the wave of harmonic resonance or intersubjectivity (see figure 4.2).

The *idiosyncratic/personal field* is rooted in the sensory image-thinking of early life and is not initially accompanied by language. This level of self-perception forms the kernel for our decisions and reactions. As previously noted, the infant's brain is dependent upon relational experience to develop properly. Each newly formed sensory-image-thinking link results in a pattern of meaning that is uniquely individual. These meanings are so deeply personal that only individuals can discover them. No one can tell another what these idiosyncratic meanings are. The *Creator* of the sand world initiates the *Witness* into his or her personal perceptions. As the pair explores the world, the *Witness* then may assist in bringing forth and exploring the *Creator*'s connections to other contextual fields. This type of unfolding occurred in the example of Renee shared in chapter 2.

The *communal field* is dependent upon the diversity of the personal one, for it is individuals who contribute to the family and society. The communal field composes the dimension of rule making. Many of our habitual beliefs, thoughts, and behaviors are based in this field. These are elements of our lives that we do not necessarily consider and decide—they are ways we implicitly know and frequently act upon as a matter of course. During therapy I frequently refer to this process as being on "automatic pilot." Examples

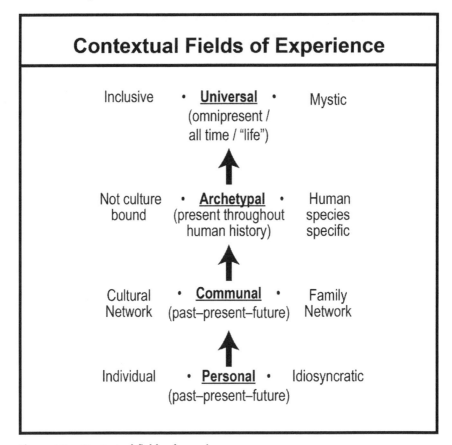

Figure 4.2. Contextual fields of experience

include the "way Mom did it," or "what the church dictates," or the "white middle-class way," or the "ghetto way." I once heard an abused child describe how she went to school every day believing that sexual behaviors between her friends and their parents were what her classmates were experiencing, too. She never thought to "tell" anyone. She had known no other way of life, and sex with an adult was her "normal." She was not aware of any right to refuse to participate in these activities.

For some of us, to be accepted by our families or communities, we must at times constrict our personal/idiosyncratic flow of experience to adapt. If these restrictions are frequent and/or become habitual, we cannot hold on to our personal selves. The degree of inhibition that may result can limit access to our personal field as we strive to meet our needs for survival for connection to and acceptance by others. The desperate need to try to "fit in" is dramatized for me by Cinderella's two half sisters as they painfully squish their feet and cut off toes in an attempt to try to fit into the coveted glass slipper.

The *archetypal field* is greater than an individual, a family, or one's immediate culture. This contextual field is the collective experience of human beings throughout time—the human way of experiencing life. According to Swiss psychiatrist Carl Jung, "There are as many archetypes as there are typical situations in life. Endless repetition has engraved these experiences into our psychic constitution, not in the form of images filled with content, but at first only as *forms without content*, representing merely the possibility of a certain type of perception or action" (as cited in Hall and Nordby, 1973, p. 42; italics in original). In Sandtray this may appear as intense experience such as one of parental compassion or multiple depictions of themes like earth mother, death, or birth. In "Sara's Story" later in this chapter, the archetypes of evil and widespread human suffering appear.

As in the "Clean Sand" story below, not every symbol is the same for all individuals or all cultures. The idiosyncratic is always embedded in the archetypal as the archetypal field is available to enhance and inform personal experiences. Since the archetypal field includes all types of human experience, no deeply personal experience is outside the archetypal.

By learning about the archetypal field we can observe where and how our personal experiences intersect, overlap, or contrast with the archetypal level of meaning. This field may provide a context to help us see where we are on our life's journey. Among the many possibilities, such understanding may provide richness, acceptance, an impetus for change, or an awareness of new resources.

At times when people are at odds with the communal field, they may find a sense of security and connection within the archetypal field. When I was a rebellious adolescent, I dove into fantasy and science-fiction literature to find an understanding for my struggles and some guidance along my path. Young and old alike eagerly devour stories as seemingly diverse as Jean M. Auel's *Earth's Children* prehistory saga (1980–2011) and futuristic civilizations like *Star Trek* (1969–2011). Such stories highlight themes of the archetypal field, bringing them into focus through popular culture.

The *universal field* is all-inclusive of "life"—plants, animals, minerals, and extraterrestrials, whether in their molecular, subparticle, or energetic forms. The universal contextual field includes what people know of the universe and what we don't know. It contains what humans identify as animate and inanimate, and existence and nonexistence. This field includes unusual experiences that often evade language. Such experiences may be considered "supernatural" or "spiritual" by some people and cultures.

Experiences contained in the universal field may be considered mystic or enigmatic. They may depict less common experiences, including pre-birth, post-death, the appearance of and communications with God, deceased persons, supernatural deities or spirits, or extraterrestrial life forms. *Creators* have described these types of experiences as "numinous," "sublimely spiritual," "enlightened," and "awe-inspiring." A few people have also considered them frightening. The universal field is not species specific. For example, it includes feeling states we share with all higher animals, "all of which exhibit similar emotional and motivational urges—[and] share very similar primary-process infrastructures in their brains" (Panksepp, 2010, p. 255). Although connections between humans and animals have yet to be fully explored scientifically, communications between humans and animals and even plant species may be included in the universal field.

The universal contextual field contains the Jungian concept of "the union of all opposites" (Hall and Nordby, 1973, p. 55). People in dire circumstances such as death-row criminals, terminally ill persons, the severely grief stricken, and torture victims may find security in this field as it illuminates that everything is part of life, death, and eternity, in the cosmos and beyond. This contextual field includes personal demons, antisocial acts, and contains all experiences without judging them.

During a Sandtray session a shift in perspective may bring internal changes as the *Creator* strengthens his or her awareness of the modes and fields that have emerged. For example, the Sandtray process may lead to an increased sense of balance within the energetic modes, or decreased self-criticism leading to compassion for self and others, and increased tolerance for life's stresses. We cannot make past negative experiences disappear; nor can we always immediately change our current reality. However, we can transform our relationship with both past and present. The psychiatrist Viktor Frankl has given us a poignant account of life in a Nazi death camp. He affirms: "What you have experienced, no power on earth can take from you" (Frankl, 1959, p. 104). Through our Sandtray experiences we can increase our own flexibility and tolerance to assimilate more and more differing kinds of events into our everyday conscious reality. In doing so, we expand our ability to recognize the choices we have in the present, their likely outcomes, and decide with greater mindfulness about how to proceed in life. The Sandtray *Witness* encourages and supports the *Creator*'s emerging capacity to abide new or uncomfortable experiences and expand his or her degree of internal integration.

Contextual Field Confusion

Distress often comes from conflict or discord among the different contextual fields, either within one person or between groups. The next two examples come from my own life and not Sandtray sessions, yet they serve to illuminate dissonance that may occur between contextual fields and the interpersonal difficulties that may arise as a result. This first vignette demonstrates a child's confusion between the archetypal and the personal contextual fields.

Donna's Story: A Wicked Stepmother

As a young woman, I was planning to marry and sat down with my fiancé and his daughter, Donna, nearly five years old. We planned to share the news of the wedding and answer any of her questions. I expected the joy that I felt to be reflected in Donna's response, as we had developed a close, positive relationship over more than a year's time. My heart sank as Donna burst into uncontrollable sobs at our news. After much listening and reassurance, I began to make sense of Donna's reaction. Her only experience with the concept of "stepmother" had been the wicked women of fairytales who were cruel to their stepchildren. Donna believed that when her father remarried, I, as his wife, would transform into such a person, contrary to her direct personal experience with me. We helped Donna sort out the person she knew from her archetypal beliefs about "stepmother" and trust her real experience.

With such confusions between contextual fields portrayed by words and meanings, it is easy to see why children needing surgery are likely to become terrified when told they will be "put to sleep" when this exact phrase may have been used to describe euthanizing the family pet. Often we believe that we are using words with a common meaning without checking with the other person. As Sandtray *Witnesses* we need to attend closely to an agreed-upon language and meaning with the *Creator*. To receive and understand the *Creator* fully we need to be sure we are speaking the same "language" they are. A lack of attunement may create conflict and discomfort for the *Creator*. Together the *Creator* and *Witness* need to be able to explore their differences without judgment. In the following instance, the conflict between individual and communal contextual fields is demonstrated by two people who are deeply imbedded in their individual experiences and cultural expectations.

My Story: Clean Sand

A friend of mine decided to become a therapist. We looked forward to the time when she would have advanced far enough in her study to attend my Essential Principles of Sandtray training. In these workshops I strive to establish a sense of safety and comfort for all participants. When she arrived for class and saw the trays of clean, new sand that I had prepared, she was repelled by them, exclaiming vehemently, "That looks like mud! My mother would never let me play in that!" Needless to say, I was surprised and disheartened. Then she explained her meaning. She had grown up in Micronesia on a small island. To her, the only sand that was acceptable to play in was pristinely white. I had supplied tan sand, perfectly normal for my northern California upbringing. The class came to learn that the children in her islands were chastised for playing in sand that was not white in color. When it rained, the tan sand became mud-like and the people believed that earthworms arising with the rain could enter one's body through the feet and attack the heart, causing death. This was a strict cultural precept infused with intense affect so that the warning would overpower a young child's curiosity and ensure behavioral compliance. Clearly *my* image of clean sand was not *her* image of clean sand—we each had our own personal and cultural meanings that were not readily compatible.

For a clinical view of how these disharmonies may impact an individual, let's examine Abra's story. She discovered how her personal desires were dampened by her family of origin's communal field.

Abra's Story: Disharmony in Contextual Fields

Abra, a bright thirty-three-year-old widow, worked in a highly skilled professional field. Over a period of nine years she sought treatment multiple times. The first treatment period came while she was caring for her chronically ill husband, Tom. Subsequently, she engaged in therapy when she and Tom became parents, and again when they separated. Later, she returned to treatment after Tom suddenly died, and she suffered from the loss of this co-parent and friend. Somatic and Sandtray methods had often assisted Abra in her growth through these difficult times.

The discovery of the conflicts between Abra's idiosyncratic and communal contextual fields came later during a primarily verbal session. She had been in a serious romantic relationship with a man and wanted to consider marriage. This warm and stable partner, however, who accepted her child and cherished her, was "only a blue-collar worker." Abra expressed an innate bodily sense that such a marriage was taboo. As we explored the origins of this deeply held belief, what emerged was that her parents brought her up to believe that attaining a college degree was her only option. Her family's ideology included a subtle, yet iron-clad, message that people without a college-level education were in some way less worthy human beings. Identifying the internal conflict between Abra's personal and communal contextual fields of meaning, and grasping how it had evolved, became helpful to Abra in clarifying and resolving the distress she had initially been only vaguely aware of.

These three examples illustrate how the clarification among contextual fields can relieve interpersonal and intrapersonal conflicts. In Sandtray sessions the emergence of modes and fields may be noted only by the *Witness*, or they may become part of verbal exploration. Sara's sand world is an example of how a *Witness* used the identification of a prevailing field to search for other levels of meaning that were also present for the *Creator*.

Sara's Story: Moving from an Archetypal to a Personal Field

A busy mental-health professional, Sara requested a Sandtray session, as she was feeling a bit overwhelmed by her work. She had a history of successfully using expressive arts methodologies to facilitate her own clarity and growth.

Sara began by making a circular sand form, like a hill, in the center of the tray. On top of it she placed people holding hands in a circle around a single candle. She then stated, "The world is so crazy it needs some harmony." Quickly she lit the candle. Then she brought in images of abuse, torture, evil, and war. She spoke of the poor state of humanity in today's world. Sara specifically referred to "evil atrocities in our world," such as "rape in the Congo, the training of child soldiers, incredibly devastating natural disasters, and the existence of warlords in many regions." She was verbally descriptive intermittently as she created her world.

Later in the session she focused on the small, black, and hunched-over devil as it crept toward the center figures and their light (see figure 4.3). Sara described this devil as the "creeping . . . seeping of evil" toward her central figures of "harmony and peace." She placed the red broken-heart figure as a barrier between the two, saying that the heart was "so tattered the evil is likely to get through." Sara made this statement immediately after pushing the heart into the sand.

I perceived Sara's expression as primarily focused in the communal and archetypal contextual fields. Through my careful inquiry and our reflection together she was able to recognize the connection between these presenting fields and her personal one.

Just like the miniature group of people in the center of her Sandtray, Sara felt bombarded by evil and negativity. She expressed feeling overwhelmed by the intense and graphic images of child abuse that she dealt with in her

Figure 4.3. The "seeping of evil" toward "harmony and peace"

psychotherapy practice with adolescents. Her heart was feeling "ragged and torn" in her attempts to hold on to her own "safe place" while being present with her clients' suffering. Eventually, she acknowledged feeling assaulted not only by her everyday work world and the "big world," but also by some family issues.

Once this realization was acknowledged between us, the focus turned to how she could strengthen and nurture herself. During that dialogue Sara placed the "Do Not Enter" and "Stop" signs in the tray. Her final adjustment was to move the "Do Not Enter" sign toward the "devil's path" and "other evils," as a way to protect her "harmony and peace" figure. She expressed a deeper commitment to strengthen herself to deal with her difficulties more effectively.

As these stories demonstrate, using this schema of modes and fields, a *Witness* may facilitate actively conscious engagement with previously implicit features of a *Creator*'s life, making what is implicit more accessible. The more modes and fields a person can experience in a balanced and harmonious way, the greater the level of integration he or she can achieve. By the use of the Sandtray process we have the opportunity to tap our own inner wisdom and explore life's alternatives. Sandtray teaches and supports mindfulness of our own processes and how they impact the choices we make within our environment. Sara was able to identify her need to work on strengthening her spiritual and social supports, on forming more effective boundaries, and on taking actions to resolve her immediate family matters.

Vicarious Traumatization

Sara's sand world demonstrates how vulnerable *Witnesses* may be to vicarious traumatization, also known as compassion fatigue. These terms generally refer to the cumulative impact of sustaining over time an empathetic life-to-life connection with trauma victims while supporting them. A *Witness's* efforts to connect to the *Creator* taps the *Witness's* own deep personal resources and may reveal deficits. The energetic intensity of maintaining affective synchrony with people who are suffering impacts us profoundly and we may become worn out. When we "burn out," we lose our spontaneity, creativity, and flexibility. Commonly we become over-identified with those we are trying to aid, negatively influencing our perspective and our ability to help. We may even become addicted to the excitement of traumatic situations, finding the routines of our normal lives dull and unfulfilling. Given these reactions, in our personal lives we may feel ill, court exhaustion, sleep poorly, or become anxious about our own or our family's safety.

The intensity and immediacy of trauma, particularly for *Witnesses* working with children, contributes to compassion fatigue. Circumstances that exacerbate vicarious traumatization include high workloads, poor supervision and training, and a *Witness's* personal trauma history and current stressors. Like Sara, we may all benefit from consultation and personal Sandtray work to combat the stressors of our chosen profession.

The human drive to make meaning is briefly explored in this chapter. Through example, we see how a *Creator's* meanings may evolve about chosen Sandtray images, even within a single session. We have sought here to understand the concepts of the energetic modes and the contextual fields. Using this basic framework aids *Witnesses* in their understanding as they support *Creators* through their Sandtray journeys. Readers may wish to apply this framework to their own sand worlds, or to other vignettes in this book to practice its usefulness.

CHAPTER FIVE

Readiness

Entering Play

Physical sensations are a major component of play, despite the difficulty in tracking them externally. Consider this example about a tactile encounter in a popular science fiction series: Data, an android, seeks to understand his human companion Picard and the experience of being human. Caught in a time warp, the pair encounters the spaceship *Phoenix*, a famous artifact from Captain Picard's own boyhood. Data asks, "Does tactile contact alter your perception of the Phoenix?" As this conversation occurs, Picard is touching the ship and gently rubbing its hull. He replies, "Oh yes. . . . For human beings the sense of touch is sometimes more important than sight or sound. It *connects* you to an object, makes it more real" (Dillard, 1996, p. 73; italics in original). We humans certainly are creatures with tactile/emotional connections to our world. Children often have favorite stuffed animals. Teens and adults alike express affection for items such as a favorite shirt. These attachments are not easy to explain rationally, particularly to the parent or partner who attempts to discard a tattered but much-loved article without understanding the meaning which it holds for the owner.

In the Sandtray process, the sand and objects evoke memories, emotions, a sense of place or movement, and proprioception. The senses of touch, taste, smell, hearing, and vision are readily stimulated. Scientists now recognize "that the use of the hands to manipulate three-dimensional objects is an essential part of brain development" (Brown, 2010, p. 185). Our sense of touch is paramount to the Sandtray process and to how humans experience their environment.

Researchers increasingly emphasize the plastic capability of the human brain to change its own physical structure, even as we age. For example, one observer of the field notes that "something as seemingly insubstantial as a thought has the ability to act back on the very stuff of the brain, altering neuronal connections in a way that can lead to recovery from mental illness and perhaps to a greater capacity for empathy and compassion" (Begley, 2007, p. 9). This new scientific information helps us see how our thoughts and experiences shape who we are.

Most therapists are familiar with the effectiveness of cognitive behavioral therapies. These therapies demonstrate that explicit thought is powerful. The Sandtray process also includes access to core affects and physical body experiences. I propose that the use of Sandtray, with its added dimensions of touch, movement, proprioception, smell, sound, vision, and implicit or image-thinking in the presence of a supportive *Witness*, offers opportunities for an exponential increase in healing, recovery, and growth. This chapter provides an overview of the framework I use to encourage the *Creator*'s connections with, and openness to, a freshly created sand world.

The following example springs from a single Sandtray session that summarizes Tanya's growth over nearly two years of more conventional therapies. Using the sand allowed her to incorporate more of her senses, further integrating her growth. For Tanya, Sandtray rapidly linked her preverbal image-thinking to her emotions and intellect, increasing her clarity about her life experience. Tanya's tactile awakening deepened her connection to newer perspectives and enabled her to consolidate her treatment gains and to verbalize her life story.

Tanya's Story: A Dry-Sand Narrative

Tanya was a single parent to four children, ages two through eleven years. Her mother, grandmother, and great-grandmother had also raised their children alone. At age twenty-nine she requested individual therapy after her three oldest children enjoyed participating in the *Dream Defenders*, a Sandtray group for healthy children of HIV/AIDS-afflicted parents. Undiagnosed for years, Tanya had contracted HIV from her former husband and the disease had recently progressed to AIDS. She reported feeling hopeless, depressed, and overwhelmed. At the beginning of treatment Tanya was unable to identify inner-body sensations or speak about her own life experiences. Yet her ability to describe her children's development seemed unimpaired.

Despite the children's persistent lobbying with their mother to use the Sandtray techniques, we engaged in "talk therapy." For me this included cognitive behavioral therapies, as well as the use of imagery and somatic-emotional exercises. Despite her compliance with medical treatment and counseling,

Tanya became increasingly debilitated and had to give up her employment. Her ongoing psychotherapy targeted her adjustment to the physical, social, and emotional changes brought on by her illness. Our primary treatment goal was to assist Tanya in becoming increasingly connected to her own experience so she could make choices from a more solid sense of self. Other treatment efforts were directed toward insuring her access to Social Security disability payments and establishing a long-term plan for her children's future without her. Toward the end of treatment, Tanya elected to move to another state near relatives who would become the children's guardians when she died.

In her last session she decided to work in the sand. Tanya expected this would be her only sand world and we discussed taking photographs and notes. Although she had seen some completed Sandtrays and many photographs of her children's work, she expressed concern that she did not "have a clue what to do" in her own Sandtray. I invited her to start by touching the sand and allowing her heart to follow whatever came next. I also reiterated that the Sandtray existed at this moment for her to express herself in any fashion she desired and that whatever was created would be exactly what was right for today.

To start, Tanya placed her hands palms down on top of the dry sand. At first she kept them still, and then she began moving them. As sand shapes rhythmically arose, words also began to flow, primarily in the emotional mode (described in chapter 4). Tanya began to speak of her family relationships, beginning with her grandmother. As the topographies of the sand changed, she shared how these images reflected the family's relational structures. For example, at one point she made sand shapes which she identified as her mother, her grandmother, and herself, moving them as she described their changing relationships over decades. At another point she poured piles of sand named for her four children, again depicting relationship changes over time. Solely using the dry sand, Tanya depicted a four-generational coherent narrative of her family, including a hopeful vision for her children's future. This event unfolded in a deep reverie with the sand, herself, and her *Witness*.

Quickly becoming engrossed in her story, with her agreement I ceased taking notes and photographs because it felt invasive. In addition, I needed all of my focus and energy to be present and to support her in her creative process. In this sand world of her family's history, Tanya summarized the major perceptual shifts that she made during two years of therapy. These included a new willingness to accept help, and to face problems rather than hide from them. At the end of the session Tanya stated that she felt very satisfied and now understood what had attracted her children to this method of expression.

Tanya's tactile awakening through her Sandtray session brings to mind the response that poet and philosopher Daisaku Ikeda expressed on finding the sculpture of a horse as he strolled along a beach: "Once the sand was touched by creative hands, it was no longer just sand. It ceased to be simply a thing. The sand became the beautiful body of a horse, a fusion of matter and spirit." He further emphasized, "That moment when something unseen becomes something visible—there we find the mystery of creativity!" (Ikeda, 2010, p. 1). This declaration begins to describe the sparkling transformation that emerged alive and fully embodied as Tanya composed her dynamic family story.

An Introduction to the Aspects of a Sandtray Session

I find words inadequate to capture the dynamic, living, creative Sandtray process. By "aspects" of a Sandtray session, I mean something more than qualities or features. Over the next several chapters I will delineate a linear structure within which a Sandtray session may be considered and its components taught. These aspects are intended to be cognitive reference points for *Witnesses* to use in facilitating a *Creator*'s growth. This Sandtray framework is not intended to be rigidly codified into a linear format that the *Witness* imposes on the *Creator*. For the first four aspects, "Introducing the Sandtray Process," "World Creation," "Silent Reverie," and "Reflecting/Directing," a *Witness* and a *Creator* sit across from each other and the *Witness* takes notes. During the subsequent aspects of "Entering into the World" and "Exploring from Inside the World," as well as the concluding aspects of "Leaving the World," "Summarizing," and "Forming a Plan," the dyad sits side by side and no notes are taken (see figure 5.1).

In some other sand-based methods, the *Witness* is primarily silent, holding a *Creator*'s experiences in the tray over time, awaiting change. For me, a *Creator*'s transformation actually begins on deciding to enter the Sandtray process. I then follow Lowenfeld's methods to actively facilitate the emergence of nonverbal material into the verbal arena. The functions of the reflections and inquiries described in these aspects are intended to foster the movement of information that the *Creator* is ready to welcome into active consciousness. Again, the purpose of accessing preverbal material is to discover the "powerful and valuable resources" that the implicit mind holds, not because image-thinking is the source of psychopathology (Urwin and Hood-Williams, 1988, p. 119).

Rather than looking at these aspects as stages or set phases that follow a sequence like those of the moon, consider the meanings of images that

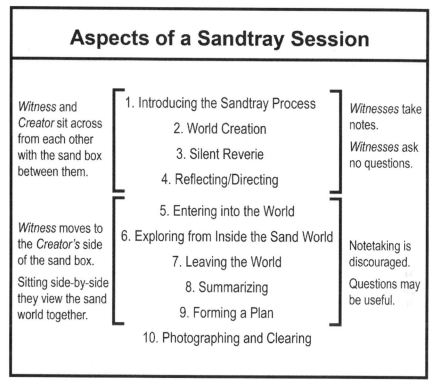

Figure 5.1. **Aspects of a Sandtray session**

emerge in the Sandtray like a bubbly stew of life. The bubbles exist and move in a wide variety of arrangements and states. For example, some of the bubbles are just beginning to form while others are bursting at the surface. All these differing events are occurring simultaneously. We can attend only to some of them in any given session, but it is helpful to be aware of the entire stew pot.

Despite the descriptions of techniques that follow, not all Sandtray sessions are verbal. That is why in previous chapters I have spent time introducing the differences between the functions of the hemispheres of the brain, the concept of intersubjectivity, and how we communicate meanings nonverbally. Sometimes a single or series of primarily silent sessions needs to occur in order to facilitate the foundation of a safe environment. Also, it is not likely that every session will include all the aspects discussed. Referring to figure 5.1, sometimes only the "World Creation" through the "Reflecting/ Directing" aspects will be available to be worked with, as in Tanya's story. At other times the "Exploring from Inside the World" through "Forming a Plan" aspects may be the main focus for the day. Some sand worlds are created quickly while others require much time. As *Witnesses* accompany *Creators* in the Sandtray process, they need to balance concerns of the direction the work is taking with the time available.

In Margaret Lowenfeld's work she functionally describes much of what I call "aspects." She did not name or organize them in a linear format, but Dr. Schubach De Domenico did so later, adding a reflective/directive technique based on Carl Rogers's work. Many of the techniques I discuss may be practiced in a micro-skills format. Such exercises may improve the comfort and ease for the *Witness*'s future application. However, to identify these aspects of the Sandtray session solely as methods to be "applied to" the *Creator*'s sand world as cognitive interventions will significantly diminish the power of this tool. These aspects are more like a series of landmarks to be aware of, not a map that must be followed.

Once a *Witness* learns to identify these aspects during the Sandtray session, supporting a *Creator* flows more effectively. The Sandtray process often unfolds in a unique and unpredictable fashion and rarely as described here. Every object in the tray (including the sand) is dynamically related to every other object, the *Witness*, and the *Creator*. Interaction and interrelatedness are fundamental features of Sandtray.

Intersubjectivity, the reciprocal rhythm of the relational dyad, is the underpinning for offering dynamic change. Gentleness, compassion, and respect for the *Creator* cannot be emphasized enough. The gentleness required to tend and to harvest the experiences that become known during a Sandtray session are analogous to that of the delicate touch needed to pick the most superb wild blackberries. A fruit appearing to be perfectly ripe is not necessarily the sweetest and juiciest. Yet in our eagerness we may pull it off the cluster. The berry will be beautiful but lack the rich depth of sweet flavor of a fully ripe berry. When we lightly touch, or softly tug, and the fruit comes to us with ease, we know it will be a treasure. This is the type of "touch" required by a *Witness* throughout the Sandtray process.

In the same way, a *Witness* will benefit from patience and the confidence that pressing issues will continue to emerge for the *Creator* over time. Concerns need not be rushed just because the *Witness* may be aware of them. Not every issue in Sandtray can be processed immediately. The direction of the flow of the session is generally governed by the *Creator*. While exploring the sand world the *Witness* invites the *Creator* to look at the tray more closely, first noticing what is present in detail, then experiencing what is there more deeply, and only then perhaps venturing a view from a new perspective.

In other words, The *Witness* invites the *Creator* to learn directly from the Sandtray that was just produced.

Although the *Witness* is ultimately responsible to hold and contain the physical and energetic environment, no one is the designated "leader" during the sand world exploration. The process is a delicate balance, tip-toeing on the edge of a sharp knife. Amy's story in chapter 2 is one example of negotiating the flow of what takes place between the *Witness* and the *Creator*. This unfolding is more akin to improvisational dance, as none of the steps are planned in advance. The commitment is only to come and work together with the tools available and a stance of openness to see what may be created and learned.

Particularly during the verbal processing, if a *Witness* never offers an invitation to a *Creator*, habitual ways of viewing the world will transform more slowly. Yet if a *Witness* is too invasive or directive, a *Creator*'s energies and meanings may be lost. Physically and relationally the arena of the Sandtray process must be felt as safe by the *Creator*, without becoming a cocoon of retreat. Ideally the *Witness* forms conditions where a *Creator* will feel free enough to explore and move to the edges of his or her tolerance or discomfort. Finding the edges of one's comfort zone encourages growth. This journey needs to occur in a secure framework so the *Creator* can test these edges without becoming dysregulated or lost. The *Witness* relies on the resonance of intersubjectivity, the landmarks of the aspects, the energetic modes, and the contextual fields to guide the flow of the session gently without taking it over.

Interpretation of Sandtrays

In Lowenfeld's approach, a *Witness* does not provide interpretations. This means that the *Witness* does not provide meanings or explanations to the *Creator* about the sand world. Any naming by a *Witness*, even a silent judgment, is a form of interpretation. For this reason a *Witness*'s accepting mental stance is as critical as silence and what is verbalized.

Instead, using the *Creator*'s own language as a basis, a *Witness* encourages a *Creator* to discover and explore his or her own inherent layers of meanings in the sand world. While interpretation may be used in other models, in this approach, the focus of treatment is on the meaning that comes forth from a *Creator*'s life. The emphasis is not based on what a *Witness* deems to be of significance, nor what the *Witness* has learned from books. It is not the *Witness*'s conceptualization that matters. The emphasis is on discovering or clarifying the *Creator*'s idiosyncratic meanings. In some aspects, as discussed later, there is a *strong* emphasis on using or reflecting the *Creator's* phrasing. Such techniques are effective in supporting a *Creator's* flow of both nonverbal image-thinking and linear thought.

Witnesses do help *Creators* decipher and clarify meanings and translate implicit features of the sand world to everyday language. At times this provides a fresh perspective for the *Creator*, like that gained when the first snow transforms a familiar landscape, making previously unnoticed contrasts apparent. It is important to note that any inquiry, idea, or impression shared by the *Witness* is done on a very tentative basis.

During a Sandtray session, it is essential that the *Creator* feels comfortable and confident to refute, correct, or refine any information from the *Witness*. Establishing this level of comfort enables *Creators* to elucidate their personal meanings and illuminate their lives as they take part in the dialogue with the Sandtray and the *Witness*. To facilitate this dialogue, *Witnesses* need to keep in mind that what they experience comes from their own perspective. A *Witness's* input may be wise and based on experience, education, and a relational resonance, yet it remains a guess. It is to be shared with caution. *Witnesses* can minimize the impact of their own reactions on *Creators* by following self-care and self-development guidelines such as using consultation. To illustrate how routinely and subtly we judge, I offer the following exercise.

An Exercise in Judgment

Consider the *Creator's* view of the completed Sandtray appearing in figure 5.2. A color close-up of this world appears on the book cover. Reflect deeply on the pictures of this Sandtray for several minutes, allowing your imagination to wonder about everything you notice. What impressions are coming forth as you sit with these images? What meanings are you beginning to define? What questions might you desire to ask the *Creator* of this world? Take note of your impressions before proceeding. (You may find it useful to take detailed notes for this exercise and repeat it again later, comparing your results.)

The initial composition of this world began with moving the sand. The *Creator* spent fifteen minutes moving the sand, first in spirals, then pushing sand to the edges and forming the "island." The *Creator* appeared to focus much effort in organizing the sand "just right" and keeping the sand out of the blue area. The size of the blue ring grew larger after a trial of a thinner one. Prior to continuing your reading, again note your impressions about this world so far.

How was this Sandtray constructed? The *Creator's* comments in parentheses follow the listing of the placement order of the miniatures. The *Creator's* statements were made throughout the session, not just during the formation of the

Figure 5.2. *Creator's* View

sand world. (1) Uroborus, a fish swallowing its own tail, in the center of the island. ("The idea to use black sand and this figure came to me prior to beginning the session.") (2) Scales of justice on a pedestal placed on a white rock. ("The pedestal alone was not high enough, I needed the rock.") (3) Brown, bare tree with snow. ("I don't want an evergreen. I want a bare tree. I don't know why.") (4) A small glass sun ("This world needs more light"); then a colorful candle was placed in the center of the uroborus. (5) Green leaves. ("It needs something green, growing.") (6) Moss. ("I wanted something that once was alive.") (7) Pod from a tree. ("An eternal sphere complexly textured.") (8) Dark-blue slice of polished stone. ("This is a pool.") A ceramic bridge was also chosen and the *Creator* considered using this to link the island to the outside sand. The *Creator* then stated, "No. A bridge will change this world too much." The last adjustment to the world consisted of lighting the candle. During the formation of the world there were no tears, smiles, or other distinct outward signs of affect. The *Creator* maintained a generally quiet and pensive manner.

Now take into account how the above information changes your initial impressions of the world. What other ideas, questions, and meanings come to you? Note these before reading further.

I will share some of the impressions and questions that came initially to my mind. Remember, these are only my personal reactions because there are no "incorrect" responses. This list does not correspond to the previous one, as my impressions came in a different order than the *Creator* placed objects: (1) Sanctuary. (2) Many apparently differing qualities appear, such as green growth/barren tree; dark sand/sun and light as well as white snow and rock on a black background; different height levels of the items. (3) The pool is a very dark color. (4) The topography of the sand: the island is notably lower than the sand outside the blue ring. (5) Circles: the island, blue ring, uroborus, sun, base of the tree, the pool, candle, pedestal, dishes of the scales, and the rock. (6) Sphere. (7) Green growth appears to be emerging from the pool, as the stem is actually anchored underneath the stone. (8) Some figures are touching each other and others are not. (9) Blue: ring, pool, and glass eye in the scales, base of the candle. (10) Contrast between the white box, black sand, and blue ring. These initial speculations led me to wonder:

- What kind of a place is this?
- Could it be isolation, security, or a restful place?
- Why did it seem important to the *Creator* to flatten the island so carefully and keep sand out of the blue area?
- How would the bridge have changed this place "too much?"
- Why are these images coming to the *Creator* at this time?
- What is going on here?
- How are these items connected to each other?
- How does the island view the sand outside the blue ring and visa versa?
- What might the meaning be for the *Creator*?

A week later I revisited these images and reflected anew. These are some of my thoughts the second time I visited this tray:

- I noticed the sparkly nature of the black sand and wondered what kind of space remained outside the blue ring. Could the outer sand be a barrier or a platform for more unfolding of this world?
- I noticed that the scales of justice were the second-tallest item after the tree. I considered that the scales may be more related to the issue of balance than to justice. I also recalled that they fell once when the world was formed, and were quickly resettled during the construction on the island.

- The island now seemed crowded to me and I noticed that the sun was on the ground. I questioned if this was a place that people can physically go to or if it is the kind of place one just thinks about.
- Are all the seasons here? I could see that idea as a possibility.
- I want to know what part of the tray is the most aware of itself and how it sees the other items in the tray.
- I want to ask about the depth of the roots of the tree, the rock, the candle, and the depth of the pool. What of the island itself: is it floating or does it reach the sea bed?

Review your notes and consider how your beliefs about this Sandtray would change if you knew the *Creator* was twelve years old, thirty-five, fifty-five, or eighty-five years old? How would your impressions change if you knew the *Creator* was male or female? How would your ideas be different if you knew that just prior to forming this tray the *Creator* expressed depression, isolation, contentment, or joyfulness? How would your judgment evolve if you knew the *Creator* had recently married, been fired from a job, lost a loved one, or received a Master's degree? Reflect on how each piece of information provided might influence your views.

As you can see from my exercise responses, I made numerous guesses, judgments, and interpretations. *Witnesses* must use their own curiosity and resonance with the *Creator* to begin to use the techniques described within the Sandtray aspects format. It is my hope that, through your personal experience with this exercise, you will see that we all routinely make judgments. It is whether we impose our impressions on the *Creator*, or use them as vehicles to aid in the *Creator*'s discoveries, that will help determine the value of the session's outcome.

Once, during my own Sandtray education, the class participants all gathered to look at each other's work. I observed a tray established by two men in orange desert sand. It had rocks in it, no apparent water source, and no green growth. Exuberantly I opened my mouth and said, "That looks barren!" The statement was my honest response, a clearly negative judgment. After a scolding from the teacher, we turned to the two *Creators* and learned *their* meanings. My impression could not have been further from theirs! They both described a beautiful, peaceful, and alive world that had not been apparent to me. I learned much from them. My memory of this embarrassing event assists me in holding back my own views and focusing on the *Creator*'s meanings.

In the Sandtray process, one goal for *Witnesses* is to become aware of their most subtle interpretations and to keep them continuously in perspective. With this in mind, I strive to use the *Creator*'s own words as directly as possible. Even when we do our best, a *Witness*'s interpretations are communicated in how accurately we state reflections and in how we phrase our questions. Even how we describe a *Creator*'s work to each other as professionals implies how we view it. It is my desire to avoid imposing my analysis of the process by using phrases such as: this figure "demonstrates," this item "represents," the image "seems to indicate," and this object "appears to represent." With vigilance about imposing our own meanings on the *Creator*, we can decrease any negative impact of our interpretations or countertransference responses on the *Creators* whom we serve.

Desirable *Witness* Qualities

Descriptions of effective *Witness* behavior and energetic stance are threaded throughout this book. I provide a summary here. These qualities assist every *Creator*, no matter what age, previous experience with the materials, or profession. The foremost requirement is an authentic belief in *Creators*' capacity for growth, inherent human dignity, and right to direct their own lives. The *Witness*'s objective is to provide a sheltered environment of acceptance and comfort. My idea of such an environment is derived primarily from two concepts. The first is the attachment-theory concept of "secure base" (as cited in Bowlby, 1969, p. 333). The other is Dora Kalff's "*free and . . . protected space*" (Kalff, 1980, p. 39; italics in original). Both of these concepts value a sense of safety as a foundation for development. Desired *Witness* qualities include:

- The willingness to enter a felt, lived experience with the *Creator*.
- A facility for authentic, attuned interaction.
- The capacity to tolerate silence and uncertainty.
- Compassion, kindness, empathy, flexibility, and respect.
- The ability to observe one's self and the *Creator* in the process.
- The capacity for self-regulation, even under stress.
- A willingness to serve the *Creator*'s needs first.
- The ability to set clear boundaries, and be reliable.
- An ability to set aside personal judgments, interpretations, and meanings.
- The capacity to explore the Sandtray with an imaginative or playful state of mind.

It is difficult for us to provide all of these qualities fully every time. Many of the qualities I identify and the suggestions I make stem from my errors over the years, both in technique and in relational issues. I continue to strive to bring these positive qualities into every session. A sincere commitment to developing and integrating these characteristics will go far toward enabling *Witnesses* to meet the needs of the *Creators* we serve.

Self-care

A *Witness's* self-care provides the foundation for the integration of helpful *Witness* qualities. Caring for one's self also fends off vicarious traumatization while insuring personal and professional advancement. Self-care includes growth, not just maintenance. Self-care requires the courage to live creatively, consistently seeking to expand our levels of tolerance through multiple means. Our limitations as *Witnesses* inhibit our capacity to help others. The Sandtray *Witness's* functions require more than knowledge and interpersonal skill. They demand abundant effort, clarity, and self-awareness for *Witnesses* to hold, energetically and emotionally, the function of a midwife to the *Creator's* meanings, without becoming caught up in those meanings or imposing our own. These *Witness* tasks necessitate an ability to stay grounded, or self-connected, in the face of all types of human experience.

Therefore, a primary ethical consideration is for *Witnesses* to engage regularly in consultation to support their own journeys for growth and self-discovery. My use of the term *consultation* includes the functions of both technical supervision and personal therapy. Readers learned earlier in this chapter, in "An Exercise in Judgment," that striving to hold a noninterpretive stance as a *Witness* does not mean that we deny our process of judgment, but rather that we become aware of how our own processes function. All *Witnesses* come with their own perceptual frameworks of meaning. We can become distracted by overconfidence, lack of empathy, collusion with *Creators* by "not seeing" what is in front of us, and other countertransference binds. The relational bond between a *Witness* and his or her consultant also serves to decrease a *Witness's* distress from compassion fatigue. Such personal work aids in protecting *Creators* from *Witnesses* who may unknowingly interfere in a *Creator's* work. Without an outside observer of our clinical work we cannot be reasonably certain that our responses are helpful to *Creators*.

In addition to consultation, the use of the Sandtray process by *Witnesses* themselves enhances our capacity to witness others. In chapter 4, "Sara's Story: Moving from an Archetypal to a Personal Field" depicts how a therapist learned to identify her own self-care resources to manage the professional stressors of intense trauma work as well as some personal emerging family problems. Just like the *Creators* we work with, we cannot always "think through" a problem solely with our intellect. We, too, can discover new ways to advance our lives, moving beyond or beneath our intellectual capacities, and harvest from the image-thinking right brain.

Even if your consultant does not use Sandtray techniques, you can do your own work with a Sandtray colleague and take the photographs and notes to your consultant to review. Working with Sandtray alone may be useful as long as you slow down your process long enough to make a clear record and take accurate results of your work to consultation. Using these methods primarily addresses the intellectual and emotional energetic modes. The *Witness's* personal use of Sandtray helps balance the physical energetic mode. For additional work with the physical mode, I also recommend the use of direct physical modalities. These may include bodily based approaches such as massage, yoga, craniosacral therapies, improvisational dance, and somatic emotional approaches such as those taught by Babette Rothschild, Stanley Keleman, Patricia Ogden, or Moshe Feldenkrais.

Preparing a Welcoming Sandtray Space

Prior to inviting *Creators* into the playroom or Sandtray studio, careful and thoughtful preparation of the environment is beneficial. Appendix A provides a detailed description of the recommended equipment. During the Sandtray process the *Creator* may require various items, so it is best to have these readily available in advance. Water, towels, tissues, matches, sand tools, and candle stick-um are some basic staples. Providing extra sand and a container to remove sand gives *Creators* additional options. As a *Witness* you will also need note-taking materials and a camera. Consider the placement of your sand boxes and your seating arrangement. It is best for the sand tray to be accessible from all sides and for the *Witness* and the *Creator* to have room to sit together on any side.

One strength of the Sandtray method is the potential to decrease the cultural bias of *Witnesses* through the inclusion of multicultural objects. To increase the effectiveness of the Sandtray techniques, *Witnesses* should include items that could depict a range of variation within ethnicity, race, socioeconomic status, sexual orientation, gender, and spiritual beliefs. No matter what the *Witness's* personal belief system may be, images of other cultural points of view must be offered. When we fail to supply specific types of miniatures, we communicate to *Creators* those experiences that we find unacceptable.

Finding multicultural objects may take effort. In past decades, play figures of non-Caucasian races appeared as clones of Caucasians, varying only in skin color. As society is becoming more tolerant, some manufacturers are producing figures that portray more accurate ethnic styles and racial traits. However, depictions of multiracial families, interracial couples, multiracial people, gay and lesbian couples with children, and transgendered individuals and couples are not readily found. On the few occasions when I have located some of these images, they were not miniatures, or were works of art that were too costly. As a society we are still lagging in providing images that embrace all multicultural arenas.

A Sandtray *Witness* also needs to gain broad knowledge about life experiences of all groups of people with an awareness of the relationship between the dominant culture and these minority groups. This includes developing a sense of each group's values, history, literature, art, faiths, and politics. We can educate ourselves about others by reading and visiting cultural venues open to the public, such as dance, music, and poetry presentations. Attending different church and temple open houses, Gay Pride Parades, or author presentations from cultures other than our own can aid in expanding our views. Joining a community organization that promotes multiculturalism and is open to all may also provide valuable interpersonal learning that is not to be found elsewhere. If these options are not readily accessible in all geographical areas, much may be learned through movies, literature, and the internet. The more *Witnesses* are able to embrace the humanity of each person, the greater are our abilities to guide and support any *Creator*.

Chapter 5 sets the stage to enter the Sandtray process in greater detail by introducing the aspects of a Sandtray session. A *Witness*'s harmonic resonance with a *Creator* contributes to a safe environment for exploring the sand world. To encourage a *Creator*'s sense of comfort, a *Witness* learns about multicultural concerns and practices authentic openness, flexibility, and the capacity to set aside personal judgments. A *Witness*'s noninterpretive approach to Sandtray aids *Creators* in discovering their own deep meanings.

The following four chapters will provide specific examples and suggestions to aid you in beginning to apply these concepts and incorporate the Sandtray aspect framework into your own clinical approach. Discussions of a variety of problems and age groups will illustrate how using the aspects can enliven a therapy session. Later chapters will specifically discuss applying these Sandtray aspects to actively moving worlds and Sandtray work with younger children.

CHAPTER SIX

Aspects 1 and 2

Introducing the Sandtray
Process and World Creation

People bond when they work and play together. Cooking, gardening, crafting, building forts, or forming Sandtrays—these activities foster a sense of "connectedness" to what is made and to the people present. This uniting force forms the foundation for using the Sandtray "aspects" outlined in figure 5.1. Although some writers suggest that well-developed trust is a prerequisite to engaging in sand work, I take a different approach. As with other methods, Sandtray requires that *Creators* perceive the sense of a "safe enough" environment to engage. In the framework presented here, when *Creators* form a sand world, they will directly experience responsiveness, respect, and warm, positive regard from the *Witness*, providing a foundation for trust.

The *Witness* and the *Creator* develop this resonant relationship as the Sandtray process directly elicits powerful image-thinking. Physical, emotional, and intellectual components blossom from deep within the *Creator's* life. A worked Sandtray is more than an allegory, a visual metaphor, or the sum of its symbols. How profoundly revealing the concrete, physical structure of a sand world can be is demonstrated in Hana's work.

Hana's Story: Configuring Family History

Hana, thirty-six years of age, came for a consultation possessing a good deal of experience in Sandtray work. She approached the Sandtray intending to address multigenerational family issues. She had recently learned "family secrets" about behaviors that suggested a pattern of depression, including that her great-grandfather had committed suicide in his early thirties. Hana had suffered from depression in the past, always feeling isolated by it within her family. She stated that she was confused by the new information, even though it clarified some family medical history.

Hana chose tan sand, and made it wet enough to shape. She created a hill that became higher as it went farther from her. Closer (lower) she formed her "middle class" family when she was a child, adding tiles as "walls." Behind this barrier she placed a "man tied to a stake", the "Wicked Witch of the West," "skeletons in the closet," a "starving woman," and "gravestones." She added "jewels" and a heart-shaped rock that she named the "heart rock," placing them beside the family prior to completing the sand world (see figure 6.1).

Hana formed her Sandtray in silence. I learned her names for the items as we processed the world using the Sandtray aspects. Hana observed that the "past" (rear) was higher and that it had considerable power over the "present" (closer). She noticed that the adults could not see the past, but that the youngest girl was being held high enough to see over the wall. This girl felt fear, knew her brother also felt it, and they could sense it in the adults. The adults acted as if there were "no problem" and pretended not to see the "scary stuff." Hana remarked, "We know we are to pretend we don't see it either," even though the little girl could see everything over the wall.

Prior to leaving, Hana expressed her astonishment at how the structure of the Sandtray revealed her family's functioning. Her parents had raised the children believing that they were "protecting" them by hiding the family history. In

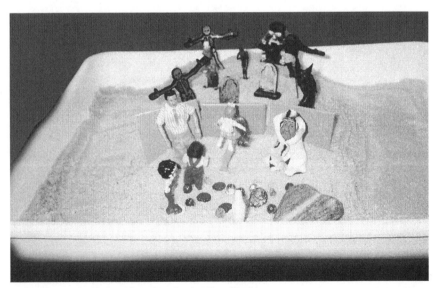

Figure 6.1.   The little girl seeing the family's history

actuality, only the children faced the history and the girl was lifted up enough to see the "skeletons of past family dysfunctions" over the barriers, while the adults remained with their backs to them. Hana said that in their efforts to shield the children, her parents provided no useful guidance on how to deal with the realities of life. The emergence into active consciousness of this new information came only after Hana formed the world and examined it closely. Even a few years later Hana stated that she still found the experience profound.

Once her images were placed into a concrete physical form, both the *Witness* and Hana were able to observe, resonate with, and learn from her sand world. As previously explored in Eddy's "war and soldier tower" in chapter 1, and Renee's landlocked "womb" in chapter 2, when *Creators* experience the physical relationships within the world, they begin to become aware of previously unknown internal processes and affects.

Many *Creators* report that they previously had some idea of the issues they brought into a Sandtray session, or that thoughts and feelings came to them during the forming of the tray that made sense intellectually. This is consistent with my image of the "bubbly stew" of consciousness—some of what the Sandtray holds is known, some may be suspected, and some is completely unknown. A resonant *Witness* providing thoughtful reflection and inquiry can facilitate the birth of what is most ready to come forth into active awareness. I have discovered that no matter how much I *think I know* about my Sandtray, there are always many other layers of meanings to be uncovered.

The First Aspect: Introducing Sandtray to Prospective *Creators*

The easiest introduction to the materials for a novice is not verbal. The availability of the sand trays and the miniatures, and how they are arranged and integrated into the therapeutic environment, can become an invitation to be curious, to touch, and to play. I prefer that my materials provide a visual and kinesthetic appeal which may elicit inquiry even from those individuals who never intend to use the sand tray apparatus. My favorite office arrangement, shown in chapter 1, is spacious and provides multiple choices of sand color and textures. A full range of table heights allows the *Creator* to stand, sit comfortably in a chair or wheelchair, or to sit on the floor.

When the tools of Sandtray are readily available, *Creators* feel freer to gravitate toward them. Like Lucia in chapter 3, some children will easily shift from other forms of play into the sand. Other children may move their play in and out of the sand multiple times in a session as if testing its qualities surreptitiously. Some therapists prefer a separate area or even a separate room for their materials. I do not. To decrease the possibility of negative nonverbal communications to the *Creator*, it is critical that *Witnesses* be at ease within their own Sandtray space.

There are no set rules about the Sandtray tools and environments. I have met Sandtray workshop participants who at first only planned to collect "artistic archetypal" pieces. I have also seen a collection consisting entirely of just thirty plastic toys. A wide variety of miniatures from many different cultures and environments is best. Both the ordinary and the exceptional are equally necessary. Sandtray can offer a contained and focused place to play out and explore one's image-thinking without constricting content. If we think of the Sandtray miniatures as the vocabulary of image-thinking, a collection limited to certain types or numbers of objects would be as restricting as severely limiting the number of words in our verbal vocabulary. The goal is to offer a full range of choices to increase the flow of image expression and to avoid an externally imposed narrowing of options. In short, images that depict many types of experiences are needed in our collection of miniatures.

Some people freely dive in and begin to create with little or no instruction. This occurs most often, but not always, with children. For example, in chapter 3, Joey's "pipeway" construction was immediate. Other *Creators* are hesitant, although they are attracted to the sand or miniatures, and may require a verbal invitation, a cognitive explanation of purpose and value, or gentle encouragement.

In our society, people often need to be reassured that there is no "right way" or "wrong way" to create a sand world. Sometimes *Creators* will ask, "Is this okay?" or "May I use this figure?" or "Am I doing this right?" *Creators* can be reassured when *Witnesses* emphasize that there are no rules or restrictions on content, and that society's rules are not applicable in the tray unless the *Creator* makes it so. *Witnesses* may reply with the reminders like "This is *your* world to with do as you please," or "Whose world is this?" or my favorite with children, "Who is the boss of this world?" The *Creator* designs the rules within the sand world, *every* experience portrayed is acceptable, and the purpose of Sandtray is to serve the *Creator*, not the *Witness*.

As with Tanya in chapter 5, I invite people to set aside their everyday thinking when they enter the Sandtray. I ask *Creators* to enter the sand world with openness and curiosity, framing the tray as a place where our everyday analysis and judgment are not typically helpful. The Sandtray can be a place where we agree to suspend our external reality when we enter. I may suggest that *Creators* move into their imaginations, like improvisational actors on a stage, letting the reality of their borrowed costumes and the live audience fade into the background. Without a script, characters and themes ripen right in the moment. Through the strength of their imaginations and engagement, they attract and hold everyone's attention as they bring to life their roles within the dynamics of the emerging story. I also reassure *Creators* that I am familiar with sand journeys and that I will accompany them.

Standing by the shelves and sand trays, I may clarify that the Sandtray process is a means to tap our inner wisdom and make it more available to our everyday frame of mind. I never direct the *Creator* to "tell a story." Asking for a linear story stimulates cognitive, left-brain processing, not the image-thinking right brain. I let the *Creator* know that the sand world does not have to make sense to them or to anyone else, and that they will not be asked to explain it, nor will I analyze or judge it and tell them what it means. I convey that both the locus of control and meaning of the tray belong to the *Creator* and that we may later choose to explore the world together to see how the *Creator*'s personal meaning unfolds.

During this introduction, I am touching the sand and some miniatures on the shelves, nonverbally inviting the *Creator* to do so as well. I am likely to verbally encourage a *Creator* to follow my example. I may explain sand work as an "awake dream" or meditation. Many people have experienced a dream in which they are falling and it seems so real that they wake up with a physical startle. Sandtrays hold elements of our reality in a manner similar to dreams. In the Sandtray we are able to look at these elements of reality that are embedded in this creative experience. At other times I describe the left- and right-brain functions and the concept of image-thinking. Explaining how Sandtray techniques can assist us in accessing our right-brain images and how we may use picture thinking to improve our daily lives can evoke people's curiosity.

Depending on my reading of the intersubjective field, I may then invite the *Creator* into the sand tray by saying, "Are you comfortable putting an item, or several, in the sand to get a feel for how this works?" When someone is internally ready, such an invitation can be the beginning of a sand world. Any decline to engage is also authentically welcomed and respected. In this circumstance, I always leave an open invitation for sand work in the future.

Once the *Creator* chooses to engage in the Sandtray process, I describe what to expect. I clarify the options to use wet or dry sand, ways to make the sand wet, or to play with or without miniatures. Explaining the need for note-taking/map-making, which helps me remember and study the important details of the play, can decrease a *Creator*'s anxiety. I also point out that I will take a photograph from the perspective where I sit and make my notes, and another of the tray from the side the world was formed. *Creators* are told that they may request pictures to be taken at any time during the session and that close-ups are available, too. They are also told that they may see my notes at any time, and have a copy along with the photographs.

Despite the technical ability to provide photographs immediately, I choose to provide them later, usually at the next session. This allows time for me to simmer the experiences and look more closely at the work as I prepare the pictures. Sometimes a significant connection or question will occur to me and then the *Creator* and I may reconsider the sand world with the photographs in front of us.

As I approach the Sandtray process, I maintain an open stance. I portray my role as an assistant who is available to help the *Creator* find a desired object, get water, fire, or other needed tools. Without words, I convey a sense of safety and respect. I also indicate that I will usually start out sitting across from the *Creator*, perhaps asking to change positions during the session. I tell the *Creator* that there are a variety of ways to consider the sand world, and explain that I may make comments later in the process. If a *Witness*'s miniatures are arranged to one side of the tray, begin by seating *Creators* on that side so they can readily access the shelves. By doing this, the *Witness* remains out of the way and can observe the *Creator*'s choosing and formation process without intrusion.

In general, I request that the sand stay in or over the box while we are inside. I offer to negotiate options for out-of-the-box sand experiences, and for breaking things, should those urges need exploration. In this way I am acknowledging these feelings in a neutral manner. My concern is for the physical and emotional safety for everyone, including future sand players and the current *Creator* at a future date.

During verbal therapy, when a client makes statements such as, "I am feeling stuck," "Something is not right, but I don't know what it is," "My life has no flow," "My life feels harder, but I don't know why," or describes a general sense of disquiet, discomfort, or unease with no discernable cause, these may be opportunities to invite the use of the Sandtray apparatus. When the focus of treatment is a particular decision or issue that does not seem to be moving forward, I often encourage the client to take an unconventional look at their circumstances by using art or Sandtray. The following case describes a shift from solely verbal to multimodal treatment.

Fawn's Story: Finding Words in Images

At thirty-three years of age, Fawn came for therapy after her third psychiatric hospitalization for depression. She was taking medication for anxiety, depression, and poor sleep. Fawn reported that her depression began during her sophomore year of high school when she recognized that she had strong sexual feelings toward her female friends. These feelings were socially unacceptable in her era and community, so she "stuffed" them.

Under tremendous pressure from the conflicts between her personal and communal fields, Fawn maintained a heterosexual courtship for two years and then married. During the marriage she worked full time and bore three children. Her distress increased. When she sought medical assistance, an antidepressant was prescribed. Her marriage eventually disintegrated and a vicious custody fight ensued.

When we first met, Fawn had been separated from her husband and engaged in court battles with him for several years. Her children were thirteen, eight, and five years of age. Fawn had become the target of a barrage of personal attacks within this adversarial setting about both her sexual orientation and her mental health.

After about six months of therapy with me, Fawn attempted to describe a sense of internal conflict or distress that had been a recurring theme for her. In one session we were "stuck" in the language, as I could not grasp what she meant. She reported feeling that she just did not have the correct words to express herself. I asked her to wander over to the shelves of miniatures and see if there were any figures that would help her express herself.

Several minutes later she returned with two objects. One item was a young Native American woman, seated. After exploring and resonating with her chosen miniatures, Fawn discovered that this figure held qualities that she valued, including calmness, assurance, and a capacity for nurturing. She related these features to her strong confidence in her parenting abilities. The other miniature chosen was a two-headed dinosaur standing with open, roaring mouths and bared teeth. For Fawn, this piece embodied a sense of being disorganized and out of control, and feelings of intense rage (see figure 6.2).

Sitting in session with these images physically in front of us, we began to explore in detail the functioning of these internal experiences and how they manifested in her daily life. The power of bringing her ideas into being using three-dimensional objects became a profound reality for Fawn. She expressed a deep satisfaction in being able to elucidate obscure feelings and "thoughts that were on the edge of thought." I used the opportunity to remind her that this image process was similar to the use of the Sandtray. Within several sessions Fawn asked to construct her first sand world.

Fawn continued to create sand worlds in her sessions intermittently throughout several years of treatment. The two items chosen above became part of our personal language together. For example: later in treatment I could ask, "Where

Figure 6.2. Fawn's images

was the calm woman when the chaos started?" Or, she was able to comment, "The dino made those decisions." In this way we had a rich manner to describe and reflect on her internal processes. Eventually Fawn's life stabilized. She increased her parenting time to 50-50 physical custody, and she returned to college.

A few people will indicate an immediate attraction to world-making solely through their actions. Their physical body mode demonstrates a strong interest, while their intellectual mode denies any curiosity. Even while these people are connecting to the materials by touching the miniatures or sand, they may indicate that they deem themselves "too mature" to use this method. They may comment, "I'm too grown-up for toys," or "I see you have kid's stuff," and other statements that devalue Sandtray as an effective approach. I strive to encourage people with this view to allow experimentation with the world materials. *Being in* an experience is not the same as *thinking about* an experience. Owen began his approach to play therapy in this doubting manner.

Owen's Story: Too Old to Play

Owen, nine years of age, came to therapy as his parents' custody dispute continued to escalate. He had been interviewed countless times over many years by mediators and custody evaluators. Physical custody for Owen and his brother alternated weekly between his mom and stepdad's home and his dad and stepmom's home. He had no history of Attention-Deficit/Hyperactivity Disorder symptoms.

Owen's school reported that he disrupted his fourth-grade class daily by incessant talking, by making annoying sounds, and by engaging in "silly" behaviors. The teacher relayed that Owen did not listen and that he vied with her to be "in control" of the class. She expressed deep concern that, even though he tried to "fit in" with the other children, they considered him "strange." In both homes, Owen became increasingly hostile toward his younger brother. Whenever an adult tried to speak with him about these problems, he collapsed into tears, cutting off any chance for resolution.

On entering the playroom for his first session, Owen maintained an adult air and style of conversation while he looked at the shelves of toys for more than twenty-five minutes. I remained nearby, calmly supporting him energetically, briefly reflecting his sounds and the few words he spoke. My goal was to be present without being intrusive. Several times I observed him reach toward an object but abruptly stop himself from touching it. Eventually, Owen guardedly queried me as to when I would begin asking questions. I clarified that this was not my function, and that I was not an evaluator. I encouraged him to choose something for play. With disdainful looks at the shelves, he moved away from them, declaring, "I don't play with toys anymore!" Subsequent information from both households revealed that, indeed, Owen did not play at home either.

I assured Owen that he would not be required to play with the toys or the sand, as these items were only for those who were interested in them. I did this in an authentic, matter-of-fact manner, letting him know that what he chose to do or not do was totally up to him. His choices were acceptable to me as long as he followed the safety rules of the playroom. He then showed interest in the foam-covered fighting swords called "Encounter Bats" and the clay. He came to the brink of engagement with each of them but pulled back. As he left the session, he told me that he would play with clay "next time."

On his second visit he came in, went to the Sandtray, and designed a complex sand world with abundant detail. His major theme was "Aliens versus Humans" in a war that has been waging for "a long time." From his initial session Owen shifted his perspective to allow himself to play. This change was the beginning of many play-therapy sessions. Owen reconnected to his ability to play and he routinely used Sandtrays as his experimental laboratory for interacting in the world.

Initially, Owen's body appeared stiff. He was wound tightly both physically and emotionally. In the beginning of treatment, anytime he began to show interest in play, he squelched his own energy. A bright child, he most easily expressed his intellectual mode. Owen's access to his emotional and physical modes initially appeared quite narrow. This mode-patterning evolved over time and he became able to describe his feelings. After five months of treatment his negative school behaviors dissipated. Unfortunately, the conflict between his parents continued to escalate. Although he remained pressured and distressed for quite some time, even when in great difficulty Sandtray provided Owen a vehicle for improved self-expression.

Once a *Creator* enters the Sandtray process the *Witness's* focus is to help the *Creator* bond to and maintain a connection with the experiences that are being formed within the Sandtray. This is done through verbal and energetic holding and guiding. When *Witnesses* release any need to know about the meaning of what is being created, the *Creator* is freer to play. *Witnesses* are helpful when they are curious and interested, but should not allow their own inquisitiveness to lead. To do so would be taking the counterproductive position of pulling *Creators* out of their own experience. *Witnesses* need to be clear about whom is being served: the *Creator* not the *Witness's* own curiosity.

The Second Aspect: World Formation

During the "World Formation" the more formal duties of the *Witness* begin. In Sandtray a *Witness* strives to be fully present and to take notes. Through careful and directed attention we take in the details of how a world is being composed and the energetic modes of the *Creator* and of ourselves. *Witnesses* observe and use their own physical, intellectual, and emotional presence to monitor intersubjectivity and to document the concrete construction of the sand world.

One of our most important functions as *Witnesses* is to help *Creators* center their focus on their own Sandtray image process. *Witnesses* endeavor to focus primarily on the sand tray while keeping *Creators* within their awareness and vision. I strive to maintain harmonic resonance with the *Creator*, the sand world, and myself, allowing the *Creator* to lead. I do not ask questions at this time. To do so would nudge the *Creator* toward linear, left-brain thinking, which disrupts image flow.

For therapists trained in a relational focus, this task may prove challenging. Initiating speech with, and looking directly at, *Creators* will tend to pull them out of their own process with the Sandtray and into a person-to-person connection. Sometimes relationally trained *Witnesses* will find that they are conducting "talk therapy" over the sand tray instead of allowing the *Creator's* images to emerge and lead in the session.

Novice Sandtray *Creators* often ask to use specific objects, to add water, or to change what they had originally formed, even when these topics were addressed during the introduction. These questions offer *Witnesses* an opportunity to encourage agency, meaning the felt understanding and knowledge that one has the ability to influence their environment. At such times *Witnesses* can remind *Creators* that the sand world is under their complete control, and that no permission is needed to use the materials or adjust their Sandtray. *Witnesses* may also choose to remind *Creators* that the *Witness's* function is to assist and facilitate the process, not direct it. Dialogue in response to a *Creator's* inquiry supports the session and is not usually distracting to them.

As a *Witness*, honoring the actual space in and directly above the sand tray as the domain of the *Creator*, I do not lean or reach over nor touch miniatures in the tray. Placing pens, clipboards, cameras, or other aids in the *Creator's* space may be disruptive. If I err in this, I apologize to the *Creator* because I consider this oversight a boundary violation. Heeding *Creators'* physical relationship to the tray itself, I notice: Are they leaning back and placing items from a distance? Are they hanging on the edge, over the tray with head, arms, or body almost touching the sand? I also attend to my own responses: Am I pulled in or pushed away? These observations may become useful in later aspects of the Sandtray process.

I endeavor to observe everything. Does the *Creator* touch or move the sand first and then choose objects? Does the *Creator's* focus go first to the shelves of miniatures? Is an actual topography formed for future placement of miniatures, or does the sand form and reform as the *Creator* configures the world? I notice which pieces are most active within the tray, which are touched the most often, and what is set in the tray and never moved or touched again. I scrutinize what is being chosen and how. Are items brought one at a time or in groups? Are some items carried while another is chosen and then the original miniature put back? Are all chosen figures used? I note if there are any "accidents"—what falls, is destroyed, found, or formed by seemingly inadvertent action. How does the *Creator* respond to and manage these? I note in what position and order items are being placed within the tray and any changes afterward.

While the tangible characteristics of the construction are being recorded, I also observe the *Creator*'s moods and behaviors along with the impact of what is being formed on me. I notice and remember the *Creator*'s facial expressions, sighs, sounds, tears, bodily states, and energetic shifts as the sand world comes together. I recognize reactions in myself: Do I feel like crying or being physically ill? Am I attracted to the visual qualities that I see or am I repelled? Am I sleepy, distracted, or uninterested? Am I feeling overwhelmed by the pace of the action or the energetic charge? I seek to track and recall when these reactions occur in juxtaposition to what is being formed in the world. As demonstrated in Amy's story in chapter 2, and in Jada's in chapter 3, self-monitoring can be the key to perceive the states of the *Creator* accurately and respond in a more helpful way. The focus of note-taking is the physical sand world, but other observations may also be jotted down.

The results of a Sandtray encounter can be rich when both parties enter the experience with openness to the three modes: physical, emotional, and intellectual. If a *Witness* is focused solely on one mode, then the *Witness*'s chosen mode is most likely to override the *Creator*'s work. Alternately, when a *Witness* is significantly inhibiting a mode, the *Creator*'s process will likewise be inhibited. Either circumstance will influence the outcome of the Sandtray process. When a *Witness* provides a sense of openness to all three modes, the *Creator* receives nonverbal permission to explore with fewer of the *Witness*'s limitations.

Of course, we are only people with our own perceptions and imperfections. So, the degree with which we can provide an optimal environment for Sandtray is likely to vary. When we review Sandtray work, either our own or that of others, it is pertinent also to review the capacities of the *Witness* at the time the world was formed. The following play describes how the *Witness*'s containment of anxiety supported the *Creator*'s ability to implement fully his own image-thinking.

Scott's Story: Waiting for a Fish

Scott sought consultation to expand his knowledge of the Sandtray process as a mental-health professional. At thirty-five years of age he had obtained experiences with a variety of treatment and personal-growth modalities. Both busy professionals, we were barely able to schedule an hour to introduce him to the materials and the process.

Scott used regular dry sand for his world. He carefully examined the shelves of miniatures, first placing what I noted as a "lioness" on one side of the tray facing across to the other side. He then brought a bin of bones and teeth to the tray, choosing and placing the bones at deliberate angles. The teeth were placed next. Saying little, his silence felt comfortable, pensive, and focused as he slowly and purposefully made adjustments, and placed the remainder of his chosen objects—except for the blue and yellow plastic fish. The communication between us was subtle and nonverbal. I resonated by matching his breaths and energies, occasionally reflecting a sigh or "ummm" (see figure 6.3).

I then noticed my watch and felt startled that we had used nearly half of our allotted time. I felt my anxiety rise. I wanted Scott to have an opportunity for an internal experience of all of the "aspects" of the Sandtray session. Then I recognized that I had become invested in the outcome of this session. I became less able to hold Scott in his experience for several moments while I processed my own anxiety. My first impulse was to ask him to finish up the formation process so that we could move on. A few seconds later, I realized what I'd done by becoming less attentive to the *Creator*. Then I breathed in and fully re-engaged with Scott. I reminded myself to "trust the *Creator* and the process."

A few minutes later Scott looked up from the tray and asked, "How do I know when I am done?" I assured him that he would have a sense of completeness and suggested that he stay with his created world and perhaps scan the miniatures to evaluate if he felt done. Being back in resonance with Scott, I felt

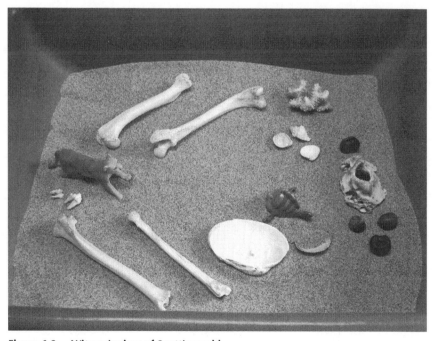

Figure 6.3.   *Witness's* view of Scott's world

authentic in encouraging his own timing. Several minutes later he brought the blue and yellow plastic fish and placed it in the tray. After several more moments of looking into his tray he informed me he knew he was done.

As a result of my own impulses and thinking that I knew best (logos), I nearly cut Scott off from the use of a highly meaningful object. The little fish, placed last, acquired pronounced significance as we progressed through the Sandtray process. Later, in the Reflecting/Directing aspect, we discovered that the fish brought qualities of youth, innocence, playfulness, and vulnerability into the sand world.

Later, the fish looked at the other items with wonder, "What's all this?" The bones and the jaguar (lioness) were ancient things, still and silent. A conversation eventually arose between the objects with these two sets of characteristics. The tray revealed how Scott can use his personal history of overcoming obstacles and difficulties with his spontaneous and playful qualities in his work of facilitating healing with the children in his professional care. This Sandtray shed light on Scott's life and budding career.

Had I remained trapped in my own intellectual mode and tried to push the Sandtray process, instead of letting it flow, Scott's valuable image-thinking meanings might have been truncated.

Scott was an easy *Creator* to witness because he demonstrated the ability to be engrossed in his "World Formation" without intellectual analysis or overt anxiety. He came with an open heart to learn these techniques as a student, not for consultation or therapy. Scott maintained an attentive mental state and readily resonated with his world. He spoke little while building the world, and then only about the process we were engaged in, not other topics.

Some *Creators* need more guidance from the *Witness* to attend to their own sand world. If a *Creator* enters a Sandtray and begins to speak of something other than what is in front of us, I may gently request that they work without words for a while, or provide some direction that helps them refocus on the tray. I may also use the "Reflecting/Directing" techniques discussed later to assist *Creators* in attending to their sand work. For example, if while forming the world Scott had stated, "These bones are ancient," I could have reflected, "The bones are ancient," perhaps then directing him, "Be with these ancient bones and see what comes to you." Again, the function of *Witnesses* is to weave the lives of *Creators* to their Sandtrays, subtly guiding them, deterring them from distractions, and redirecting their attention to the sand world here and now.

When *Creators* talk about the Sandtray during the "World Formation" aspect, the *Witness*'s response depends upon whether the *Creators* are describing or explaining. Descriptions are offered in a manner that supports resonance with, and attachment to, the Sandtray and the *Creator*'s experiences. A *Witness*'s intellectual explanation of the *Creator*'s world is discouraged.

Sandtray uses words to reveal and clarify our nonverbal image-thinking. In one respect this appears to be a paradox. Yet our words about sand worlds need to be the kind of words that invite implicit material to come forth. Dr. Siegel aptly describes two different ways to speak of experiences. "Aren't words the left brain's specialty? Yes and no. When we *explain* . . . we are relying heavily on the left. When we *describe*, rather than explain, we are bringing the experientially-rich, right side into collaboration with the word-smithing left hemisphere" (Siegel, 2010, p. 114; italics in original). As gleaned from Scott's sand world, this framework relies on experiencing and describing what is immediately in front of us.

Some practical points in taking notes come into view from Scott's session. First, notes are recorded from the *Witness*'s viewpoint despite the fact that it is upside down from the *Creator*'s perspective. Second, I use compass points to describe object placement along with the numbering system shown (see figure 6.4). Third, *Witnesses* often must use *their own* words for the objects that a *Creator* chooses. For Scott, I called his "jaguar" a "lioness." Once the *Creator*'s name or meaning for an item is stated, *Witnesses* need to shift and *only* use the *Creator*'s reference word. As previously discussed, even naming a figure is an interpretation. So, I avoid doing so. When *Witnesses* repeatedly use their own framework, ignoring that of *Creators*, *Creators* then have more difficulty sensing respect, responsiveness, and positive regard.

Playing in a *Creator*'s Sand World

At times a *Witness* is invited to play in the *Creator*'s world. Since the norm in play therapy is for therapists to engage directly in the play activities *with* children, this request is often made by children. The Sandtray apparatus is an exception to this standard because once a *Witness* physically enters a *Creator*'s sand world, the relational dynamics are profoundly changed. A *Creator*'s perception may shift to the view that the tray is "our world" instead of "my world." In the Sandtray process, *Witnesses* consistently strive to allow *Creators*' meanings and experiences to come forth. Meeting this goal becomes more complex and elusive when we move our clinical perspective from one in which the therapist's approach is primarily cognitive, to one

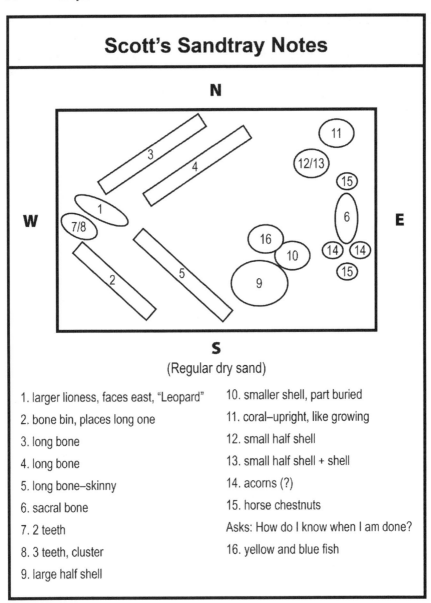

Scott's Sandtray Notes

N

W

E

S

(Regular dry sand)

1. larger lioness, faces east, "Leopard"

2. bone bin, places long one

3. long bone

4. long bone

5. long bone–skinny

6. sacral bone

7. 2 teeth

8. 3 teeth, cluster

9. large half shell

10. smaller shell, part buried

11. coral–upright, like growing

12. small half shell

13. small half shell + shell

14. acorns (?)

15. horse chestnuts

Asks: How do I know when I am done?

16. yellow and blue fish

Figure 6.4.   Scott's Sandtray notes

which includes intersubjectivity. Playing together in the physical reality of a *Creator*'s sand world is akin to drawing on another's picture, or changing a *Creator*'s clay formation. When *Witnesses* play in the Sandtray we are within the personal boundary of the *Creator*, which can be easily violated. I therefore discourage novice Sandtray *Witnesses* from playing in the sand world with *Creators*.

Therapeutic interactions can more easily become muddled when a *Witness* works directly in the sand world of a *Creator*. The difficulty of learning to track both the flow of the content and of the multidirectional nonverbal communications, while at the same time taking notes, prohibits beginners from competently joining the *Creator* in a Sandtray. I am not speaking of requests by *Creators* for help to hold something up or a request to aid them to tie items together with a string. I am referring to a request to enter into a period of unstructured play within the *Creator*'s sand world. *Witnesses* often report losing track of the play or the therapeutic focus while playing in a *Creator*'s world. *Witnesses* risk succumbing to the view that the interactions are "just play" and mistakenly believe that their play cannot be harmful.

And yet, when a child invites us, we need to find a supportive reply. During my training, my teacher suggested complying with such requests and then becoming inept at carrying out the functions directed by the *Creator*. This can be a useful response for some *Creators*. In my case, now that I am experienced in Sandtray, I am cautiously open to playing with *Creators*. I do tell them that I need to know the context and the qualities of the items that I am to direct in the sand. In effect, I need them to instruct me so that I can move the items in the tray in a way that is useful to their worldview. Particularly, if the scene is a war, I may be able to glean from the *Creator*'s instructions some history of the world and an anticipated outcome. My inquiries in these interactions are similar to those outlined in chapters 7 through 9. My fundamental stance is that the sand world belongs to the *Creator* and that I am an assistant to carry out his or her wishes. When a *Witness* makes the choice to engage in interacting with a *Creator* through touching and moving the sand and images, a *Witness* must be aware that greater responses will be evoked within him or her. This internal stimulation inside a *Witness*, in turn, impacts the harmonious resonance of intersubjective communication, often on an unconscious level, increasing the potential for a *Witness* to respond without self-awareness. *Witnesses* should be cautious.

I have found routinely playing in the sand with a *Creator* to be useful solely in a handful of cases. When I have worked in a child's Sandtray, each session was monitored weekly with a consultant. The session dynamics, including my motivations and responses, were closely examined and evaluated. The following questions were part of a detailed examination of the work:

- Why are you pulled to play in the Sandtray with this child?
- What makes you hesitate to do so?
- What are the child's developmental needs that may support your choice to engage directly in the world?
- What kind of experience is the child asking for? (For example: Is the child seeking companionable play, or competitive play? Is the child testing your stated limits using the Sandtray? Is the child trying to practice friendship skills?)
- How are boundaries being formed, maintained, and negotiated? Is the child asking to work with you in the tray with a distinguishable boundary between "sides," and how does this evolve?
- What are the risks for this child in working together with a *Witness*?
- How will you know when you have overstepped the child's boundaries?
- How will you manage the child's violation of your boundaries?
- What is the most effective way to enter this *Creator*'s play?
- What is this child forming, not only in the sand world, but between the two of you?
- How will you know when it will be appropriate to remove yourself from playing inside the tray, allowing the child to advance alone?
- How will you make the above transition? What might it mean to the child, and to you?

I routinely addressed these questions as a way to form an ongoing assessment of the appropriateness of my work. Through this intensive review, I became more confident in witnessing *Creator*'s Sandtrays.

In chapter 6, we have seen how *Witnesses* may introduce the Sandtray process and invite *Creators* to begin the aspect of "World Creation." When *Witnesses* are alert to opportunities to introduce the idea of image-thinking to *Creators*, the move from verbal therapy to Sandtray can be made smoothly. The times when *Creators* struggle to describe authentic experiences can be cues for *Witnesses* to offer a nonverbal method. As demonstrated by Scott's story, when *Creators* make a concrete form in the sand tray, much more may be revealed than what *Creators* initially had in mind while the world was constructed. Cautions for *Witnesses* who play in the sand worlds of *Creators* complete this chapter. Next, we will explore the functions and the tasks of *Witnesses* during the aspects of "Silent Reverie" and "Reflecting/Directing."

CHAPTER SEVEN

Aspects 3 and 4

Silent Reverie and Reflecting/Directing

Speech often obscures our thinking as well as our awareness of our bodily states. Silence allows us to dwell in our senses, inspirations, and the musings of our hearts. The artist and poet Kahlil Gibran reminds us that "you talk when you cease to be at peace with your thoughts" (Gibran, 1923, p. 60). Yet not all silences hold the same qualities. Silence may serve as a place in which vague ideas, feelings, and images begin to clarify. Many writers have described silence as pensive, suspicious, loving, and tense. Sandtray *Witnesses* begin by specifically cultivating a silence of acceptance, safety, and honesty, recognizing that these qualities may shift moment-to-moment, as described later in this chapter in "Sandy's Story."

Silence assists *Creators* in moving from their everyday perspective to focus on the reality of the sand world in the present moment. While *Creators* form the world, they project ideas, feelings, and sensations into the sand tray. Sandtray offers opportunities for *Creators* to explore mindfully qualities in the sand world that were previously unavailable to them. As *Creator* and *Witness* contemplate the newly built world, a focused silent period assists both of them to experience and nurture what is implicit in the sand world and the intersubjective relationship. This concentrated silence also enhances the ability of *Creators* to make connections between their more familiar experiences and those that are less known. A *Creator* can access all three modes, physical, intellectual, and emotional, and all four fields, personal, communal, archetypal, and universal.

During the "Silent Reverie" and "Reflecting/Directing" aspects, *Witnesses* facilitate a *Creator*'s attention into the sand world in a softly directed manner, while they gently invite less familiar ways of perceiving. Although a *Creator* may have thought through the world's formation, assigning explicit meanings to each item, additional implicit meanings are also present and await exploration. Lowenfeld herself reminds us that when a world is created it "is a presentation of an aspect of his [the *Creator's*] inner state" of life (Urwin and Hood Williams, 1988, p. 360). As *Witnesses* energetically join *Creators* in these silent periods, the *Creators* are able to reach a deeper state of reverie to experience the Sandtray and, through this work, their own inner selves.

Both of the aspects discussed here are accomplished with few words while the *Witness* and the *Creator* continue to sit across from one another. This positioning allows the *Witness* to monitor more easily the *Creator*'s bodily stance, facial movements, and minor sounds, facilitating harmonic resonance between them. When the *Witness* mirrors the postures and the affects of the *Creator*, it is important not to exceed the *Creator*'s level of intensity of expression. As with the two previous aspects of "Introducing the Sandtray Process" and "World Creation," questions from *Witnesses* at this time are not helpful. Although the *Witness* looks into the sand world with the *Creator*, the *Witness* always keeps the *Creator* within his or her awareness and peripheral vision.

A subtle shift of language is introduced by the *Witness* as the *Creator* finishes the formation of the sand world and begins "Silent Reverie." While the *Creator* makes the world, the *Witness* may use such terms as "*your* world" or "*your* Sandtray." Subsequently, "*the* world" or "*this* world" are suggested phrases. This minor change in viewpoint nudges the *Creator* toward greater projection. Although the *Witness* accompanies the *Creator* into the imaginal reality of the Sandtray, the *Witness* must simultaneously be grounded in the reality of the therapy session and the external world.

The Third Aspect: Silent Reverie

The aspect of "Silent Reverie" is pivotal for what is to come later in the Sandtray processing. The term *reverie* refers to a state of abstract musing or daydreaming. I use this term to indicate a state of undifferentiated biological and emotional connection with the sand world. "Silent Reverie" includes a meditative, deeply engrossed state of mind that is not primarily based in linear thinking. Silence allows the *Creator* to begin making sense of the sand world differently, perhaps by starting to reconnect to forgotten memories and unacknowledged or rejected parts of the self.

Once a *Creator* completes the "World Creation" aspect, the *Witness* asks the *Creator* to look at the Sandtray again, in silence. The *Witness* accompanies the *Creator* in doing so, noticing details anew. One goal here is to relax the intellectual mode and allow the physical and emotional modes to come forth. When the *Creator* is in this reverie state, sensations and thoughts are not being processed through routine linear pathways. Reverie provides an opportunity to perceive in less habitual ways, as though we are using a different camera lens or filter for our mind's eye. In "Silent Reverie," as when in a daydream, a person may appear to be inattentive. In reality, the *Creator* may be highly attentive to deep internal states, or may be focused on the experiences that are arising from the sand world's images.

Usually no words are spoken while the *Creator* is actually in the state of "Silent Reverie." It is only after the fact that glimpses of this state may become verbal. Reverie is based on both what is implicit between the *Creator* and the newly formed Sandtray, as well as the dynamic energies between these two and the *Witness*. A period of reverie serves to simmer and blend this mix nonverbally.

Describing "Silent Reverie" is challenging since, as compared with a photograph or a video, there is nothing visible. Vincent's example may begin to provide some clues to the depths of this aspect.

Vincent's Story: Safety in Silence

When Vincent entered treatment at age fourteen, his parents were two years into their intractable custody conflict. Mom was alienating his younger brother from their father. She had recently proposed splitting custody, moving to another state with his younger brother, and leaving Vincent with his father.

During the initial session, talking of his relationship with his mom, Vincent stated that she "leans on me." He further described being pressured to reveal his feelings and thoughts and he expressed his concern that his mom would press him to reveal what occurred in treatment. Vincent was immediately attracted to Sandtray, and seemed relieved when I assured him that it required no talking.

In the next session Vincent walked over to the sand trays, chose the top one, and began moving the sand. Silently he placed castle walls, a black dragon, and many pewter and fantasy figures. These included knights, monsters, and gargoyles. He also set a wizard, a large warrior, a small soldier, and a giant coin within the castle walls (see figure 7.1).

Vincent said nothing as he worked. I observed him to be fully absorbed in his "World Creation." I strove to join him energetically in his process and watched closely to what was occurring in the Sandtray. He worked steadily, sometimes pausing to ponder his tray, sometimes adding or changing the world after

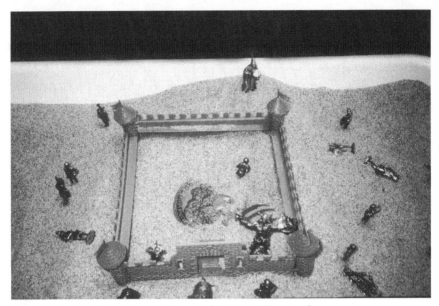

Figure 7.1.   Conflict between Athens and Sparta: *Witness's* view

examining it for a while. His breathing and actions were calm and his focus was in the world. At times Vincent looked carefully at the tray and experimented with various positions and interactions of the objects. At other times he only looked at the world, silent and meditative, appearing fully absorbed in his inner process.

In the last minutes of the session Vincent revealed that the place he formed was "ancient Greece, with conflict between Athens and Sparta. Neptune was present as the God of War." Vincent stated that "the immortals" were responsible for killing people and that the dead (indicating the figures lying down) "rise up and fight to kill living people to make them dead" and to "make them be on their side." He also said, "Neptune protects everyone's rights."

Vincent moved in and out of "Silent Reverie" during this session. His silent and intense focus appeared reflective. One way I guessed his state was through the intersubjective flow. He "felt" to me like he was in a state of reverie. Of course, I could not confirm that this was the case until later.

Over time Vincent made many silent wars in the sand while I tracked details, reflected verbally, and took notes. Little by little we developed a language for the experiences occurring inside his Sandtrays. Later in his treatment, he became able to connect the experiences in his sand world with those of his everyday life. Once he had made those links, he began to be able to share his Sandtrays, to process them verbally with me, and to learn from them as they unfolded. Eventually Vincent became able to articulate his needs, wants, and feelings clearly in his everyday life. Some helpful statements for initiating "Silent Reverie" include:

- "Take a few minutes to be with what is in this world silently."
- "Look at the Sandtray again and just be with what is here."
- "Relax your mind and just notice whatever floats by."
- "Sit with this sand world and just notice what is evoked in you."
- "Look again at this world."
- "Pay attention to anything new that you may not have noticed before."
- "Just notice the positions and relationships of what is here in the tray."
- "Allow your impressions to float by without needing to make sense of them."
- "Notice everything that is here."
- "Try not to think too much and just let your body experience what is here."
- "See if you can just be with these experiences and be aware of where they take you."
- With teens: "Spend some time hanging out with what's in the tray."

Additional statements may also be used to prolong "Silent Reverie" offering *Creators* more opportunities to form a connection with the sand world. In chapter 6, one vignette demonstrated how Scott readily moved into "Silent Reverie" solely with the invitation to observe the world. This is all that was required with Scott. The type of prompting a *Witness* uses will depend on the relationship between the *Creator*, the *Witness*, and the intersubjective flow of the moment.

Some *Creators* need much clearer guidance to refrain from speech. It is suggested that the *Witness* gently interrupt the *Creator* who talks immediately after making the world, redirecting him or her into "Silent Reverie." Some *Creators* may need to have these promptings repeated. And, for some, multiple Sandtray sessions may be required for them to develop the ability to tolerate silence.

Even though some phrasing has been offered here, it is important that *Witnesses* not push, even in their own thoughts. When needed, some further suggestions may include:

- "I am interested in those events, and we will talk about them later. Right now I'd like you to be silent with your sand world and just notice what comes to you."
- "See if you can let go of any need to speak, and sit with this world in silence."
- "It is not necessary for you to describe what the world means right now. It will be more valuable for us to just sit with this world in silence for a few minutes."
- "We will be talking later, but for the next few minutes I want you to look at the world quietly."

Statements like these are offered as trial balloons that can be sent up to see which way the wind blows. *Witnesses* need not invest in moving *Creators* in a specific direction. For some people an entire minute of silence with the world is enough.

Creators may move the sand or objects in the tray when they are in "Silent Reverie," and notes are taken of these adjustments. Once something changes, the *Witness* may find the opportunity to invite the *Creator* to look again in silence, perhaps noticing the difference the change brought to the world, and asking him or her to get a sense of how it feels *now*. This suggestion is recommended whether the adjustment is a minor turn of a single figure or a major repositioning of the sand and multiple objects. In chapter 5, the *Creator* of the judgment exercise tray worked diligently forming the sand. Though slight, each different width of the blue ring held a different meaning and, like Goldilocks, the *Creator* worked until the sand form felt "just right." Every alteration in a Sandtray impacts everything else that is there, the *Creator*, and the *Witness*. In the same way that a stone thrown into a small pond moves all the droplets of water, any change in a world sends ripples throughout the system.

The Fourth Aspect: Reflecting/Directing

The "Reflecting/Directing" aspect can be facilitated by the *Witness* so that it flows quite naturally after the *Creator* has spent time in "Silent Reverie." Maintaining sensitivity and responsiveness, the *Witness* directs the *Creator* to look at the world again, suggesting that this time the *Creator* begin to share verbally what is seen in the world and what is evoked by the world. In the "Reflecting/Directing" aspect the *Witness* withholds questions and interpretations so as to maintain the flow of a connected intersubjective experience. Questions and interpretations disrupt the sense of affect synchrony that has been established.

In this aspect the *Witness* directs the *Creator* to resonate with and verbalize fragments of experience in a nonlinear format. The *Witness* does *not* ask the *Creator* to tell a story. Such a request activates the linear left-thinking hemisphere, not the image-thinking right brain. The intention here is to encourage the *Creator* to associate freely, in the presence of the *Witness*, while both are looking into the sand world. One *Witness* function is to foster the *Creator*'s abilities to remain present with the world. The *Witness*'s authentically attentive stance and focus into the tray will become an implicit directive for the *Creator* to follow. The "Reflective/Directive" aspect entices the *Creator* to awaken to previously unknown images, presentiments, and sensations. These meanings emerge by slowing down habitual perceptual mechanisms.

Suggestions given by the *Witness* are not stated in question form. Instead, they are soft directives. The *Witness* needs to listen to his or her own voice inflection to be sure the tone does not go up at the end as questions do. Examples of directives for *Witnesses* to use to initiate the "Reflecting/Directing" aspect include:

- "Look at the world and tell me what pops into your head."
- "Now take some more time with this world and see what you notice now, and say whatever comes to you."
- "Be with this world and tell me what is here and what it brings to you."
- "Look at this world again and share anything that crosses your mind."
- "I want you to look at the Sandtray again and see what ideas come to you."

After the *Creator* answers the *Witness*'s initial prompt by sharing information from the sand world, the *Witness* continues this aspect by verbally reflecting back the words or phrases of the *Creator*. The *Witness* then directs by asking the *Creator* to stay engaged or move deeper into the newly identified experiences within the world. When the *Creator*'s next verbalization comes, this sequence repeats itself with the *Witness*'s reflection and subsequent direction. Working in this way facilitates a more profound encounter for the *Creator* with both the world and what emerges from it. The *Witness* proceeds to reflect and then direct in a careful, connected, and rhythmic manner. The "Reflecting/Directing" aspect is *not* just parroting the *Creator*'s words. When done effectively, a harmonious cadence between the *Witness* and the *Creator* arises.

After the *Creator* begins to speak, the *Witness* needs to find a space to reflect. Generally, the *Witness* uses the *Creator*'s *exact* words and phrases for the world and its contents. The *Witness* may need to interrupt the *Creator* with care, to offer reflections. At the end of the reflection the *Witness* provides directions for the *Creator* to deepen an experience right in the moment. Noting the *Creator*'s statements in writing can be helpful in maintaining accuracy. It is also acceptable to direct the *Creator* to slow down, to request that he or she honor his or her nonlinear mind and see what emerges. For example: "Please slow down a bit and spend more time with what is here." "Take your time and allow yourself to stay with this experience of (use the *Creator*'s specific name for the experience)." Other suggested directives include:

- "Be with this experience of (use the *Creator*'s words)."
- "See if you can learn more about this."
- "Notice where this resonates in your body."
- "Stay with it and see what happens."
- "Allow yourself to recognize the importance of this."
- "See if you can experience this more deeply."
- "See if you can allow yourself to value this experience more deeply."
- "Allow yourself to open up to this."
- "Let yourself be with this and remember it."

Along with these phrases, I find it useful to include the *Creator*'s words while "Reflecting/Directing." Doing so makes the reflection specific and personal, enhancing the *Creator*'s sense of being sincerely heard, felt, and valued. Doing so supports in the *Creator* a developing sense of attachment to the experiences in the sand world, and communicates to the *Creator* a message of being acknowledged and taken to heart by the *Witness*.

The *Witness* continually observes what emerges with the *Creator*, striving to stay attuned and follow whatever comes up. The "Reflecting/Directing" aspect continues with further statements. The *Witness* may link the newest experiences to those just previously shared. The *Witness* and the *Creator* are beginning to form a shared language about what is seen in the tray. The "Reflecting/Directing" aspect may be several minutes long or may become the bulk of the Sandtray session. The processes described above may be more easily grasped from the following vignettes.

Sandy's Story: Imperative to Safety

Sandy, an accomplished therapist, participated in an advance training that included exercises of the Sandtray "aspects." Each participant created a Sandtray with several miniatures. Sandy chose red sand. She then placed a large oak tree, with a Native American "storyteller" figure under it, in the northwest corner of the tray (see figure 7.2).

Figue 7.2. *Witness's* **view of a woman sitting under the tree (close-up)**

During the class I circulated to each *Creator*, demonstrating the Reflecting/ Directing technique. The therapists in the class learned the technique from their own internal experience as well as through observing my approach to each of the other participants. To provide the reader with an idea of how this two-person process unfolded, I have put my internal reactions to Sandy's work in parenthesis.

Sandy: "That's a woman sitting under the tree."

Witness: "Allow yourself to be with this woman sitting under the tree and learn more about her."

Sandy: "She looks asleep, but is really very alert." (I have no idea what this experience is for Sandy, but I feel positive about this place. It is visually pleasing to me and I like the figures she chose.)

Witness: "Get a sense of this experience of looking asleep, but really being very alert." (As we continue to resonate with this Sandtray, I stay with my own sense of this place as a peaceful and calm one, while following Sandy.)

Sandy: "She is anxious, concerned about her safety. At first I thought she was just relaxing there, but she can't relax; she feels unsafe." (The latter phrase is a firm statement. I am aware of Sandy's frown and an increased tension in both her voice and body. There is an energetic shift that feels abrupt to me, as I see no danger here. I am a bit confused, but much more alert for what may come next.)

Witness: "Try to stay with her anxious concern about her safety, her being unable to relax." (Perhaps five to eight seconds pass as Sandy's tension increases to the degree that I feel a definite sense of alarm throughout my body.)

Sandy: "Oh, she must get up and move! This place (by the tree) feels very UNSAFE!"

Sandy reaches for the figure of the woman, picks her up, then moves her to the southwest corner, a place in the tray far from the tree (see figure 7.3).

Since this interaction occurred in a teaching setting, I never investigated what this experience meant to Sandy or how it linked to her daily life. However, she assured me that the exercise assisted her in moving from a vague and theoretical understanding of the Reflecting/Directing aspect to a deeply felt and readily remembered sense of its application.

Figure 7.3. Sandy's world prior to moving the woman to the southwest corner

The Exception to Exact Reflections

The exception to using the *Creator*'s exact words in the Sandtray process occurs when the *Creator* uses the personal possessive form to reference an item in the sand world. Instead, the *Witness* then reflects with neutral language. Using Sandy's example, had she stated, "This is me sitting under the tree," my reflection could have been, "This woman is sitting under the tree." In this framework, "my mother" becomes "the mother" or "this mother." Being totally in the present means to be with "this mother" that is here, now, in the Sandtray, not "my mother," who is somewhere else. So "my house" becomes "the house" or "this house" and "my child" may become "this child." As the *Witness* responds with a non-possessive form, the *Creator* is more likely to form an expanded perspective. This technique increases the tendency of the *Creator* to project into the tray. The *Creator* may or may not change his or her own language. It is not useful to attempt to change the *Creator*'s language.

When the *Creator* names a specific person or thing, the *Creator* is bound by the limits of what he or she knows about that exact person or thing. As a *Creator*, if I am stuck with the limits and abilities of "my son," I tend to impose those on "the son" that is in my Sandtray. This decreases flexibility in my view of possibilities. It also confines the exploration of relationships within the imaginal field of the sand world. If "the son" is not "my son," a greater range of characteristics and situations may be explored than I believe to be possible if the figure is "my son." This linguistic change is another area in which the *Witness* entices the *Creator* to expand into new and less familiar ways of viewing the Sandtray. Again, the intent is to move into fresh areas without straining the authentic and safe connection between the *Witness* and the *Creator*. Despite the offered phrasings, Sandtray is a journey that is "felt" together, and cannot be scripted.

Mismatches in language, sequence, tone, and energy may cause ruptures similar to those in other forms of treatment. In Sandtray these breaks can often be repaired immediately by the *Witness* re-repeating the *Creator*'s exact words and tone in sequence, while striving for harmonious energetic resonance.

No set rule exists as to when to move from one aspect to another. This is mainly determined by the intersubjective flow. The "Reflecting/Directing" aspect will often end naturally when the *Creator* stops providing statements. When the *Witness* wants to finish or slow this flow and go on to another aspect of the Sandtray process, the *Witness* stops making "Reflecting/Directing" statements. The *Witness* may cue the *Creator* nonverbally by looking up from the world to look directly at the *Creator* more frequently. When the *Witness* attempts these techniques, and the *Creator* continues to speak, then the *Witness* needs to rejoin the *Creator* by continuing the "Reflecting/Directing" aspect. Some experienced world *Creators* have asked the *Witness* to cue them to move on. For example, a *Creator* may ask in advance to limit the formation of the world to fifteen minutes. Another possibility would be to agree that during a protracted "Reflecting/Directing" the *Witness* may directly ask, "Do you want to have time to go inside the world today?"

Let's consider Natalie's story, which provides a more elaborate example of the "Reflecting/Directing" aspect.

Natalie's Story: Volcano Power

Natalie, fifty-eight years of age, came for a Sandtray consultation when we had worked intermittently together for nearly a decade. She requested a double session, as many external events were changing in her life. Natalie was divorced, worked full time, and had adult children living away from home. Accomplished in Sandtray herself, she recognized a sense of feeling overwhelmed by several recent deaths within her circle of friends. Natalie also stated she was aware that the anniversary of her father's death was in two weeks. At the beginning of this session she was very talkative, moving to the sand trays only after sharing her sense of loss verbally.

Natalie asked for water, adding some right away. She began moving all the sand with scoops, shovels, and her hands. Initially she pulled the sand together in a large pile. Then she added more water, mixed it in, and spent fifteen minutes creating a variety of sand forms. Then she formed a large mountain in the center. She grabbed sand from the top and let it fall like rain all over the world, leaving a crater in the center. Later she told me that this action was the "volcano spewing its stuff." Next, Natalie reshaped the volcano. She then formed the sand to surround the volcano with blue in all but one section. It appeared to be an island with a small land bridge.

When Natalie began to add objects, she started by placing the rocks in the caldera. She then carefully placed sharp rocks going down one side of the volcano. A woman in a hammock was placed next on the only piece of land connected to the volcano. Next, fire was placed near the mountain's crown. Then she placed hearts, followed by the other items. One of the last figures placed was a woman in a boat filled with fruits and vegetables.

Natalie: "The volcano is erupting."

Witness: "Let yourself stay with that volcano erupting and see what comes."

Natalie: "It is flowing down one side and into the ocean (the sharp rock area), yet the fire wall is all the way around."

Witness: Be with its flowing down one side as you notice the fire wall all the way around."

Natalie: "The lava is flowing but it is only going into the ocean. The volcano is alive and active, but it is not damaging anyone, or the trees, or life."

Witness: "Continue to stay with this volcano that is alive and active, but is not damaging anyone or anything."

Natalie: "Well, it doesn't appear to be damaging anything, but some things under the water have to be killed." (Note: As she becomes more deeply connected to the sand world, a shift in Natalie's awareness is occurring.)

Witness: "So allow yourself to take in that some things under the water will be killed."

Natalie: "It's changing the ocean (pause), restructuring that part of the ocean (pause), but the volcano doesn't see it."

Witness: "So take in this change, restructuring, that the volcano does not see."

Natalie: "Nature (pause), like a natural wildfire (pause), it creates a balance."

Witness: "Breathe in and embrace this sense of balance."

Natalie: "Eruption is an important function. The lava may be developing another smaller island that will create new forms of life and habitat, even under the water."

Witness: "Remember knowing how this eruption is an important function, and that it may create new life and habitat" (see figures 7.4, 7.5).

To provide further perspective on Natalie's work, a summary follows. Later in this session, Natalie filled in a sand bridge from the volcano to the land mass behind the woman in the fruit boat. She discovered that the woman in the hammock wanted to "get away from it all" (the volcano experience) but couldn't. We noticed how Natalie had placed this woman reclining on the only part of sand that was connected to the volcano when the world was first formed. Natalie then stated, "The natural flow cannot be escaped." We learned that the woman in the boat is the wise sage who knows and is aware of all that is occurring in the world. She goes about her business in a calm

Figure 7.4. Natalie's view of her volcano world

Figure 7.5. *Witness's* view

manner. This boat woman is planning to go to harvest apples (northwest corner) and take her nurturing elements to the woman in the hammock. Part of Natalie's treatment plan was to increase her awareness of when she exhibited characteristics of each of these two women in her everyday life.

Although we briefly went on to explore this world with the other aspects, Natalie reported to me that the "Reflecting/Directing" portion of the session was very meaningful to her. She believed that what occurred subsequently during the session could not have happened without the foundation of the "Reflecting/Directing" aspect.

Natalie's example provides instruction on matching and sequencing a *Creator*'s language. What, when, and how statements are offered cannot be known by either party in advance. The aliveness of the interaction determines the words that emerge. My relationship with Natalie cued me as to when it might be more valuable to ask her to "breathe in" an experience versus "observe" or "remember." *Witnesses* can practice recognizing the qualities of the "Silent Reverie" and "Reflecting/Directing" aspects. They can learn both the practical and implicit ways to support a *Creator*'s abilities to become more attuned to their own sand worlds.

I have established in this chapter the significance of a resonating silence in the aspects of "Silent Reverie" and "Reflecting/Directing." *Witnesses* hold *Creators* in "Silent Reverie" to deepen their personal sense of the sand world's meanings. The "Reflecting/Directing" technique illustrates another way *Witnesses* facilitate exploration of the Sandtray. This aspect is a skilled weaving of words among the silence. With gentle prompts, *Witnesses* encourage nonlinear verbalizations of experiences as they float by the *Creators'* awareness. Statements have been suggested and vignettes offered to demonstrate the implementation of these Sandtray methods, emphasizing that preconceived scripting is discouraged in this process. Once again, we see how intersubjectivity functions as the basis for interactions between the *Creator* and the *Witness*.

CHAPTER EIGHT

Aspects 5 and 6

Entering into the World and Exploring from Inside the World

Sandtray *Creators* play when they create a Sandtray, look at it closely, and then adjust or move the sand and the objects. *Creators* become deeply involved with the Sandtray images, using their intellectual, physical, and emotional modes. As *Creators* move the sand and the objects, they are dwelling in these images and energies, integrating them, first nonverbally. The act of forming a Sandtray, and following one's inner promptings to arrange the world in a manner that seems "just right," begins a transformative process made possible by integrating the *Creator's* image thinking, bodily sensations, and his or her everyday consciousness. Sand-world-making fulfills the counsel from Jungian analyst Marion Woodman: "If you take the image and dance it, sing it, paint it, write a poem about it, the image is integrated into your life, into your body. If you don't do anything to integrate it, the energy is lost. And, the transformation that is possible through that energy doesn't happen" (Woodman, 1994). Using Sandtray combines many senses and levels of meanings within the same moment, affording greater opportunity for change.

Thus far in the Sandtray process a *Creator* has been encouraged to form a world, to sit in "Silent Reverie," and to enrich his or her connection to the experiences that the tray contains by "Reflecting/Directing" with a *Witness*. This chapter explains the aspects of "Entering into the World" and "Exploring from Inside the World." Further imaginative perspectives are stimulated when *Witnesses* invite new subtle changes in point of view that cue *Creators* to project more readily into the sand world.

The Fifth Aspect: Entering into the Sand World

To initiate the "Entering into" aspect, the *Witness* encourages a shift to exploring the experiences in the sand world from the context of being within it rather than looking at it and talking about it from the outside. This adjustment in perspective assists the *Creator* in discovery into the sand world in yet another manner. Together the *Witness* and the *Creator* explore present experience from the vantage point of being *inside* the world, as if it were real, and not imagined. The *Witness* may have gleaned some understanding of the world from the previous aspects, yet *Witnesses* must not make assumptions. It is true that "nature has designed our brain and mind so that we can directly intuit others' possible intentions," yet until the *Witness*'s guesses are acknowledged by the *Creator*, they are not addressed as facts (Stern, 2004, p. 96). Names of miniatures, depicted events and places, or relationships between items will only be definitive if the *Creator* has stated the meaning. As previously discussed, the *Witness* continues to refer to the world and its contents in neutral and/or third-person language.

"Pretending" is a means to relax the *Creator*'s linear thinking and allow implicit material to surface more readily. This mindset is facilitated by the nonverbal communications of the *Witness* who maintains his or her own connections to the imaginative qualities of the sand world. However, no matter how much one "pretends," the physical, intellectual, and emotional events, with their associated explicit and implicit memories, portrayed in the Sandtray, are authentically experienced. This is one reason that the Sandtray process can help bring about profound change in a person's views and, therefore, actions.

The *Witness* initiates the perceptual shift of moving into the world by looking up out of the tray at the *Creator* and requesting permission to move from across the tray to a position next to the *Creator*, usually sitting but occasionally standing. Most often this happens during a pause or when a sense of winding down of the previous aspect occurs. Once this move is made, the *Witness* actually sees the sand tray from the same position as the *Creator* for the first time. It is important for the *Witness* to request a few minutes to view the world in silence. An invitation to join the *Witness* in this second reverie gives the *Creator* another opportunity to delve into the sand world.

The *Witness* then asks to be taken into the sand world by the *Creator*. Suggestions to begin this aspect include:

- "Will you take me inside this world?"
- "Let's use our imagination to become tiny and go inside this world and see what is here."

- "Let's go into this world as if it were real. Where would you like to start?"
- "Pretend I came from another planet and need to know everything about this place."
- "Let's look at this world and pretend that you and I can go inside it as if we were small."
- "Now we will move our awareness inside the Sandtray, experiencing it as if it were real."

Creators may need time to adjust to such a request. If they are uncertain where to start, the *Witness* may suggest that they enter into the area of the tray that feels the most comfortable. If words were provided by the *Creator* in the previous aspect, referring to them again may be effective. For example, the *Witness* may suggest: "When you first used words here you began with (use the *Creator*'s words). Does it feel right to start here again?" Use the precise word or phrase which the *Creator* actually provided. Consult your notes to insure accuracy. From this point on in the Sandtray process, *Witnesses* may refer to their notes, but note-taking is discouraged. A more productive focus is on the intersubjective field and being with the *Creator*. The *Witness* assures the *Creator* that the *Witness* will be entering the experiences inside the sand world with him or her. These perceptual shifts are subtle, yet significant. The *Witness* needs to allow the *Creator* time to consider any invitation or request, answering questions or concerns as they arise.

The Sandtray journey is an unrehearsed one. These explorations are co-created and the outcome is determined by both parties. The *Witness* accompanies the *Creator* wholeheartedly into the world without pushing or being invested in the outcome. The *Witness* continuously monitors the sense of attunement within the dyad. This connection is facilitated by the *Witness*'s focusing his or her energy into the sand tray itself. The *Witness* simultaneously maintains contact by keeping the *Creator* within view. One value of exploring from inside the world with a *Witness* is highlighted in Janet's story.

Janet's Story: Becoming Tangible

Janet, a confident forty-two-year-old businesswoman, was a survivor of early childhood sexual abuse. She became widowed through a car accident when her only son was a toddler. Now that her son was an adult, Janet felt free to focus on her own needs. She had received several years of treatment for Posttraumatic Stress Disorder (PTSD) and had a history of panic attacks well managed without medication. Janet initiated treatment with the request for Sandtray sessions, having been encouraged to do so by a friend.

Janet came to therapy stating that she was "in turmoil" over choosing one of two men she was dating, if either. After her marriage to a violent drug abuser, she avoided intimate relationships for nearly ten years. She stated that she had only vague memories, tied to her grandparent's home, of her childhood abuse. She shared that what felt clearer to her at times was a sense of terror.

During early treatment sessions Janet demonstrated difficulties allowing herself to be fully present with me or the worlds she created. A bright woman, she readily talked about the world, rather than being present within the experiences that she formed there. I sensed that Janet did not trust me or the Sandtray process, in part by her reluctance to enter the experiences that she, herself, created.

In her fourth session, Janet placed a variety of items that she later called "just things I like." She initially claimed that she chose these objects without reason, and that they had nothing to do with her life. I proceeded with the Sandtray techniques presented in this book, not knowing then that this world had been created to "test" me and the Sandtray work. Later we discovered how these objects were, indeed, connected to Janet's life. This tray assisted her in forming the question, "How do I enter a relationship with a man and still keep myself?" At the end of this session, Janet told me that she had "thoughtlessly" placed items in the tray to try to "trick" or "test" me. We acknowledged together how the objects that enter the sand world must somehow carry a link to the *Creator*'s life.

Several sessions later, and in her next Sandtray, Janet formed the world shown (see figure 8.1). She placed the items in the following order: (1) garbage

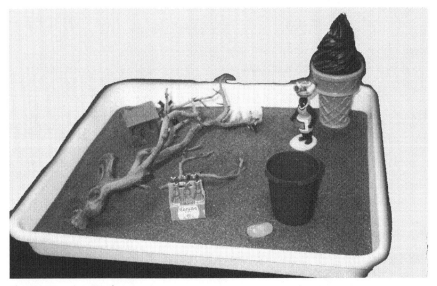

Figure 8.1. Janet's view

can with lid on top (empty); (2) black woman with fruit basket on her head; (3) St. Kitts house; (4) windmill, with her stating, "It makes a pretty sound when it turns;" (5) large branch; (6) six-pack of Corona beer; (7) giant ice cream cone; (8) wolf in sheep's clothing; (9) large pink quartz.

During the Reflective/Directive aspect Janet's statements included: (1) referring to the can and the rose quartz, "Throw the kid away in the garbage can, [pause] but something beautiful is nearby;" (2) gesturing to the woman with the fruit basket and the windmill, "It's a third-world country, foreign;" (3) pointing to the branch, "Desolate;" (4) staring at the wolf in sheep's clothing, "The bad wolf already killed a sheep [pause]. The sheep fence. [pause] The sheep had bells, [pause] something scary about that."

Janet made several other descriptive statements which I also reflected, including: "This is not a safe world, even though it says, 'Safe-T-Cup' on the ice cream. Don't believe everything you read! It is a foreign and desolate thing. Foreign could be good, but? There is no place to go for help. Only the quartz is beauty. This is a place about hypervigilance; be guarded; it's unsafe. You have to walk there but you have to deny who you are. To be here is a terrible world. I am living in a garbage can."

Then we began to explore the world from within. This is only a piece of the work Janet did that day:

> Janet: "I'm in a desert, but not really. The woman has fruit and looks domestic, not mean."
>
> *Witness:* "Stay with her. See what comes."
>
> Janet: "She's out of place." (No response to my reflection/follow-ups to this statement.)
>
> *Witness:* (Trying another approach.) "What else can she see?"
>
> Janet: "She sees the wolf but has no fear. He is not a threat to her. He is a threat to me—in the garbage can." (Notice the change from third to first person. At this point the can is still empty, though clearly she feels like she is inside.)
>
> *Witness:* "What's really in the garbage can?" (Pause) "Take a look."
>
> Janet: (Unscrews the lid and looks in.) "Nothing."
>
> *Witness:* "Does something belong here?"
>
> Janet: Gets up, scans the shelves, returns with a figure, and lays it in the garbage can, leaving the lid off. It is a small dark-skinned girl in a red dress. Together we look at her in silence (see figure 8.2).
>
> *Witness:* "How old is she?"
>
> Janet: "Five or six. Her mom can't see her now, because she's in the garbage can. The wolf knows she is there. Mom doesn't know the wolf is bad."

Figure 8.2. The real girl comes into the world

Witness: "Stay with her there in the garbage can."

Janet: "She is helpless. The wolf is going to get me. (Notice her shift from talking about the girl, to being the girl.) I feel like an animal trapped in a cage, waiting to be killed. I can only see inside the garbage can. I can hear everything. I can't see or talk to anyone [pause]. I listen to the wolf coming, [pause] footsteps. He will knock over the garbage can to get her. (Notice her shift back again to the talking about, third-person perspective.) When she's older she will see the quartz."

Witness: To provide distance from the intensity of the trauma she just expressed, and because she just spoke of it, I directed Janet to experience the beautiful qualities of the quartz. This is primarily silent. Janet briefly describes that the quartz provides a "grounded and nurturing contact" for her.

Janet: (Redirects us to the wolf.) Referring to an evil character from the Star Wars saga, she says, "He has a 'Darth Vader' voice. He wants to take me over so that I don't exist. He says forcefully, 'I came to destroy you. You must make an alliance with this monster, and become a zombie.' Get him away! Mom hears none of this. She will only hear what is pleasant and secure. (*Witness* is in synchrony with Janet, making encouraging sounds.) No one acknowledges the danger except the quartz."

As we begin to wind down this aspect, we notice how the girl in the garbage can started without any form, then became more real when the figure was added. Once the girl figure came into the world, the girl (and Janet) found a voice for her. Among other observations was that the quartz being placed closest to Janet, between her and the garbage can, functioned like a buffer. As we talked more about the experiences in the tray from the outside, Janet turned to me and said, "I could never have gone in there alone; it's too scary. I knew you were with me."

This was the first tray in which Janet was able to enter the perspective of being inside the world. In future work she remained more comfortable talking about the worlds, yet she had gained the flexibility also to explore the view from inside the tray at times.

Sometimes *Creators* are unable to enter the frame of reference, demonstrated above, of being inside the world. If the request to engage the sand world together is not taken up, there are no "tricks" to use. The *Witness* accepts the *Creator*'s direction and continues to examine the world from the perspective of looking at the world, perhaps talking about what is there, or sitting together in silence. The Sandtray process is dynamic and the *Creator* may shift back and forth from the "looking at" and the "being inside" perspectives, as Janet did. These two views provide different information. The *Witness* tracks when the *Creator* initiates each perceptual shift, following and supporting the flow of exploration.

The Sixth Aspect: Exploring from Inside the Sand World

Once the dyad moves to the "Inside the Sand World" perspective, the *Witness* may facilitate the Sandtray process using tactful and tentative questions. As illustrated with Janet, *Witnesses* will find the use of "Reflecting/Directing" techniques in conjunction with inquiries beneficial. In this sixth aspect, continuing the connection to the flow of implicit thinking is important. Since questions tend to pull for the logical, linear-thinking aspect of our minds, the *Witness* avoids a series of questions. Instead, the energetic focus remains inside the world and many periods of silence may fill the spaces between the words. The *Witness* is facilitating a rhythmical dialogue between the *Creator* and the world as well as between the *Creator* and the *Witness*.

Most questions are designed to solicit further descriptions of an object, relationships, or experiences within the world. The *Witness*, without contradiction, accepts any description that the *Creator* provides. For example, if as a *Witness* you see a "horse," and the *Creator* calls it an "ox," or you see a "princess" and are told it is a "soldier," use the *Creator*'s word and mindset for the object. The *Witness* is not teaching consensual reality here, but is learning the *Creator*'s idiosyncratic frame of reference.

The *Witness*'s desire for information, or to facilitate a solution, should not occur at the cost of disrupting relational harmony. With practice, the *Witness*'s self-monitoring skills increase and the *Witness* becomes better able to attend to his or her own internal states. A mindful *Witness* will be alerted to tendencies such as becoming too interfering in the *Creator*'s Sandtray process or being overly invested in the outcome within the tray. The following story highlights how a *Witness* may become overly controlling and committed to a specific outcome for the *Creator*.

Liam and Vicky: Pulling versus Accompanying

During a Sandtray "Essential Principals" workshop that I offered, Liam was filling the *Witness*'s role for Vicky, the *Creator*. A therapist with excellent training in solution-focused treatments, Liam stayed in resonance with Vicky until they came to the "Exploring Inside" aspect. He then became excited, believing that he could see a solution in the sand world for the dilemma of the female figure which Vicky and he had been learning about.

In the sand world, the woman began crossing the bridge. She was aware of the "skeletons" and "evil ones" down in the "river." They were trying to impede her progress, but she had overcome their influences so far. She was close to accomplishing her goal and advancing in her life despite their efforts to block her. The woman knew that the treasure chest was nearby, yet was unable to look at it. She felt stuck on her journey and peered over the edge of the bridge and looked into the river. She began to talk about the obstacles that these figures in the "river" created for her (see figure 8.3).

At this point Liam began to ask Vicky (as the female figure) to move back from the edge of the bridge, to look at the treasure chest instead, and then to move toward it. Vicky didn't move the woman. She was unable to comply with Liam's direction and be true to herself. She did not "feel" that it was correct to move away. Subsequently, Liam asked Vicky to place the woman in front of the treasure chest to "see what would happen." She did so yet stated that she felt pushed by the flood of questions and directions Liam was giving her. The move to the treasure chest "didn't feel right," so she put the woman back on the edge of bridge where she had been. Vicky then sat back from her Sandtray and pulled herself further out of connection with the experiences in the world.

A bit later, Vicky agreed that I could lead her back into the world. We began by summarizing what had occurred until the figure of the woman reached the

Figure 8.3.   Being on the bridge, looking into the river: Vicky's view

side of the bridge. I then asked Vicky to reenter this female figure using her imagination. Rather than asking the figure to leave this place, I then asked Vicky to learn more about being in this place of looking into the river from the side of the bridge.

After further work, utilizing Sandtray techniques from the perspective of where the woman is vs. where she needs to be, Vicky began to illuminate relationships between the woman and the forces impeding her. Eventually she became authentically able to turn the figure away from the edge of the bridge. The woman could look away from the river and see the treasure chest, but not move toward it yet. The physical images portrayed in the tray reflected Vicky's actual internal state at that moment. She truly shifted her intense sense of being "stuck" in the engagement with historical and familial forces, to breaking from them, and looking ahead to her own goals.

Vicky did the work that she could do that day. To have complied with the *Witness*'s original requests may have led to an apparent resolution during the session, but it would have been only external compliance to the *Witness*'s directives. Liam "lost" Vicky, in terms of holding their relational synchrony, when he shifted to "thinking" a solution for her and trying to manipulate her toward it. Once Vicky, through the figure, actually experienced the pull within her of the scary, evil figures, she also sensed how to move away from them from an internally felt place. Vicky created a real change in her own experience, albeit not the dramatic resolution Liam sought for her.

Once Liam recognized the value of helping Vicky stay present inside the world, he also admitted that considerable effort would be required for him to change his habitual approach to therapy. More effective statements that Liam might have chosen to keep Vicky's perspective inside the world are:

- "I am wondering what feelings come to this woman as she looks at the 'evil ones' and the 'skeletons' (pause); let yourself stay with that until you really know it."
- "How does she experience them, and they her?"
- "Tell me how, in her body, she experiences the feeling of being 'stuck' in this place." After a pause, "Let yourself become more aware of these feelings."
- "Notice the connection between her 'feeling stuck' and the 'evil ones.'" After a pause, "Please tell me how they influence her to stay here near them."

Both Vicky and Liam experienced the difference between processing the sand world intellectually vs. processing it experientially. The *Witness's* task is to help the *Creator* be mindfully present with, and learn from, what is presented in the sand world. It is not to move the *Creator* away from what is real, even if the experiences in the world are uncomfortable. By allowing herself to profoundly experience facing "the evil ones," Vicky illuminated the internal processes that sustained what she called "the pull of control" by them. From that awareness, she began to gain an internal sense of how to change her own distressing pattern of engagement with them. The *Witness* can learn to be patient, trusting that the *Creator's* most pressing concerns will repeatedly return until they have been resolved or are no longer distressing.

A Living World

As the aspect of "Exploring from Inside" proceeds, the *Witness* continues to encourage the *Creator* to describe in depth what is seen, experienced, or sensed within the sand world. When the *Creator*'s meaning is unclear, the *Witness* inquires carefully about the experiences, working toward a full sharing and understanding that resonates within each individual and between *Witness* and *Creator*.

The *Witness* continuously monitors relational harmony and does not use gestures that put hands, body, or equipment in or over the sand tray's space. The examples offered throughout this chapter demonstrate the type of statements that illustrate how to best facilitate this aspect. There are often many silent pauses as the world is explored. During these silences the experiences from the world are being absorbed by the *Creator* and the *Witness*. The dialogue is one of shared experience, not just words.

Throughout the "Exploring from Inside" aspect, the *Witness* notices the modes and fields that are most accessible for a *Creator*. The *Witness* may gently ask about the less obvious modes and fields, being careful not to strain the *Creator*'s tolerance level. In practice, this exchange often takes place as a teaching dialogue that includes both directives and questions from either participant. The *Creator* teaches the *Witness* the experiences in the sand world. The *Witness* assists by clarifying the details so acutely that the *Creator* expands his or her own understanding. This intense focus provides an amplification of experiences, allowing for a deeper connection to and a greater awareness of them. For example, in Sandy's tray consisting of the tree and the Native American "storyteller" in chapter 7, after the woman was moved to the southwest corner, the "Exploring from Inside" aspect could have included an exchange like this:

Sandy's Exploration from Inside the World

   Witness: "Let's learn some more about this woman."
   Sandy: "Okay."
   Witness: "We know she is in a more comfortable place here. Let yourself move into her, to become her in your imagination. Tell me what you become aware of."
   Sandy: "I am sitting. I am bundled up, although it is not cold here."
   Witness: "Stay with the sense of being bundled up, although it is not cold here."
   Sandy: "My blankets help me feel warm, comfortable, and safe."
   Witness: "Stay with feeling warm, comfortable, and safe as you remember a while ago when you felt compelled to move." (Here the *Witness* is seeing if the *Creator* has the ability to touch an uncomfortable experience while grounded in a safe place.)
   Sandy: "I had to move. The tree or something in it was really a threat."

Witness: (Picking up on Sandy's use of the past tense, clarifies) "So it *was* a threat, but is not now?"

Sandy: "Yes, it was. I am safe now that I am not close to the tree. I am still wary of it."

Witness: "Stay with the sense that the tree is not a threat to you here. How does your body feel now as you look across at the tree?" (The *Witness* is continuing to ground Sandy in her sense of safety as Sandy is asked to stretch from the emotional mode to the physical mode. The *Witness* is essentially inquiring about the availability of Sandy's physical mode.)

As illustrated above, the *Witness* and the *Creator* immerse themselves in the object's thoughts, feelings, sensations (taste, touch, smell, vision, hearing, and internal and external bodily awareness), knowledge, dreams, intuitions, hopes, and other experiences that emerge. The *Witness* may ask, "What does (the item) look like (focus on the physical properties such as color, shape, pose, size, etc.)?" "What is it doing (use verbs such as sitting, standing, jumping, running, being alone, searching, etc.)?" The *Witness* may also ask about what a figure senses regarding the history or future of the world and that figure's place in it. Not only do the objects that are placed in the tray have these potentials, but also the sand forms and spaces or "empty" areas may assist in our learning. As an example, consider how a *Witness* might explore the blue circle surrounding the black sand mound in the "Exercise in Judgment" in chapter 5.

The *Witness* may guide the *Creator*'s awareness into the sand world by asking the *Creator* to engage mentally with an object or figure and experience it from its own point of view as if it were alive and/or aware. Sandy's, Janet's, and Vicky's worlds demonstrate these techniques. The Sandtray process is similar to that of Jungian active imagination. The *Creator* is enticed to bring the fullness of his or her active consciousness into the dramatic aliveness of the Sandtray's reality. Barbara Hannah, a Jungian analyst, states that this type of creativity "gives us the opportunity of opening negotiations, and in time, coming to terms, with [the] forces or figures in the unconscious. . . . It differs from the dream, for we have no control over our behavior in the latter" (Hannah, 2001, p. 16). Unlike Jungian active imagination, which is practiced alone, Sandtray works both to assist and to protect the *Creator*. Sandtray exploration is also under the control of the participants. At times the *Creator* and the *Witness* may be in a deep resonant link of imagination, but they are not unaware of the external environment. In this Sandtray technique the *Creator* and the *Witness* journey together. Their bond holds the promise of what is yet to be discovered in the sand world. This joining provides a safe foundation for the *Creator*, decreasing fears of being engulfed by the unknown.

The Language of Discovery and Exploration

As the Sandtray work continues, use the guiding framework of the energetic modes and the contextual fields discussed in chapter 4. This approach will open exponential possibilities for exploration into every sand world. Identify and explore the modes and fields most easily accessible to the *Creator* first. After this step has been accomplished, seek to learn about the others.

During a Sandtray session, the *Creator* may point to an object and say something like, "This one is trying to figure out what to do." When the *Creator* has not yet identified the figure, the *Witness* has more difficulty talking about the object. A *Witness*'s response to this type of *Creator* statement may be, "Tell me more about this one." When the *Creator* still does not label an item, the *Witness* may request information in a neutral and objective manner, without naming the item. In this process, the *Witness* will likely observe and sense where the *Creator*'s gaze and energies are focused in the sand world. If no name is given to an area or item, the *Witness* may attempt several techniques at an appropriate time. In "Language Box A," any of the statements in upper left section may be paired with any of the statements in the right portion.

"Tell me about"	"the one in the (corner, center, on the mound, etc.)."
"Let's spend a minute with"	"the item in the blue space."
"I am wondering about"	"the figure that seems to be sitting down."
"Let's learn more about"	"the green one that may be lying down."
"Let's get to know more about"	"the one closest to us."

"Teach me about the characteristics that . . . brings into this world."
"Please describe . . . to me."
"Let's be with . . . a bit longer and see what we can learn."

Language Box A

Those phrases in the upper-right section may also be interjected into the three sample sentences in the lower segment. Phrases structured in this manner may be mixed and matched as ways to enter into the living realities within the sand world. These statements are only examples. The precise details you choose will arise from the world that confronts you. The *Witness's* descriptions are always suggested in a very tentative tone, as even the color of an object may be a matter of opinion. Once knowledge of the figure is shared, the *Witness* may ask, "Do you have a name for this figure?" or "What do you call this?"

Further examination within the sand world becomes easier once an item is labeled. The *Witness* can more readily ask about other objects, also not yet designated, by describing their relationship to the named one.

"Language Box B" offers these phrasing samples. Beginning with the upper-left section, the statements may be mixed with the ones in the right or bottom portions. These phrases provide the Sandtray *Witness* an initial framework for using these techniques.

The *Witness's* tasks include staying attuned to the *Creator* to assure that the new information arises in a manner that is natural for the *Creator*. For the best flow, the *Witness* moves with the *Creator* from one object or area to

"Tell me about"	"the one to the (left, right) of the (named item)."
"Now let's see about"	"the (shorter, taller, bigger, smaller) one."
"Let's learn about"	"the one (above, below) the (named object)."
"What's it like for"	"the one to the (side of, inside, outside) of it."
"Now let's explore"	"the (closer, farther) one."
"What do you know about"	"the one (named item) is looking at."
	"the one (next to, on top of, under) the (named item)."
	"the one looking at the (named figure)."
	"the one that seems to be (hidden, exposed, peeking out from) the (named object)."

Language Box B

another only after acknowledging what has emerged first. Suggested invitations to assist the *Creator* in broadening his or her focus include: "See if you can sense what feels connected to this area." "What does the man see in this world?" "What does the fairy know of the rest of this world?" The *Witness*'s goal is to assist the *Creator* in deepening both verbal and nonverbal connections to the sand world. The *Creator* is best served by learning thoroughly about one item or relationship, rather than jumping haphazardly from one area to another solely for the purpose of identifying objects. The latter does not easily bring the *Creator* to an in-depth association with his or her own work.

When the *Witness* maintains a perspective that is in the present and inside the sand world, as if it were real and alive, this energy leads the *Creator* into the world as well. The shared journey into the sand tray helps hold this view for both parties. Inquiries that support this frame of reference are numerous. In an actual Sandtray session, such questions as those below and reflective/directive statements by the *Witness* will be intertwined with silence and comments by the *Creator*. For example:

- "What does the woman see?"
- "Tell me about what is there."
- "Where is the dog going?"
- "What does it expect will happen next?"
- "Who is the man facing?"
- "Does he know who she is?"
- "Does he want to communicate something to her?"
- "How is he feeling about how she may respond?"
- "Can you guess his internal bodily state?"

When the *Witness* observes a shift in the relationships between objects in the world, the energy or mood within the *Creator* or within the dyad's harmonic resonance, the *Witness* may consider asking about this change. Here are examples of how the *Witness* may focus on a change:

- "Was (the named object) always in this place?"
- "Has this been here the whole time?"
- "Where was it before it came here? (pause) How was it different when (use a neutral or reflective description of the previous position)?"
- "Do you recall what occurred that it needed to move or change?"
- "Do you remember what it was like before?"
- "How is it different now?"

As the Sandtray process unfolds, it may become evident that objects need to be moved or changed. The *Creator* may realize that what is concretely visible in the tray is not an accurate depiction of his or her actual experience. Both Sandy's tray in chapter 7 and Renee's tray in chapter 2 illustrate how these changes may evolve during a Sandtray session. Some phrases a *Witness* may use to indicate to the *Creator* that change is acceptable are:

- "I am wondering what (the named object) needs now."
- "Think about a way to fulfill this need."
- "Is there anything here (indicating the collection of miniatures) that may assist them?"
- "I am curious to know where the (named object) would prefer to be now."
- "Please show in the Sandtray the changes that you are now describing to me in words."
- "Would you feel more comfortable if you found another figure or object that better depicts what you are describing to me now?"

The last two suggestions are most useful after the *Creator* and the *Witness* acknowledge together a shift of meaning or position. In another instance, if the *Witness* strongly senses the *Creator*'s need for change while the *Creator* seems hesitant to act, the *Witness* may gently, yet more directly, invite such a change. Sometimes *Creators* need to be reminded that the sand world is theirs to change.

On occasion, a conversation between figures or objects in the world may be appropriate and this type of interaction is encouraged in the same exploratory manner, from inside the world. Such invitations are most suitable *after* the current circumstance is thoroughly explored, and when such an exchange flows naturally from the work. For example, it would have been possible to invite Vicky's figure of a woman to initiate a conversation with one of the miniatures in the river, or even the river itself. Directing a *Creator* to engage figures in a dialogue solely as a technique does not provide the same result as when the discourse emanates from the aliveness of being inside the world.

Witnesses seek to remain curious about the sand world throughout the Sandtray process. *Witnesses* strive to connect with *Creators* without becoming overwhelmed by *Creators'* experiences, or so repelled by them that the harmony between the pair dissipates. Witnessing accounts of torture, chaos, abuse, grief, and other painful human experiences may be difficult. Authentically resonating with the elation of love, joy, or enlightenment, without being swept away, may also be challenging. Either reaction by the *Witness* may make the task of holding a connected therapeutic environment harder to meet.

This chapter addresses the aspects of "Entering into and Exploring from Inside the Sand World." We have seen how subtle techniques that entice *Creators* to enter into the imaginal field of the tray also facilitate a greater capacity for projection. Gentle questioning facilitates the *Creator*'s journey from within the internal perspective of the sand tray. Despite the increased verbal nature of these two aspects, silent periods remain valuable. In silence, *Creators* may contemplate experiences that have been formed in the sand that as yet have no words. For *Creators* whose experiences may be ready to be verbalized, many suggestions have been provided to aid *Witnesses*. Without leading or manipulating, *Witnesses* tactfully influence *Creators* to stretch their capacity to inquire into the experiences which they, themselves, formed in the Sandtray.

CHAPTER NINE

Aspects 7–10

Concluding a Sandtray Session

As the *Creator* and *Witness* leave the aspect of "Exploring from Inside the Sand World," the aspects of "Leaving the World," "Summarizing," and "Forming a Plan" often intermix to harvest the fruits of earlier discoveries. Sandtray encourages the *Creator's* immersion in direct experience, as this is the best way for humans to learn. Daniel Siegel reminds us that "experience means neural firing" triggering brain change and growth (Siegel, 2010, p. 42). Integrating new learning from the Sandtray now comes into focus.

Building a Bridge from Sand Worlds to Daily Life

The glimpses of the *Creator's* experiences from the depths of the Sandtray may feel unbounded by time and space. We see only a brief look at our implicit image-thinking with each sand world. In these concluding aspects *Witnesses* assist *Creators* in returning to their everyday awareness, safely bringing with them the knowledge and experience from the Sandtray's journey.

Thus far, the *Creator* and the *Witness* have looked at, resonated with, and then lived within the experiences in the Sandtray. As the pair continues to sit side-by-side, the dyad's intimate journey winds to a close. Now the *Witness's* task is to assist the *Creator* in accessing value from this excursion into the realm of imagination. The focus remains on the experiences that materialized in the sand world, not on the symbols used by the *Creator*. Noting the energetic modes and the contextual fields (discussed in chapter 4) may be of use in this dialogue. *Witnesses* strive to aid *Creators* in recognizing the interface between the Sandtray and their real world.

When attention shifts away from inside of the tray, the *Creator*'s relationship to the events that were just shared with the *Witness* begins to change. Some of the experiences the *Creator* projected into the sand world are brought out of the tray, and begin to integrate into the *Creator*'s everyday consciousness. *Witnesses* prompt *Creators* to engage in a dialogue about the Sandtray process. Together, they weave the nonverbal senses and images from the sand world into verbal ideas and concepts, more easily encoded by the linear mind, or left brain. Interpretations from *Witnesses* are avoided, as they are more likely to instill confusion in *Creators*. The Sandtray therapy goal is to link the *Creator* to his or her own authentically felt experiences, not to symbols or to archetypes. Instead, *Witnesses* strive to assist *Creators* in the process of gathering, containing, and holding the accessible portions of his or her own experiences that were previously projected into the sand world.

The Seventh Aspect: Leaving the World

A *Witness*'s task during the "Leaving the World" aspect is to support the *Creator* through the perceptual shifts of moving from inside the sand world, to an overview of the sand tray, and then back to inside the *Creator*, who is looking at the world. When it is near the end of the session, this aspect can naturally flow from a *Creator*'s comment made from the outside of the sand world's view. The *Witness* then follows the *Creator*'s lead, maintaining the external perspective. This aspect ushers in the return of the *Creator*'s awareness to his or her present time and current reality. *Witnesses* may initiate this evolution by asking *Creators* to share their internal experience of having formed and explored the Sandtray. To illustrate, Janet in chapter 8 had adjusted her view to speak of the world outside herself. The *Witness* could then readily ask, "What's it like for you now, to create this experience as a grown woman?" Such a question moves the focus out of the tray, back inside the *Creator* in the present.

A *Witness* may also bridge the internal and external perspectives by saying, "We'll need to end the session soon. Is there any other part of the world that you need to visit today?" When the time comes to leave, the *Witness*'s questions and statements are framed from the vantage point of being outside of the sand world, peering back at the journey the two are finishing. The *Witness* gradually leads this change verbally and nonverbally. Speaking directly to the *Creator*, and turning one's body slightly to face the *Creator* rather than the tray, the *Witness* shifts the energy away from the sand world and to the *Creator*. Other questions to prompt this adaptation are:

- "How is this experience of (use the same description used when exploring the world from within) inside your body?"
- "How does this experience of (use the same description used when exploring the world from within) play out in your relationship to others in your daily life?"
- "What issues emerging from the Sandtray might have something to do with your life right now?"
- "What messages do you sense from your inner wisdom?"
- "Do you have a sense of why this experience is coming forth in the sand world at this time?"
- "What awareness is this world bringing to you today?"
- "Is this a past issue? If so, what do you believe is bringing these feelings/thoughts/memories into the present right now?"

Blending these techniques with those of the "Summarizing" aspect can smoothly shift *Creators'* perspectives from imagination, helping to prepare them to return to their daily lives.

The Eighth Aspect: Summarizing

The "Summarizing" aspect is generally a synopsis of the experiences noted while inside the world. However, any portion of the session may be included. These highlighted incidents may also be used in combination with the "Leaving the World" aspect. At times a summary is used to leave the interior view of the sand world. A *Witness* may say, "Before we leave this world, let's remember what has happened here." Then the pair could discuss the sequence of events from entering into the tray until the present. If the *Creator* does not begin to speak when invited, the *Witness* may start, using the *Creator*'s words provided earlier in the Sandtray aspects. In chapter 7, Natalie's volcano tray was processed something like this:

Leaving and Summarizing Natalie's World

When Natalie's session began, we were sitting away from the Sandtray apparatus. She shared that she felt shaken by her recent loss of several friends and her acute awareness of the anniversary of her father's death in two weeks. After talking, Natalie spent much of her Sandtray session creating in the Sandtray. After a long "Reflecting/Directing" aspect, we had a short "Exploring from Inside the Sand World" aspect. As we were running out of time, I took Natalie's cue, when she made a statement from the external worldview, to wind up the session.

Natalie: "Wow, I really needed to make this world today."

Witness: "Yes. Let's talk about how these experiences in the Sandtray may be working in your life."

Natalie: "I came in feeling so disrupted by so much loss."

Witness: "Yes, we talked about that for a while when you first arrived. Then you came to the sand tray and started to move the sand."

Natalie: "Yes. The sand was going all over the place, just like the feelings inside me. I felt so much turmoil. It was good to move the sand about so much. It took the edge off my erratic energy."

Witness: "Then you seemed to focus when you made the mountain."

Natalie: "Yeah, then the volcano began to spew its stuff all over. And then I put the miniatures in, starting with the rocks. Then the hammock woman and the other items."

Witness: "Then later, when the volcano was erupting, at first you were unconcerned, and then you realized that it did do damage. You said that nature created a balance, and the possibility of another island with new life and habitat came up."

Natalie: "I thought of resilience within change. I chose to observe rather than ignore. I began to observe with the confidence that something new was also forming, that change is not all bad."

Witness: Where else in this world might the tendency to ignore be present?"

Natalie: (Laughing) "The woman in the hammock, she's relaxing right next to an erupting volcano!"

This exchange took little time and yet it summarized Natalie's experiences from when she entered the session through creating and exploring the Sandtray. A bit later, together we identified the connections between her personal expressions and the communal, archetypal, and universal contextual fields. She commented on her religious views of death and how death is part of life for all humans. She then shared her beliefs about a never-ending cycle of life and change that allows her to feel confidence in all the changes. The formation of a plan for Natalie grew out of our summary including the functions of the woman in the hammock and the woman in the boat.

As in Natalie's case, the *Creator* is best served when the review of the world is done jointly. When *Witnesses* initiate "Summarizing," they continue to entice *Creators* to engage with them, perhaps asking, "Then what happened next?" or "Where did we go from here?" Some *Creators* are unable to articulate a coherently sequenced narrative about the world. The *Witness* needs to assess if a *Witness's* summary alone will be useful to the *Creator*. Both knowledge of the *Creator's* history and the dyad's relational synchrony will provide clues for this decision.

The *Witness* may use some of the questions in the "Leaving the World" section to help form links between the reviewed experiences from the tray and the *Creator's* present state. The experiences from the sand world are summarized first. When appropriate, the *Creator* may be asked about the familiarity of the identified experiences, or their presence in the *Creator's* daily life. Suggested phrases a *Witness* may use to invite the *Creator* to reexamine the world's experiences are:

- "Let's review what we've just experienced."
- "How might we summarize what just happened?"
- "Let's go over the journey we just had in the sand world."
- "What's happened in this tray so far?"
- "Let's put together what happened here."
- "What do you sense is the key message of this work we did today?"
- "What is the essence here, and what might this have to do with you?"

Some areas or experiences in the sand world may remain a mystery and can be acknowledged as such. Not every item or event in the tray is clarified at once, and some never are. A summary is not necessarily a linear story with a beginning, middle, and an end. By framing the Sandtray process coherently, *Creators* and *Witnesses* jointly weave word pictures about what occurred in the Sandtray. The result often incorporates further translations of image experiences into words.

At times new information emerges in the summary. For example, the changing meaning of miniatures—from when chosen, to being placed in the world, to being inside the world, and again looked at as the *Creator* leaves the world—may be identified. Also an overview may clarify harmonies or incongruities between *Creators'* concrete expressions in the tray and their words, or between in the energetic modes and the contextual fields observed. For instance, I once created a Sandtray choosing a pewter figure of a woman striding forward. For me she exhibited qualities of strength, determination, and tenacity. The training session had gone more than an hour and I thought I knew all about my world by the end. As we were exiting the world, my *Witness* had me look at this woman again, asking me to describe what she carried in her right hand. I remember feeling a sense of shock to see the head of a man, carried by his hair. Until that moment, that physical reality had been completely out of my awareness. As this story illustrates, both *Creators* and *Witnesses* will benefit from remaining attentive to new information whenever it comes forth.

Reminding the *Creator* how he or she arrived at the present moment is useful in initiating the "Forming a Plan" aspect. In each of these three aspects—"Leaving the World," "Summarizing," and "Forming a Plan"—*Witnesses* track the perspective being used by both *Creators* and themselves, seeking cues to inform the most advantageous responses within the time remaining.

Aspect 9: Forming a Plan

A plan is developed after the *Witness* and the *Creator* have taken stock of the events in the tray and their impact on the *Creator*. When the sand world has strongly moved the *Witness*, this view may only be tentatively shared when to do so is clearly in service of the *Creator*. This situation was demonstrated when sharing my welling of tears in Amy's Sandtray in chapter 2. All other intense reactions by *Witnesses* are explored elsewhere, such as in consultation or self-reflection.

Throughout the Sandtray process, *Creators* learn to identify experiences and explore options presented by the implicit and explicit functions of their own minds. This aspect is not based solely in cognition. The pair does not just think up a plan. Together they discover what the *Creator* need, informed by the Sandtray journey. Nor does the *Witness* impose a plan on the *Creator*. Most often, "Forming a Plan" entails arriving at an agreed-upon mental or physical action that the *Creator* will implement to promote integration of a new facet of awareness or learning.

To illustrate, with Natalie's volcano tray in chapter 7, she decided to observe the times that she exhibited the thoughts and behaviors of the woman lying in the hammock desiring escape, versus the wise woman in the boat who takes action. To prepare her to self-observe, we discussed the people and environments in her daily life that were most likely to evoke each set of responses. Natalie stated that sometimes she behaved like the lounging woman when she needed to invoke the skill set of the wise woman. Aware that both of these thought and behavioral choices are available inside her, she eventually began to identify them as they emerged in her everyday life. Once her reactions were no longer habitual and outside of her awareness, Natalie could better choose her responses in any given situation. An example of arriving at a plan with an adolescent is provided below.

Mason's Story: Identifying Feelings

Mason, fourteen years old, witnessed severe domestic violence between his mother and her boyfriend. The police removed him from her home and he was permanently placed with his father and stepmother. Mason lived at his father's house for more than a year before beginning therapy. Mason had a highly conflicted relationship with his stepmom, often provoking her anger.

As we got to know each other, I discovered that while in his mother's custody, Mason had suffered many years of neglect, as well as emotional and physical abuse. While he was growing up his mom had been abusing drugs and exhibited a variety of confusing and scary behaviors. Mason demonstrated anxieties and insecurities. He reported feeling socially awkward and generally distrustful. When he felt strong emotions, Mason stuttered.

In one session, Mason began to describe the qualities of his relationship with his stepmom. She could be a warm and nurturing woman, yet she habitually yelled loudly when upset. Mason wanted to be close to the stepmom who behaved in a loving way, but he feared the angry stepmom, even though his reason informed him that he was safe from the type of harm he had received in his past. As he began to speak of the relationship with his stepmom, his stuttering became severe and he could not continue. Since he had worked in the sand during many previous sessions, I asked him if he would like to show me using the sand. He got up and formed this world. As he moved the sand and figures, Mason's ability to speak returned to normal. Later, we were able to converse about the different characteristics of his stepmom and how he related to them. By this time we were both sitting on the same side of the tray (see figure 9.1). Using the "Language of Discovery and Exploration" described in chapter 8, we reentered the sand world.

The "boy" between the "mom with her arms out" and the "mean skeleton" feels very confused and does not know what to do. He often feels stuck. Mason moved him around in the tray, trying out how the various relationships felt with many differing configurations. With inquiry, he identified the feelings and bodily states of the boy figure clearly in each position. When the child got close to the skeleton, his legs were set even deeper into the sand and he felt fearful and less able to move. When the boy went to the "stepmom with her arms out," he was picked up and held in her lap, feeling "great" about it (see figure 9.2). Mason revealed that this was the relationship that he desired, but did not find often.

Figure 9.1. Mason's view of the confused boy

As we left the sand world, I suggested that a person could pay attention to different subtle experiences within the real world, just like the boy in the Sandtray did. I shared with him that this kind of awareness was one that I also used and learned from. We chatted about how this might work for him. Prior to leaving that day, Mason agreed to pay attention to when he felt the "close to the mean skeleton" feelings, when he felt "close to the stepmom feelings," and when he felt "stuck in the middle." He also agreed to monitor both these internal senses as well as to report back what was going on externally in the family that coincided with each of his feeling patterns.

Some ways in which a *Witness* may introduce a dialogue about a plan between sessions include:

- "How might you support this newly developing part of yourself after you leave today?"
- "Can you think of a way to nurture this awareness in your everyday life?"

Figure 9.2.   Mason's desired relationship

- "When these experiences that were in the Sandtray emerge in your daily life, how do you react, both internally and externally?"
- "How can you create this experience (that you need more of) for yourself, on a regular, ongoing basis?"
- "What choices have you made in the past? How do you see yourself taking a different path? How can you begin to recognize your choice point? Was any part of that revealed in the tray today?"
- "Now you have clearly identified what you need. How can you go about giving this to yourself in a realistic way?"
- "Take some time to consider the kinds of experiences that came up in your Sandtray today. Notice your choices about them as you recognize these experiences coming to you in your everyday life."
- "How can you use what you learned today in the outside world?"
- "Do you have any ideas about how to avoid this kind of experience?"

When *Creators* learn to identify events from the sand world within their daily lives, they are developing mindfulness and self-observation skills, increasing their active consciousness. Another Sandtray goal is to assist Sandtray *Creators* in seeing that they are creating everywhere, all the time, and have options other than the automatic reactions they have previously learned. When *Creators* consider what actions were taken to generate an outcome that occurred in the sand world, and evaluate if that result was the desired event, such reflection may assist them in determining what action to take in their present lives and what results they may reasonably expect. Another treatment plan is illustrated here.

Bella's Story: Spring Blooms

Bella, forty-two years old, initially came to therapy with chronic depression after multiple childhood traumas, including incest and multiple hospitalizations from type 1 diabetes. She made a great deal of progress using expressive arts therapies, including Sandtray. Bella came to see me on and off for many years. At the time of this incident she was an executive in a small firm and we had a well-established therapeutic relationship.

One day, deep into winter, and after many gray and stormy weeks, Bella dragged herself into my office and flopped on the couch like a rag doll. She stared at the floor, yawned, and said that she felt "very sleepy." Bella then stated in a near whisper, "I'm probably depressed." I found her difficult to engage verbally. I was stunned and somewhat at a loss as to what to do, as I had never seen her in this condition. After a silence, I asked her if she thought she had enough energy to make a Sandtray. Lifting her head to make eye contact, she replied, "Yes."

Bella remarked that she had no idea what she wanted to create as she began to choose items and set them on the table outside the sandbox. Physically and verbally, she became more animated. Then Bella went to the tray and silently set the miniatures into the sand world. She moved the sand, making the blue show at one end. When finished she announced, "It's spring! This is the opposite of where I am now." Gesturing to the windows, she described, "Here (in the real world) it is all rainy and dark. I feel it will be a long winter." Next, she laid her right arm on the edge of the sand tray, putting her head on top of her arm. (I got the impression that Bella wanted to crawl into her spring world.) I had reflected her above statements and no more were forthcoming. I asked her if I could move to join her and we could experience the world together (see figure 9.3).

Once she took me into the world, Bella and I conversed about the following experiences: (1) fire brings "inner warmth, 'smoos,' and snuggles"; (2) grasses "remind me of lying on the grass, relaxing, and chewing the sweet long pieces"; (3) blue sphere "is for the times of laying back, when I was a kid, looking at the shapes of clouds, and imagining them to be different things"; (4) balloons are "for going to parties"; (5) "corona, I hate beer, but I wanted something yellow. I wanted a feeling of relaxing and sipping margaritas. That's a sort of adult form of 'grass sitting'"; (6) the "lotus carries the same feelings as the others"; (7) this tray was "not right until the ocean came, when I made the blue show."

Figure 9.3. Bella's longed-for world

After our dialogue to deepen and explore these experiences, in despair Bella blurted out, "I am longing to feel this!" Then she allowed her tears to fall. After a time we discussed how she could reconnect to these nurturing experiences, or readily create them in her everyday life. Bella decided to pick up a plant for her office as she returned to work from the appointment. She identified friends and family who would willingly give her affection. She considered purchasing some balloons and we discussed the possibility of a day off of work for self-care. As a longer-term plan, she considered a trip to the ocean, always a point of renewal for her. As this plan unfolded, Bella recognized that she had been isolating herself from those people who would support her. This old, habitual pattern of not reaching out had crept in and become harmful to Bella in her current circumstances.

Weaving the Personal into the Archetypal and Universal Fields

Thus far in the Sandtray process, we have focused on an individual's personal, idiosyncratic experience. The most appropriate time for *Witnesses* to stimulate a dialogue about the archetypal or universal contextual fields (discussed in chapter 4) is during the "Summarizing" and "Forming a Plan" aspects. This process is not an intellectual "figuring out" or "thinking up" how a *Creator's* experience is related to one of these fields. Rather, the archetypal and universal fields emerge from the intersubjective synchrony and the images and events the *Witness* and *Creator* share. As in the earlier aspects, the *Witness* offers comments or questions as a bridge to these two fields, and then responds following the *Creator's* lead.

Learning about the archetypal field can aid *Creators* in viewing their lives in relationship to other humans. This broader perspective may provide *Creators* with increased tolerance, a decreased sense of aloneness, and increased compassion. History, art, stories, songs, poems, movies, and all forms of human expression may provide encouragement, clarity of where one's life fits within the whole of humanity, or models for how others have met challenges or managed suffering without self-abandonment, and with dignity. From the nonjudgmental universal field, *Creators* may draw strength, support, and a sense of normality. This field fosters an awareness of the continuity, vastness, mysteries, and flux within the cosmos. Connecting one's personal experience to this field may help *Creators* to live in greater harmony with their experiences, be they struggle, grief, regret, ecstasy, or contentment. Often the flow of the session moves to the universal field after first touching upon the archetypal field. Natalie illustrated this sequence when she discussed death as a fact of human existence prior to sharing her beliefs about an eternal cycle of life and death within the universal field.

The opportunity for a *Witness* to introduce material from the archetypal and universal contextual fields does not present itself with every session. This technique is used only when the experiences from the sand world are exceptionally clear. This means that the *Creator* has fully explored them, made implicit concepts verbal, and thoroughly taught the *Witness* these experiences. As the *Witness* becomes deeply moved by events that may have archetypal or universal elements, and observes obvious overlaps between the *Creator*'s personal expressions and one of these fields, the *Witness* may venture the following types of questions:

- "Is there anything about these experiences that brings to mind a myth, song, television show, or movie, etc.?"
- "Do you know what other people call (use the *Creator*'s name for the object)?"
- "Are you interested in what other people call this particular figure?"
- "Do you know what kind of experience this is in general?"
- "Do you know who in history or stories had this kind of experience too?"
- "What can you tell me about (name an experience pattern or a category that is in the sand world, for example, betrayal, mothers, guardian angels, evil ones, loss of a treasured object, or torture) in general?"
- "What can you share with me about (name a category or experience) that you know?"
- "Do you have a sense of who in history or stories this figure was made to represent?"
- "Would you like to know more about this object?"
- "How do you see these experiences fitting into a cosmic perspective?"
- "What might some other being in the universe think or feel about these experiences?"

Witnesses first prompt *Creators* to share connections to the archetypal and universal fields that come to them. The *Witness* then fosters a dialogue to learn more about the *Creator*'s views. The energy needed in this method is that of gentle curiosity, not of probing or analyzing. If the *Witness* has a clear image that has come to mind through the Sandtray work, that idea may be tentatively put forth to the *Creator*. When the *Creator* expresses curiosity about a topic, researching the figure or concept together may be desirable.

Although not discussed until "Leaving the World," *Witnesses* consider the contextual fields throughout all of the aspects. As *Witnesses* hold the framework of the Sandtray process, they notice and remember when links to the archetypal or the universal fields occur to them. *Witnesses* use these observations and their experiences from within the intersubjective relationship as a guide for later in the session.

Aspect 10: Photographing and Clearing the World

Photographing the World

In general, photographs are taken at the end of the Sandtray session, but are allowed anytime. When working with a new *Creator*, this is the description usually provided and followed. Using a camera offers yet another opportunity to see the sand world differently. *Witnesses* may want to suggest that *Creators* walk around the sand tray to consider various shots, as this provides an expanded perspective. A digital camera with an adjustable view allowing both parties to see a planned shot is advantageous. Keeping a camera at hand during the entire session is expedient to respond to *Creators*' requests for photographs. *Creators* often request pictures just prior to making changes in the world. The more the *Witness* is able to comfortably incorporate photography, the easier it is to combine this aspect with summarizing or discussion of possible plans.

When a *Creator* becomes comfortable with a *Witness*, and with using the Sandtray apparatus, no limits apply to this aspect. Even videotaping a session would be reasonable as long as the equipment does not distract from the work and the use of the material is clarified in writing. It may take several video sessions for both the *Creator* and the *Witness* to become completely comfortable.

Should *Creators* choose to take the pictures themselves, *Witnesses* need to make sure to take one photo of the world from the frame of reference that their notes were recorded, and to retain an overview shot from the *Creator*'s side of the tray. Maintaining records of a *Creator*'s Sandtray journeys assists *Witnesses* in tracking the *Creator*'s growth and change over time. Pictures may also provide a form of object constancy to some *Creators*. Both notes and photographs are useful to *Witnesses* who desire to improve their skills through study and consultation.

Photographs are kept with the Sandtray notes and copies are provided to *Creators*. When the *Creator* is a child, I emphasize that the pictures belong to the *Creator* when speaking to parents. If a child does not want to share photos with their caregivers, or decides to leave them with me, I comply. If a *Creator* does not want to photograph, I do not do so. Depending on what transpired in session, I may ask permission to take pictures after the *Creator* leaves, for my records and future use.

For use in therapy, I prefer to give pictures to *Creators* at the beginning of their next session so that I have time to reconsider the work after the session. Sometimes an important element will be noticed while reviewing the photographs on the computer. At the next session, while both parties are looking at the pictures, the *Witness* can easily share new observations with the *Creator* and discuss possibilities. Bella taught me the value to *Creators* of viewing pictures between sessions. She kept her photos readily in sight, used them to focus on her plan, or to contemplate them for their soothing properties. Some *Creators* keep a scrapbook including their Sandtray stories, poetry, art, journal entries, and other works that support their personal growth.

Clearing the World

"Clearing the World" refers to the *Witness* removing the Sandtray miniatures from the tray, cleaning them, and replacing the items on the shelves. The sand is then flattened out to make a "clean slate" in preparation for the next *Creator*. In therapy or personal-growth consultations *Witnesses* take apart the Sandtray after *Creators* have departed. Dismantling the world gives *Witnesses* another opportunity to reflect on the work and notice more about it. Sometimes buried or covered items are found for the first time. New connections between figures or areas of the world may also be observed. This information may be added to the session notes.

On occasion, *Creators* may request to take apart their own worlds. If possible, allow them to do so. If time does not permit this, ask the *Creator* to begin to remove items, and to allow you to assist after the first four to six objects are removed. Placing the removed miniatures in a basket rather than back on the shelves will expedite this process. This method of undoing the Sandtray is also most practical during groups and trainings.

A Summary of the Sandtray Aspects

We have now looked at each Sandtray aspect separately. The aspects of "Introducing the Sandtray Process" and "World Creation" encourage *Creators* to take action in the sand tray. The quieter aspects of "Silent Reverie" and "Reflecting/Directing" allow time to consider the sand world in a different manner. "Entering into the World" and "Exploring from Inside the World" are aspects that stimulate a deeper experiential perspective for *Creators*. Throughout the narrative in the concluding aspects of "Leaving the World," "Summarizing," "Forming a Plan," and "Photographing," there is a two-way communication between implicit and explicit information. This exchange occurs both between the *Creator* and the *Witness* as well as within each of them. Stern states: "Images, feelings, intuitions in the implicit domain must get rendered into the verbal explicit domain by the speaker. And in the opposite direction, words must get rendered into images, feelings, and intuitions by the listener" (Stern, 2004, p. 187). These activities assist in bringing a new awareness or a fresh point of view. Through this dialogue the *Creator* can consider how to apply the wisdom gained from the Sandtray process in everyday life.

Since allowing *Creators* freedom of expression is fundamental to the Sandtray process, these aspects rarely unfold in the linear fashion described here. When they do so, it is most likely to be with an adult who is a practiced sand player. Creating and looking at a Sandtray is not necessarily the same as *experiencing* and being able to learn from the sand world. *Creators* must become aware of their own processes, consciously learn about them, and perhaps experience them viscerally. The Sandtray aspects, applied within a resonant relationship, facilitate the connection between *Creators* and their patterns as revealed in sand worlds.

Witnesses do not need to implement the Sandtray aspect framework in full. Readers may desire to experiment piecemeal with these techniques. Some may find it useful to begin with reflecting statements while working with a *Creator* who occasionally speaks, adding directive invitations as deemed helpful. For a sand player who is chatty and analytical, a *Witness* may suggest "Silent Reverie," and then decide how to proceed. When a *Creator* asks, "What does this mean?" a *Witness* may reply, "Let's use our imaginative perspective and see what we can learn," as a prompt to enter the sand world. Harmonic resonance between the *Creator* and the *Witness* is essential for the *Witness* to identify how best to support the *Creator* in gaining from this work.

The focus in chapter 9 is on the concluding aspects of the Sandtray session—those aspects that build bridges between the experiences within the sand world and the *Creator*'s everyday life. The Sandtray affords opportunities to glimpse implicit or right-brain functions in our lives. The degree to which image-thinking processes become available is, in part, determined by a *Creator*'s and a *Witness*'s ability to resonate with and contemplate the sand world in front of them. As stated earlier, the aspects of "Leaving the World," "Summarizing," and "Forming a Plan" are often intermixed and rarely sequential as described here. These three aspects support the translation of implicit thinking material, as depicted in the sand world, into linear-thinking verbal language, more accessible to both *Creators* and *Witnesses*. In the final aspect of "Photographing and Clearing" suggestions are offered to enhance further the Sandtray process.

CHAPTER TEN

Children's Active Sandtrays

Self-initiated play cultivates human imagination and curiosity. These abilities promote the creative learning of social, intellectual, and emotional skills. Our fast-paced culture nonetheless values achievement-oriented activities and devalues play. The pleasure-in-the-doing that play holds remains underutilized in our daily lives. In our utterances about play, we say that anything mindless or easy is "just child's play" or a "waste of time." Yet, for humanity to flourish we must meet our challenges with flexibility, resilience, and creativity—all qualities promoted by play.

Within a society that underrates play, as we grow older and move into the world of work, creative play often recedes under the hectic demands of life. While academics are praising the value of play, opportunities for American children to engage in creative, interactive play with other children have diminished. Peter Gray, research professor of psychology at Boston College, asserts that the decline in play correlates to the increase in psychopathology in both children and adolescents. "Play, especially social play with other children," he has written, "serves a variety of developmental functions, all of which promote children's mental health. In the absence of such play, children fail to acquire the social and emotional skills that are essential for healthy psychological development" (Gray, 2011, p. 458). Scientists of various fields, including neurology and sociology, are studying the "simple" play of children and increasingly recognize it as critical for healthy human development.

While playing, children are enacting their image-thinking as they experiment, explore, form, destroy, and form anew. Play provides an interface between the implicit (right) brain and the explicit (left) brain functions and builds connecting pathways between them. As we play, a welling-up of image-thinking evolves until portions become accessible to our more conscious, linear-thinking mind. The neurobiology maxim is that all experience changes the brain. Therefore, play experiences must be included whether or not they are goal directed or well understood.

Play therapists must find a way to leave the highly valued cognitive stance of our adult world, and become spontaneous, resonant, and reflective with children. Authentic play requires that we loosen our judgments and persona, as we mirror and validate children's internal and external experiences without encroaching on their sense of self and spirit of creativity. Sandtray *Witnesses* model self-regulation and implicitly provide interactive regulation within the therapeutic relationship.

The most frequent question I am asked is what a specific type of play means. This is a question I cannot answer. Using the Sandtray aspects helps to clarify a *Creator*'s meaning, both for a *Creator* and a *Witness*. Although the topics of a *Witness*'s judgment and interpretation are addressed in chapter 5, let's briefly examine here the sand world of seven-year-old Frank. Standing in front of the Sandtray, he pushes a miniature Peter Pan deeply and deliberately through the sand toward a boat with a Captain Hook figure on board. Peter Pan's course is an "S" curve, following the boat's trajectory, not heading directly toward the boat. What might this mean? What part of this image and action captures the *Creator*'s focus? Here are just a few possibilities:

- The boy is striving to get to the boat. He is swimming as fast as he can. He was left behind and he is fearful that he will never see the boat or the people again if he does not catch them now.
- The boy is pretending he is a dolphin having fun and is swimming and playing with the ship. They are friends.
- The boy is sneaking up on the guys in the boat to attack them. They are bad guys who deserve it!
- The boy is swimming to get away from the sharks, hoping the people in the boat will see him and help him escape. (No shark figures are in the tray.)

Notice that the action that Frank creates is the constant here, but the feelings, meanings, and foci may all be quite different. Frank's facial expressions, energies, and affective resonance during the play are likely to stimulate different perceptions in the *Witness*, depending upon Frank's personal meaning. Some of his play may be fantasy while some may relate to real-life experiences. How is one to know the internal experience of the play without entering into the world of the child? Sandtray founder Margaret Lowenfeld asserted that adults need to leave their roles of parent, observer, or teacher behind and adopt the function of "a comrade instead" (Lowenfeld, 1991, p. 26). Even photographs or videos of a Sandtray cannot reveal the *Creator*'s meanings for an activity. Through harmonic resonance and the judicial use of the aspects, *Witnesses* become able to form a bridge between a sand world's action and a *Creator*'s meaning. Later in this chapter, the stories of Tyrone and Gordy provide details of these interventions.

As Sandtray *Witnesses*, we have great knowledge of child development, psychotherapy, play, and the Sandtray process. Yet our abilities to be with the child inside the play, while honoring what is coming forth and facilitating the emergence of meaning, may be the more useful skill set. When *Witnesses* join in the aliveness of the play, they can effectively invite *Creators* to link different parts of play together and link feelings and situations in the play to daily realities. When *Witnesses* fail to enter the child's perspective and suggest solutions or meanings from outside the play dynamic, these interpretations can be disconcerting for *Creators*. The value of following a child's lead, even when a *Witness* does not know the point of the play cognitively, is illustrated in the two cases below:

Josh's Story: Making Food
Nearly four years old, Josh led me in making Play-Dough food during a session early in his treatment. At three years, he had abruptly been taken by his mentally ill mother to reside in another state when she separated from his father. Josh was removed from her care by Children's Protective Services and returned to his father, whom he had not seen for over six months. Following Josh's direction to "make food," I did my best to form realistic pizza, burgers, and cookies as we played together. No matter what Josh told me he was making, the results looked like smashed up Play-Dough to me. I could feel that Josh wanted me to understand something that I clearly did not. I continued to resonate with his play, reflecting and inquiring using the Sandtray aspects framework. As we chatted, I casually began to mirror the type of food he was forming with my own Play-Dough. Eventually I got his message that his play food looked like the food he really ate, which was not like the food I had first formed. Josh began to describe how his mom put him inside of dumpsters behind grocery stores and restaurants to find food. The food he formed in the playroom was this "mashed-up" food that he ate while in his mother's care.

Once I understood his experience, I was able to reflect, empathize, and explore with him how pressured, hungry, and scared he felt when his mom required him to get food in this manner. As I struggled to understand what Josh attempted to communicate, my efforts encouraged him not to give up on me. Finally, I understood him and we had a meeting of hearts. This shared play interaction became one pillar in building our relationship for future work.

As with Josh, a *Witness*'s sincere desire to understand and learn is not lost on preschoolers. They know when we are "with" them or trying to be. For survival, children are born biologically prepared to attach to adults. They have the innate sense to recognize authentic attempts by *Witnesses* to connect and empathize with them. Like adults, child *Creators* hold their own internal healing powers. Our task is to assist in the unveiling and implementation of their healing, recovery, and growth through an attuned play relationship.

There are times when *Witnesses* never discover the explicit meaning of what is taking place in the sand world. One task for *Witnesses* is to find a way to hold and honor this type of play without pressing children to satisfy our curiosity. When a strong relationship exists between a child and a *Witness*, sometimes meaning may be guessed, even quite accurately. These assumptions are the initial guides *Witnesses* use to initiate reflections and inquiries. The following vignette portrays one sand world in which the *Witness* does not cognitively understand the content of the world.

La Shell's Story: A Working Well

La Shell first came to me as a toddler after a period of life-threatening, terrifying abuse. Brought to treatment by her father and stepmother, she had been victimized by her mother and the mom's boyfriend. We had worked together for several years, and she occasionally returned to treatment for a variety of reasons during later developmental periods. By the time she was twelve and a half years of age, I thought I knew La Shell quite well. Therapy had always been useful to this child and her family. She returned now due to her family's impending move out of state. The employer of both her parents closed its California operation and the family needed to move with the company to maintain the parents' employment and the family's financial stability.

La Shell was not very talkative as we renewed our relationship. After all, she was nearly a teenager and displayed less eagerness to see me than when she was younger. La Shell both looked and stated that she felt sad about the family's move. Her stability and nurturing had all been linked to her current geographical area, as her abuse took place in another state. La Shell warmed up to therapy and to me within a few sessions. Soon she worked in the Sandtray again, silently forming a sand world that looked very much like this one (see figure 10.1).

While moving the sand, she was intent, focused, and appeared to know exactly how she wanted her world to look. Once she created the hill she carefully dug and secured a deep well shaft within it, clearing out any sand that caved in and firming up the inside. She then placed the well securely on the top, and began to add water a bit at a time. I gently reflected that action verbally ("The water is going into the hole"). Repeating this action, La Shell frowned, described her intention to fill the well full of water, and indicated that she was not sure how this could work. We discussed the properties of sand and water, using her past experiences with them as a reminder. She soon realized that filling the well would likely make the sand very wet without holding the water in the well as she desired. La Shell stopped adding water. She stated that she did not want the water to leak through the sides of the well and make it cave in.

After problem-solving La Shell's dilemma, we looked through the miniature collection for a container to fit under the well. None satisfied her. What was available was not deep enough, did not fit seamlessly to the bottom of the well, or was not the correct shape. I could sense her intense frustration. Prior to the end of the session, we stood together viewing her sand world. She was able to tell me that she knew she needed to have the well hold water, but did not understand why this was so. La Shell was able to describe the qualities that she needed

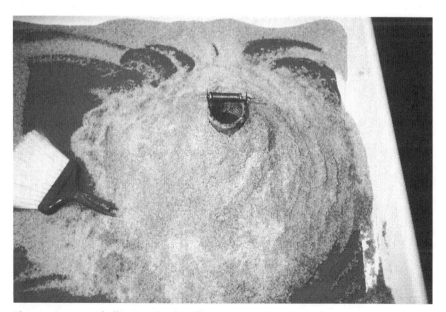

Figure 10.1. La Shell's contained well

in a container. I suggested that we both look for something that might work, and she could experiment with what we discovered during our next session.

For years I had supported this child and her family through very difficult life events and I wanted her to feel satisfied in her current work. Although I did not know why La Shell needed to create her experience in just this way, I trusted that to do so would be healing for her. Racking my brain, I spent a busy week looking in shops to find the "right fit" for her well, but to no avail. Just prior to her next session I noticed an everyday item that held some of the properties she required. I went to my pharmacy and asked them to sell me the tallest available pill bottle of a certain diameter.

The photograph shown is La Shell's second Sandtray with a mound and well. Created in much the same way but more quickly, she was able to use the pill bottle as a water container. The well worked, with the little bucket bringing up water when called for. She repeated this action numerous times. As we explored the world, she shared a sense of satisfaction, contentment, and "rightness" about how her world came together.

We still had no explanation for her intense need. However, we were able to establish a shared narrative about the process of these two sessions. This dialogue included identifying La Shell's deep sense of knowing what she wanted and feeling thwarted in her initial attempts to create her desired world, a framework of how she experienced the transformation of her frustration and dissatisfaction during her first attempts, and her shift to enjoyment and completeness that came with the successfully functioning well. Toward the end of this session, using her Sandtray experience as the key, we talked about the concept of not giving up when what one wants does not come readily. This theme also emerged in future sessions. As La Shell recognized and accepted that her family needed to relocate, she also formed her own goal to return to California once she was old enough to attend college.

La Shell did not respond to my attempts to invite the Sandtray aspects of "Entering into and Exploring the World." She was able to reflect on the process more than the content. Much could be stated about this Sandtray if seen as an allegory or metaphor. Wells are symbols often associated with females, healing, and shafts that connect the surface to what is beneath it. We could analyze La Shell's actions as a connection to deeper consciousness, or focus on the meanings of her need for containment of the well's water over the bottomless pit that would suck up all the water and cave in her hill. Had I sensed her need to look at these issues, I may have introduced symbol dictionaries and studied these with her. Instead, I focused on what was occur-ring and the energies that moved with her actions of creation. I remain allied with J. R. R. Tolkien's views of allegory. He stated, "Many confuse 'applica-bility' with 'allegory'; but the one resides in the freedom of the reader, and the other in the purposed domination of the author" (Tolkien, 1987, p. xvii). Not knowing the purpose of the *Creator*, for I believe that she did not know explicitly herself (logos), I am unwilling to apply meanings for her. The min-iatures La Shell chose may be related to the meanings available from symbol research, yet for her at that time, those meanings were not in focus. My use of the Sandtray aspects as my guide allowed La Shell to lead us to a shared narrative of her needs, feelings, and the transformations that took place both internally and externally from those two sessions. Although I continued to see La Shell, I never learned more about this tray. Such inconclusiveness can be the outcome of the Sandtray process.

First Steps with Children

Children who come into the playroom for the first time know that I have already met with their parents or guardians. Prior to the intake interview the caregivers have completed forms and questionnaires. Having been told only why others think the family needs help, I seek to discover the child's point of view. In preparation for the child's first session, the parents have described both me and the playroom to their child. I tell the children that they will be able to choose our activities almost every session. Sometimes I will choose, particularly if the child and parent come in with an immediate problem that we need to work on together to resolve. Routinely, I intermit-tently see the parents separately from the child both to evaluate the child's progress and to assist the parents in facilitating positive interactions at home that support treatment goals. Parent and child sessions are usually planned with the child's input.

Young children will often gravitate eagerly to the Sandtray apparatus. Some dart to the tray, working immediately to move the sand or form a world. In these cases I usually manage to state "the rule" that the sand stays in or over the box, providing additional introductory information as needed. Young children's brains process differently and much faster than adult brains. As adult *Witnesses*, to accompany the activity level of youngsters, we need to be prepared for their abundant energy with our tools at the ready.

No matter how concerned or attentive *Witnesses* may be, we will miss plenty of details that busy young *Creators* present. I emphasize to the child that my notes help me to remember the important world the *Creator* makes.

Active nonverbal play relies principally on implicit communication, particularly in early stages of treatment. The fewer words available to a child, the more difficulty the *Witness* has in verbally confirming information and the greater the *Witness's* dependence on relational intersubjectivity for information. Our notes and maps of the Sandtray with soft reflective sounds are clues to intensely working *Creators* that we are attending to them. As I have struggled to follow lively *Creators*, some have offered to slow down while others have tested me with questions or wanted to see my notes. *Witnesses* need to be good enough to resonate authentically with *Creators* and their play, inviting them to deepen their work by using the Sandtray aspects framework as the *Witness* deems useful.

For preschool *Creators* in particular, some physical preparations will be useful. For example, I make it a point to sit on the floor for preschoolers, placing myself in physical proximity. I provide smaller and deeper sand trays for them to choose from. Many miniatures are in baskets low on the shelves, ready to be pulled out, explored, or dumped into a tray. Youngsters are also provided the option of low sand tray tables, or using a tray on the floor. I am clear to preschoolers, as with all *Creators*, that they may use any of the items they see and that I will either help them get what they need or reach it for them. I encourage them to use everything that is available in the miniature collection.

The playroom emphasizes playing "freely and safely," which addresses what most adults would consider "limit setting." I describe my job as keeping the playroom safe for everyone including myself, future players, and this child on future visits. I may suggest that if everyone who had taken a turn before the child had broken or removed objects then he or she would have fewer items to play with. I assure children that I understand feeling the need to destroy something at times. I confirm that I can provide them an opportunity to destroy items if they let me know. Smashing aluminum cans, popping balloons, mixing different colors of sand, and tearing up a complete city phone book are some activities that children have negotiated. The playroom includes target shooting, bean bags, punch balloons, and many other ways to channel physical energy outward safely. I may also suggest acceptable messes, such as cards, plastic chips, or wet Sandtray play, as long as we clean them up together. Ideally these topics are covered in the first session, and referred to as needed. With a variety of art and craft supplies, *Creators* can make many items to take home. This fulfills the need of many children to form a concrete connection between their experiences in the playroom and their home environment.

Despite my agreements with child *Creators*, "the rules" may be ignored or overtly tested. Closely following the flow of the play helps *Witnesses* anticipate a child's actions. A reminder of a boundary is best prior to an infraction. For example, the point at which the sand piles up close to the edge of the tray may be the opportune time to remind a *Creator*: "Please keep the sand in the box." Also, as shooting moves to the edge of the safe zone, or the *Witness* feels the *Creator*'s energy rising close to the edge of containment, a reminder of the agreed-upon boundaries or an implicit direction to deescalate is preferable to dealing with infractions.

When a *Creator* routinely has trouble with any rule, I think about what need the child is expressing. I wonder about the qualities of experience this child seeks and consider how I might provide them. Should I remove some of the sand from the tray prior to the next visit? Do we need to go outside and throw sand, or something else? Do I need to provide a deeper tray or a floor covering so that this behavior does not become an issue for me? Could the behavior be an issue of visual/spatial perception? I often discuss these concerns with the child, attempting to discover how his or her needs can be satisfied while following the playroom rules. The first choice is to make the play possible. The last choice is to limit access to the play. The latter is rarely required, and is always time specific.

Young *Creator*'s worlds are often filled with constantly changing sand shapes and objects. As stated in previous chapters, both adolescents and adults will alter sand worlds, but their trays are rarely characterized by the fluid movement common to young children. At times, youngsters will narrate their play action, perhaps providing *Witnesses* an opening for verbal interaction. Young *Creators* are also more likely to play both in and out of the sandtray within a single session, requiring the physical space to do so.

Applying the Sandtray Aspects to Shifting Worlds

In working with moving sand worlds, the elements of the Sandtray aspects described in previous chapters tend to feel more like a kaleidoscope than the linear format that has been presented. The age of a *Creator* does not change a *Witness*'s response to an active Sandtray. Not all of the aspects are useful in all sessions or with all *Creators*. With practice, *Witnesses* can identify when the aspect of "Silent Reverie" occurs or when "Reflecting/Directing" or "Summarizing" might be advantageous to *Creators*. As *Witnesses* apply the Sandtray aspects, their ability to recognize each one increases, just as easily as learning to discriminate which shapes are green or red, or triangular or round in a kaleidoscope's design. *Witnesses* can learn to distinguish when *Creators* use the perspectives from inside or outside the sand world and to respond in an effective manner.

A Sandtray reflects the *Creator*'s life in some way. However, as the Sandtray is being formed, neither *Creator* nor *Witness* may immediately recognize how the experiences in the sand world fit into the *Creator*'s real life. Historically, mirrors of stone or metal were used as reflectors, although images were distorted. There are times when the Sandtray process feels just as unclear. Initially, until implemented, the Sandtray aspects remain only possibilities in the background. Verbalizations tend to come in pieces and parts, with a coherent narrative developing only over time. When I feel unsure, confused, or unclear for any reason, I speak and initiate less often, not more. The *Creator* sets the pace of the play and the relationship. How a *Witness* proceeds depends on the historical impression received from the intake session with the caregivers, the content of the sand world, and the intersubjective "feel" of what is observed, particularly in terms of the *Creator*'s sense of safety.

During the first couple of Sandtray sessions, when I witness a new *Creator*, I am likely to do little verbal initiating. Following the social work maxim: "Start where the client is," I follow the *Creator*'s lead. I watch closely and observe the child's patterns of organization and energy, while noting how much and when he or she verbally shares on his or her own, including such sounds as singing and vehicle noises. My goal is to respond helpfully to verbal and nonverbal communication, composing a safe feeling relationship with *Creators*. For some children the *Witness*'s focused attention and note-taking is enough for them to open a conversation.

Other young *Creators* need *Witnesses* to use reflective techniques or interested inquiries to help instill a greater sense of being seen and respected. Through therapeutic play encounters, *Witnesses* strive to give children a sense of agency, or the power to have an impact on their environment. Agency can be experienced in all play, but being the absolute *Creator* of a defined world in the sand enhances the *Creator*'s skills to influence his or her everyday reality. *Witnesses* commonly sit a foot or two away from the edge of the tray, checking the *Creator*'s comfort level verbally. Some *Creators* will ask *Witnesses* to be closer. To feel comfortable, a few children will need the *Witness* to be more distant from their play. *Witnesses* always use their interpersonal skills to read the intersubjective relationship and determine the best action or even inaction. Deva's example is just one reason why I do not provide "rules" for *Witnesses* to follow about these details of Sandtray:

Deva's Story: Deva in Charge

Deva, age nine, tested my assertions that the sand world was hers and that she had lots of choice in the playroom. After telling me that she wanted to play in the sand, I helped her set up what she needed to work. Then Deva sat me well across the room, where I could not possibly see her Sandtray as she worked. I was sitting more than thirteen feet away, but I looked toward her and stayed energetically focused on her. As her "World Creation" proceeded she began to report events as they evolved in the Sandtray. Each time I thanked her, adding comments like, "I can't see, but I am glad you are telling me this," or "I am using my imagination to try to follow your creation." Once Deva realized that I would allow her the comfort to determine how close I could be, her desire to share and be witnessed prevailed and I was not banished again. Had I insisted on sitting close enough to take notes, Deva may have dismissed me as a hypocrite instead of accepting me as someone she could begin to build trust with.

At the beginning of a Sandtray session with a child, as with adults, I seat myself across from them. Subsequent positioning is directed by the child, or it emerges from our interactions together. *Witnesses* often actively assist young *Creators*. While continuously respecting the boundaries of the tray, should the *Creator* request assistance, such as holding two sticks together while they are being taped, I ask for permission to put my hands or body over the tray. Respecting this boundary continues even while photographing a bird's-eye view from the step ladder. This consistently reinforces the message that during the session the Sandtray is the *Creator*'s personal space to use in any desired fashion.

If a child is describing a scene that I cannot see, perhaps because it occurs behind a big rock, I reflect that fact and offer to move. Sometimes I will ask *Creators* if I can come and look from their view. Most preschoolers assume that we can see everything they are doing. Children often will move to other sides of the sand world as they create. Young *Creators* will come to work beside *Witnesses* and may even lean their bodies into the *Witness* as they work. I notice what is being formed as these changes take place. During treatment, if a *Creator* never initiates a move from the starting perspective, at some point I may invite the *Creator* to switch sides with me, or to walk around the tray as we are composing a summary or photographing the world.

For bustling *Creators*, even a brief stop in action to look at what is there may indicate "Silent Reverie." Following the *Creator*'s lead the *Witness* also stops to look, perhaps deciding to prolong this reverie with a comment such as, "Oh," or "Let's see," or "Look at that." If a *Witness*'s reflective statement is responded to by the *Creator*, the *Witness* may then attempt to continue the verbal engagement with a fragment of the "Reflecting/Directing" aspect.

Alternatively, a conversation may spring up about the action or experiences from the context of inside the world and a piece of the aspect of "Exploring from Inside the World" may occur. All of the Sandtray aspects are available tools at any given time in actively flowing worlds.

As *Witnesses* engage with *Creators* in the various Sandtray aspects, minor shifts in the play may take place. The *Witness* may use the aspects to facilitate minute perceptual alterations between the *Creator* and the world so that the *Creator* is able to experience what is being formed in a different, less habitual manner. At times, fresh perceptions of the world may be sparked by seemingly simple statements such as:

- "Wow, look at what just happened."
- "I see how the blue one just covered the black one with the sand."
- "I'm wondering how the orange one feels about being run over."
- "How did that one get there?"
- "The little one went under the sand. Oh, it popped up again!"
- "I'm curious to know how the biggest one feels now."

In each of these samples, the *Witness* would use a specific name for figures used if these had previously been named by the *Creator*. Consideration of Tyrone's sand world will clarify the use of these skills within a session.

Tyrone's Story: Car Therapy

Tyrone, age eight, had been diagnosed with Juvenile Onset Diabetes at two years of age. After hospitalization he began daily insulin shots. His parents felt guilty and distressed, unable to help their toddler understand the necessity of this painful ritual to save his life. His medical condition and his emotional reaction to the treatment negatively impacted his life. Tyrone became an irritable and oppositional child with very dysregulated affect. He had been in treatment with me two earlier times in his life. He returned this time because his parents had divorced and were both in new relationships. Tyrone was now living with his grandmother.

After several months Tyrone's Sandtrays remained focused on the use of vehicles. After several primarily silent sessions during which Tyrone used a similar set of vehicles to enact a similar pattern of action, it occurred to me that Tyrone may be feeling stuck. He had not been responsive to exploring these worlds with me. Of late, he had seemed to puzzle over Sandtray activities in which vehicles went around and around in circles and then crashed. Other vehicles remained within the center area.

In this session, in addition to the cars, he also chose a boy in a wheelchair as his "speedy guy" going in circles (see figure 10.2). After awhile, I began to reflect some of Tyrone's vehicle sounds. Then I reflected the activities I saw in the sand world with words. Tyrone responded to these attempts positively. As we looked into the tray together, initially from opposite sides, a dialogue unfolded. Our interactions went like this:

> *Witness*: (Reflecting the action in the tray) "That one keeps going around and around."
> Tyrone: "Yes, the boy keeps going until he crashes."
> *Witness*: "He goes around and around until he crashes over in that corner." (I indicate the position with my eyes and head posture.)
> Tyrone: "Yeah, he goes faster and faster and then he crashes."
> *Witness*: "I watched him crash over and over again, just like the cars. I kept wondering what that was like for him."
> Tyrone: "He knows he's going to crash and he's trying to figure out how not to."
> *Witness*: "Oh, he really wants to know how not to crash. How might he do that?
> Tyrone: "I don't know." (Sighs, sounding discouraged.)

Figure 10.2. Tyrone's "speedy guy" crashes: *Witness*'s view

Witness: "Maybe there is something we can do to help him figure this out. Do you want to try?"

Tyrone: "Yeah!"

Witness: "Let's look at this together. May I come and sit by you to see from your side of the tray?" (He nods affirmation and I move next to him and focus my attention on the boy in the sand world.) "When does he suspect that he may crash?"

Tyrone: "He starts out okay, but he gets going so fast that he can't stop, and he knows he has to crash to stop." (Perking up, interested.)

Witness: "Wow, that must be hard."

Tyrone: "Yeah." (We pause here a moment to take in the boy's struggle.)

Witness: "Does he notice when he's just beginning to go too fast?"

Tyrone: "No."

Witness: "What do you think would happen if he did?"

Tyrone: "He could slow down because there is a brake on his wheelchair."

Witness: "Oh, I didn't know that!"

Tyrone: (Pointing.) "Yeah, it's right here."

Witness: "I am guessing that by the time he notices what is happening, he is going too fast to stop and he has forgotten about the brake."

Tyrone: "Yes that's right!" (Clearly he is excited.)

Witness: "Let's look at this again and see if we can help this guy remember the tools he's got that he can use so he won't have to crash."

At this point Tyrone spontaneously recreates his actions in the tray in a slow motion, instant replay style. Together we take a detailed look at the process of the boy in the wheelchair and the other cars who watch him. Tyrone began to articulate how the boy in the Sandtray was like him going around and around the family members, whom he named. He notices that just like him the boy does not know how to reenter the family interaction without crashing first.

Then we began to form a plan for Tyrone that included some homework of bodily based mindfulness exercises. These targeted self-soothing, anger/energy management, and identifying feelings accurately. He was now eager to begin to learn these, as the concepts came directly from his own play. He began to "pay attention" to himself in a completely different fashion. Once he experienced a link between his Sandtray and his daily reality, Tyrone became fully engaged in exploring his sand worlds using the Sandtray aspects.

After more "car therapy" and problem-solving sessions, we identified his need to remind himself routinely that he had control of his own internal "brake." He became most successful by starting his day with a self-care exercise when he got up. Eventually his family learned to help him by cueing Tyrone empathetically and without criticism when they sensed his energy accelerating. In this way the caregivers and Tyrone could be on the same team, addressing the problem together as opposed to battling each other.

As with Tyrone, *Witnesses* may need to experience many "car therapy" Sandtrays before they are able to find a way to make a bridge to language, or find practical solutions. What is useful is for *Witnesses* to stay in tune with the play without becoming bored or feeling helpless. Sand worlds that appear similar may or may not be the same type of experience for the *Creator*. We may conclude, by looking at popular television and books directed at very young children, that preschoolers seem to thrive on repetition. So what looks like the same play to adults may be experienced differently each time by youngsters. Despite adult impressions, vehicle play has great variety. To assist *Witnesses* in staying present during "car therapy," I offer some considerations of the value of this play:

- Who makes the roads and paths?
- Who leads and who follows? Who is in charge? What is the nature of any power struggles?
- Which vehicles interact and how? What multiple and changing relationships are forming and reforming? What boundaries are being formed and reformed? What happens when these boundaries cannot be held?
- What moves in harmony, and what does not?
- What are the functions of different kinds of vehicles?
- How are rules established and followed?
- How are obstacles managed? Are they moved, crashed through, or do they stop the vehicles altogether?
- When a crash occurs, who gets help and who does not? Who instigates the crash and why?
- Who provides assistance, how effective are they in this task, and what type of relationship ensues afterward?
- Who survives and who dies and what happens afterward?

In "car therapy," like all moving worlds, the Sandtray aspects are briefly entered, left, and then perhaps later reentered. There may be multiple short summaries and perhaps an overall summary. "Forming a Plan" may occur at the end of a session or a series of sessions. With youngsters, the aspect of "Leaving the World" is often very brief, and summaries are often made during the photographing of the tray. *Witnesses* may initiate summaries by making statements using the *Creator*'s previous words, or by inviting the *Creator* to join in the summarizing. This technique not only pulls together the actions in the world, but also indicates to *Creators* that *Witnesses* were engaged with them throughout the journey of making the world. The following comments offer some options:

- "I remember when the big lion came and the other animals went behind the rock pile. Do you recall what came next?"
- "The pirates started out as bad guys. Then they went through lots of adventures and each one learned that he had a good quality inside him. Each pirate was surprised that he wasn't all bad, as he had thought. Do you think that's pretty accurate?"
- "There are lots of families here. All the families have a mom and a dad and two children, a boy and a girl. They all went to a big park for a picnic. There was lots of food and nobody was hungry. The kids all had balloons and balls and had a good time. Everyone was friendly. Did I miss anything important?"
- "I saw that the green robot started hitting the red one. They fought for a long time. Then what happened?"
- "Let me see if I've got the idea of today's work. At first the green army lined up and no one else was there. Then the silver army started to come in and began shooting right away. Then all the soldiers were shooting, and exploding, and most soldiers died. Their bodies were left bleeding on the sand. Each side's few survivors crawled away but in different directions. They are going to find their friends and tell them what happened. The survivors will find other people and the two sides will meet to fight each other again."

Witnesses need to be prepared to be corrected in their recapitulation of the play. *Creators* may talk about something new and important not mentioned earlier or change what they reported earlier. Reflection of these fresh perspectives is encouraged. If the *Creator* has been silent, and the *Witness* believes that words will be useful, the *Witness* may then make a brief and neutral description of the play.

"Forming a Plan" for young *Creators* often includes collaboration with their caregivers. Parents may need to be alerted that a child may require extra nurturing during a challenging time, or to be educated in how to support a child's emerging skills. A plan for young *Creators* between sessions may be to consider a sand world character's dilemma and the figure's options. While the *Creator* is making the world, all of the short interactions, identifiable as Sandtray aspects, occur very quickly, in no particular order, and often simultaneously.

In a rapidly changing Sandtray, *Witnesses* must decide at every turn of events if and when to interject. The goal is to deepen the experience for *Creators* without interfering in their process. All interventions are offered in a manner that maintains intersubjective synchrony. While the sand world is being built, the *Creator's* verbal statements and sounds, or the action in the Sandtray, may be mirrored verbally by the *Witness*. Let's take a brief look at applying the Sandtray aspect of "Reflecting/Directing" with a preschool *Creator*.

Gordy's Story: Godzilla Wars

Gordy, a bright and verbal three-and-a-half-year-old, landed in the center of a highly conflicted custody battle. The parents had been divorced a year and had not resolved their differences involving Gordy and his younger sister. The parents fought about the toddler's clothes, haircuts, preschool, and doctors, as well as the visitation and parenting plans. During the marriage Gordy had been exposed to domestic violence. He had not been shielded from the verbal hostilities of his parents' ongoing war. When I began seeing him, he was being directly pulled into parental conflict by being told mean things about the other parent, and by being prompted to say specific statements about his parents to the teacher and the therapist. By the time we met, Gordy presented as a confused and sad child who had begun to act out aggressively at home and school.

The tray shown was created three months into treatment, when parental animosity was escalating over the approaching winter holiday custody plan (figure 10.3). Previously, Gordy had been minimally verbal when he engaged in Sandtray play. He had a Godzilla video at home and spoke about the story in the previous session. He chose all the Godzilla figures available, which included: two large matching Godzilla figures, one medium-sized one, and a baby Godzilla in a shell that opened up into two pieces.

Gordy prefaced his play by saying, "I don't want to make any story!" After I reassured him that no story was needed, he also emphatically told me he was "mad" about his parents saying mean things about each other and telling him what to say. Gordy chose a 16 x 20 x 6-inch tray and wanted it placed on the floor with water available. He made the sand wet, shooting the water from a turkey baster and poking this into the sand like a sword. The two large Godzillas

Figure 10.3. Gordy's view of the "mommy" and the "daddy" fighting

were set in the tray side by side and the medium one was placed to the side and partly buried. The baby Godzilla sat up in its shell. The following is a sample of our exchange during his constant action:

> Gordy: (Squirting all but the baby with sandy water) "All Godzillas are bad so I have to shoot them all."
> *Witness*: "They must all get shot."
> Gordy: (Forcefully pushing the medium Godzilla's head deeper into the sand) "Other." (As the two big ones fight more actively, throwing and stirring sand, he is very engrossed in this play.)
> *Witness*: "They are hitting each other and moving the sand a lot." (The *Witness* makes several more brief direct reflections of the interactions as they change. The *Witness* senses that the comments are acceptable to the *Creator*.)
> Gordy: (He identifies one of the large matching Godzillas as the "mommy" and the other one as the "daddy." As they fight he is pouring more water in the tray. The mess is getting sloppier and he uses a shovel, rake, and other sand tools to stir the tray and objects.)

Witness: "The mommy and daddy keep fighting, the sand gets wetter, and now the baby gets sand all over him too." (The Godzillas are being buried and unburied as they continue their fight, and sand is flying—mainly within the tray.)

Gordy: (He buries the baby Godzilla without force and the baby's shell is tossed around during the hostilities. The mommy and the daddy keep fighting. This action continues and at the end he brings in two two-headed monsters to join the war.)

Witness: (At the end of the session Gordy is asked if the words the *Witness* used today seemed right. He nodded affirmatively.) "So when the mommy and daddy Godzilla fight, the sand goes all over and even buries the baby one." (He nodded repeatedly up and down to this summarizing comment [figure 10.4].)

In this example, Gordy was better able to communicate verbally than many of his age mates, including being able to state his angry feelings.

Figure 10.4. The sand even buries the baby

He also acknowledged the *Witness*'s summary, seemingly satisfied that his message had been received. War play has many nuances and is often far more than just an "expression of aggression." When wars become a focus of Sandtray action, *Witnesses* may want to consider the following issues:

- What are the types of rules being demonstrated in this war? Are they fair and equitable? Do the factions agree to them or not? How is dissent managed?
- Are there sneak or terrorist-style attacks?
- Who is in charge and what is the locus of control, self or other?
- How are boundaries formed and violated?
- Who is hiding and who is attacking and when do these actions occur?
- Are there negotiations (yours/mine/ours/encroachment/peace/war)?
- Who is winning, losing, being friends, staying friends, or isolating?
- How are hope and despair depicted?
- Does anyone not want to fight or want to be a pacifist?
- Does anyone express being tired of fighting or wanting peace after war?
- How are the above themes depicted and how is surrender viewed?
- Are the concerns of life, death, rebirth, compassion, or its lack present?
- Who determines the value of lives, if they are equal or not, and who survives?
- What do survivors report of the war? How are prisoners treated? Does healing take place? Who does this and how?

In "war play," like other energetic worlds, *Witnesses* need to respond actively in real time as the Sandtray is being constructed. When *Witnesses* wait to say something until the end of a constantly shifting Sandtray, they can't easily address what was formed twenty or forty minutes previously. Applying the aspects is most useful during the moments that the *Witness* and the *Creator* both see the Sandtray together. Meaning is diminished or lost when the *Witness* and the *Creator* are trying to remember thousands of previous configurations. Major shifts are more easily inquired about immediately after the fact.

Although many verbal options are provided in this chapter and others, timing and relational resonance must determine their use. The harmony of the intersubjective relationship must be safeguarded at all times. If attempts by *Witnesses* to reflect or invite dialogue are met with signs of negativity or irritability, this is likely a manifestation of a rupture in harmonic resonance. *Creators'* behaviors to watch for include:

- Ignoring the *Witness*'s verbalizations.
- A dirty look.
- "No" or negative head-shaking.
- Turning his or her head or body away from the *Witness*.
- Crouching further over or leaning more into the tray.
- Physically moving to block the *Witness*'s view of the tray.
- Any behavior that evokes a sense that the *Witnesses* is being closed off or cut off from the *Creator*.

Witnesses can alleviate these ruptures by lessening their energetic intensity or physically moving back slightly from the tray to help the *Creator* feel safer. Sometimes a quick "I'm sorry" will also help. When these disruptions occur, the suggestion is for *Witnesses* to remain silent, not verbally engaging, unless or until *Creators* clearly invite or initiate words. During these times *Witnesses* continue to focus on the nonverbal qualities of the interactions. These cues are not "resistance" but are *Creators'* attempts to regulate themselves and stay within their level of tolerance. Any forcing, pushing, or display of frustration on the part of *Witnesses* will be counterproductive. Developmentally younger children often have less access to the intellectual mode and are more likely to express themselves using the physical body and emotional modes. *Witnesses'* sensitivities to these nonverbal interactions are particularly advantageous when working with preschool-age and developmentally delayed children.

Chapter 10 describes the use of the Sandtray aspects with the active sand worlds of young *Creators*. *Witnesses* require a creative and playful state of mind to accompany children in their play. Initially this is done nonverbally and sometimes evolves into a conversation. In working with child *Creators*, *Witnesses* generally rely more heavily on relational intersubjectivity than with adults. The fewer words spoken, the more *Witnesses* must use conjecture as the basis for forming inquiries and supporting the play. When treatment lasts long enough for a child to develop the ability to communicate his or her experience in words, previous sand worlds may then be discussed directly. Common nonverbal cues that children use to indicate discomfort during a Sandtray session are identified. *Witnesses* may not always perceive *Creators'* meanings for specific play actions. Cognitive awareness by either party, however, is not required for *Creators* to experience deep and meaningful transformations leading to problem resolution and behavioral change.

CHAPTER ELEVEN

Traumatized Children

Many children survive life's difficulties, including poverty, divorce, and mental or physical illness in the family. Even those children raised in loving, stable homes must learn to negotiate illness, loss, and disappointment. As affirmed by famed children's author Maurice Sendak, "Childhood is the very, very tricky business of survival" (Sendak, 2006). How these occurrences shape our lives depends on a complex web of factors. Any two people will react quite differently, even to the same event. In the assessment of children, behavioral reports from caregivers are essential. The designation of trauma, however, is ultimately determined by an individual's subjective experience. *Witnesses* must find ways to discover a child's viewpoint since only he or she can convey to us the impact of any ordeal.

Young children who encounter abuse and neglect prior to forming an organized sense of self, become impaired at a fundamental biological level. The framework that infants form in early life, to make sense of themselves and their environments, is developed through daily interactions with caregivers. This early organization occurs primarily in the right hemisphere of the brain—a brain that is dependent on nurturing environmental interactions for adequate maturation. When no loving care is provided, or when a child is met with hatred and abuse, the basic framework for human interaction remains unformed or grossly distorted.

Infants and young children must rely on their caregivers to survive even when these caregivers are the source of harm. Unlike Eddy in chapter 1, who was the victim of a single-incident trauma within a loving and organized

163

family, many abused and neglected children suffer multiple layers of trauma. They cannot develop healthy foundations for recognizing and regulating their own internal states nor the ability to perceive accurately the emotional states of others. These skills are essential to successful engagement within our human community.

The abusive incidents which brought children to my playroom were often found to be only a part of a pervasive pattern of abuse, neglect, and unhealthy parent-child interactions. Recently, Julian Ford and Christine Courtois described complex psychological trauma "as resulting from exposure to severe stressors that (1) are repetitive and prolonged, (2) involve harm or abandonment by caregivers or other ostensibly responsible adults, and (3) occur at developmentally vulnerable times in the victim's life, such as early childhood or adolescence (when critical periods of brain development are rapidly occurring or being consolidated)" (Ford and Courtois, 2009, p. 13). When a child encounters safety and acceptance, growth and experimentation with the environment is stimulated. In the absence of basic safety or when the child is harmed, deadened withdrawal or a hyper-alertness or activity level are the likely survival responses.

The children presented in this chapter lived extremely chaotic lives deprived of a fundamental model to make sense of their own impulses or their environments. I began treating children with complex interpersonal trauma without the clear definition above. Due to their flawed ability for authentic interaction, these children require relationally based play as a primary reparative treatment modality. To be emotionally met in a rich play environment provides these wounded children a context in which to access their innate healing capacities.

Infants and young children harmed by abuse and neglect have not yet developed language to express themselves. One adult survivor of early life abuse stated that "I realized that I was afraid to feel the actual hurt that was festering in my heart. I ran away from it. . . . I thought that if I really felt the full force of my emotions, I would die or go insane" (Gaudioso and Martin, 2007, p. 26). This woman articulated her feelings after years of effort to heal. We need to find ways to assist very young neglect and abuse victims to communicate. Often, however, their development of language is actually delayed due to their maltreatment.

What these children do have is an active image-thinking process. Since trauma is primarily recorded in the right or image-thinking hemisphere of the brain, Sandtray aids these young *Creators* in self-expression. The *Creator* and the *Witness* share image narratives. Initially incoherent, and often tumultuous, these image narratives become a shared language between them. Emerging from the chaos, some images may begin to form a wisp of communication, disconnected yet recognizable as such. Eventually some of these wisps will twine together to form more recognizable threads that then become available to be woven into a language-based coherent narrative.

Helping young *Creators* become the masters of their sand worlds assists them in distinguishing between the "me in here" and the sand tray "out there." They gain a sense of agency assisted by their control of the sand world and what goes inside of it. The Sandtray process and the *Witness* form a container for the raw, nonverbal expressions of experiences and emotions that engage the ability of these young *Creators* to make sense of their life's chaotic events. Cognitive therapies alone cannot build a bridge to these youth that are internally tumultuous and fragmented. The Sandtray methods encompass all of the energetic modes—physical, emotional, and intellectual—providing incalculable opportunities for *Witnesses* to connect to and harmonize with these struggling young lives.

In chapter 3 we met Lucia, a girl with complex trauma. Lucia entered foster care at four and a half years of age with her siblings after they witnessed the death of her stepsister Susie in a bathtub. Lucia suffered from Posttraumatic Stress Disorder (PTSD). Lucia made the candlelit bathtub memorial previously shown when she was six and a half years old, two years after Susie's death (see figure 3.1, chapter 3). That sand world became a piece of Lucia's coherent narrative that both she and her *Witness* could refer to, furthering communication about her real experiences. Now let's take a look at a later portion of her play therapy. By this time Lucia had developed language that included emotional concepts, allowing her to talk about experiences she had avoided in the past. This vignette also demonstrates how Sandtray aspects may be applied to other forms of art or play therapy.

Revisiting Lucia's Story: The Volcano and the Snowman

Just over one year after Lucia's memorial Sandtray, the court began to prepare a plan to return the children to their mother's and stepfather's home. Once Lucia's mom became clean and sober again, she was able to work actively toward regaining the custody of her children. Parent and child visitations became routine and positive. Both mom and stepdad were working with increasing success on their individual and couple goals as outlined by their therapists and the court. The reunification plan included family therapy at another clinic and the use of Parent Child Interaction Therapy (PCIT) with Lucia's younger siblings. Lucia continued her individual treatment with me.

Now seven years old, and two years into treatment, Lucia openly talked of her abuse experiences, withholding no secrets about her past. Often we discussed the plan to increase visitation and the goal of returning the children home. I also made it clear that if reuniting with her parents looked too unsafe to the court, she could grow up with other, safer people taking care of her. On this particular day, Lucia mentioned that her mom used to hit them but does so no longer. I told her why I did not want the children hurt. She chimed in, "or like Susie."

That day, Lucia asked to play with a bake-in-the-oven clay material. She started making forms, destroyed them, and then recreated something else. Lucia was intent and silent. Clearly, she was not in the mood to talk. We continued our clay work side-by-side at the art table. When she reformed her clay, I also reformed mine. In this way I generally mirrored her process without copying her work.

This play pattern went on for two sessions. Each time Lucia was talkative as we prepared to play, becoming silent and completely engrossed in her work as soon as she started forming the clay. Despite our nearly two years of treatment, I had no idea what this play could mean to her. Our harmonic resonance was companionable as she led the play. I felt confident that this activity was meaningful to her, but I would not find out just how significant for some time to come.

Lucia created a small, white, narrow volcano-looking form. Lastly, she made a tiny nondescript figure, which she stuck at the base of the volcano. Then she told me she was ready to have me take her creation home to bake it. I still had no idea as to the meaning of her sculpture. In a later session when Lucia had completed this piece, we sat together in a relaxed mood to look at her sculpture. The following dialogue ensued (see figure 11.1):

> *Witness*: "Wow, you have worked long and hard to make this." (This was my authentic perception of her efforts.)
> Lucia: "Yeah. It's a volcano." (She looked relaxed, sat back in her chair, and appeared ready to talk.)
> *Witness*: "Of course, I wasn't sure, but I had guessed that it might be one." (Gesturing toward the little figure,) "Can you tell me what this is?"
> Lucia: "He's the snowman that lives at the bottom of the volcano."
> *Witness*: (Focusing both eyes and energy on the tiny figure) "Oh, I had no idea who he was. I have been wondering about him."
> Lucia: "Well, he is really scared." (A few moments of silence follow.) "All the time he is waiting for the volcano to blow up. He knows it used to blow up all the time and he's waiting for that to happen. He is stiff and holding his breath." (Here, her mood changed, becoming very somber. I mirrored that shift of feeling tone.)

Figure 11.1.   **Lucia's snowman near the volcano**

Witness: "That must be hard for him." (She nodded in acknowledgment.) With puzzlement I then asked "What happens when the volcano blows up?"

Lucia: "He melts." (I reflected this statement and we sit in silence at the thought of the snowman's demise.)

Witness: (Speaking softly) "Right now he is still there though."

Lucia: "And so afraid." (I also reflected this statement, and we allowed the sense of fear to be present in the room. We were near the end of her session and Lucia shifted her attention away from her work. No attempt was made to draw Lucia's attention back to the snowman.)

At the end of this session the *Witness* did not choose to bring in a problem-solving approach. A shift to linear cognition could have been easily stimulated by asking, "Is there anything that could help the snowman feel less afraid?" or "Let's think about what we can do to help the snowman." As described in earlier chapters, times exist when the *Witness* and the *Creator*

problem-solve together. However, timing may be the key factor in the effectiveness of using cognitive techniques like "Summarizing" and "Forming a Plan." For Lucia, it was enough to allow her previously unstated experiences to come forth to a mental image that could become concrete, and then to begin to explore the figure's qualities. As with Vicky in chapter 8, the *Witness* could sense that it was too soon to move to problem-solving. Both *Creators* and *Witnesses* need time to consider new material, or material that is brought forth in a fresh manner, prior to seeking cognitive solutions. When play springs spontaneously from the *Creator's* inner life, the *Creator* of the play regulates the topics, pace, focus, and intensity of the play.

I pondered Lucia's work deeply. Her early encounters while in the care of her mother and stepdad included extreme violence. Subsequently, they worked hard to parent and relate to each other without brutality. Lucia was experiencing these changes at her weekly visits. During later sessions the terror of the snowman was referenced as we talked about her struggle to trust and to feel safe as she anticipated the return home. Despite the peril of reuniting this family, doing so honored the deep and increasingly positive attachment bonds between the children and their mother. The alternative risk for Lucia and her younger brother was to grow up in the foster care system.

Posttraumatic Play

For more than four decades, therapists have noted the different qualities between posttraumatic play and normal play patterns. Basic features of posttraumatic play include the lack of joy, creativity, and spontaneity accompanying a compulsive repetition of play actions. Also, *Creators* often do not find relief from anxiety, nor do the play activities depict resolutions to threat, danger, or a sense of terror. I have observed that the judicious use of the Sandtray aspects decreases the compulsive repetition of traumatic play. Minute changes in the way *Creators* view their worlds begin to break the constricted constellation of posttraumatic play.

Following the *Creator's* lead, both directive and nondirective approaches to play can be useful. For me, being directive is not the same as being controlling. I may make a verbal suggestion or prominently put out items that I suspect will be useful. I invite but, in doing so, I do not restrict the *Creator's* play. I trust the life force in even the most dispirited child to move toward health. To suggest is not the same as to manipulate the *Creator* to comply with the ideas of the *Witness*. The energy in the treatment session and the experience for each party are different in each case. The *Witness's* mental, emotional, and spiritual stance forms the foundation of this work. Again, the *Witness*'s harmonic resonance with the *Creator* renders the *Witness* more able to perceive accurately what is most helpful in the moment. When the *Witness* approaches the encounter solely intellectually, this task is far more difficult.

The Sandtray aspects, whether used in or out of the Sandtray, are meant to serve as guidelines to assist *Witnesses* in recognizing opportunities to engage with *Creators*. Due to the nonverbal presentation of many young traumatized children, I rely heavily on observing the energetic modes as well as the contextual fields of their play. *Witnesses* seek to be engaged and attentive without being invasive. *Witnesses* must continuously monitor the *Creator*'s level of comfort, maintaining the awareness that, for some children, even minimal reflections may feel like interference.

The following two case studies are examples of preschoolers who, at the beginning of treatment, were using only a few words. The first case introduced is Jana, a victim of severe sexual abuse in early childhood. Many nonverbal play sessions occurred early in her treatment. During these sessions I worked to be authentically attentive, to reflect and validate her experiences as appropriate, and aid her affect regulation through our relationship. As treatment progressed, Jana became more interactive and verbal in her play therapy.

Jana's Story: Caging Fear

The police removed Jana from her parents' home at three years and seven months of age along with two younger siblings. She was a victim of neglect, beatings, and sexual abuse. Her older half sister had previously been placed out of the home and her parents were on felony probation for abusing that child. The police reported that the home was filthy and that there were mice nesting in Jana's crib. Her fifteen-month-old brother suffered a head injury and had multiple healing and untreated fractures. The authorities knew her parents for previous domestic violence and drug abuse violations. Although she was free from fractures at that time, clearly Jana had experienced an abusive environment since birth.

Jana was brought to me for treatment at four years of age by a relative caregiver. This home also had custody of Jana's seven-month-old sister. Jana was cute, acted sweetly, and wanted to play with the toys. Her foster family reported that she was aggressive and cruel to others, particularly her infant sister and a fragile elder also in the home. Jana initially showed extremely restricted affect with no remorse. Jana was defiant and irritable. She had difficulty falling asleep and she had nightmares in which she screamed and swore every night. She had killed another child's pet frog and smeared feces on the wall. She had a superficial friendliness to all strangers and exhibited sexually suggestive be-haviors with all men, rubbing up against them, pulling down her top or lifting up her dress. Jana met the criterion for both PTSD and Reactive Attachment Disorder-Disinhibited Type.

When treatment began, helping Jana feel safe was in the forefront. Her play was initially based in the physical energetic mode and very disorganized and fragmented. As time passed her play developed some recognizable coherent fragments. She portrayed many tales of isolation and loss, including those of babies who got left behind and forgotten by their mothers, and babies who had no home. Despite beginning treatment and the love and care from her relatives, her symptoms worsened. Jana appeared to be extremely jealous of the care needed by her baby sister and the elder in her relative foster home. She required constant supervision and would attempt to startle, frighten, or attack these two family members with any minor lapse of attention. Within six months, and after a psychological evaluation, Jana moved to a highly structured therapeutic foster home with no young children.

Although this change was initially difficult for her, within six months of her weekly sessions she began to show improvement. Jana's nightmares decreased to once a week and she began to show signs of attaching to the foster mother. She started to exhibit a greater range of affects and was effectively learning to use words to express her needs and desires. Jana's observable dissociative behaviors decreased, but she continued to be manipulative, oppositional, and aggressive.

During this six-month period of play therapy, in her play Jana started acting out people who were fighting and then began beating the baby dolls. At first I tolerated this behavior. Soon her behavior repeated, becoming an intense pat-tern of beating and yelling mean statements at the doll, such as, "You're a bad baby!" My intersubjective sense was that Jana was replaying the abuse she had both witnessed and experienced, and that she might be dissociating with these actions. Her play followed no process or resolution, only a spiraling escalation. My discomfort grew to a sense of impending danger.

This baby doll beating ended my career as a completely nondirective play therapist. I intervened by removing the doll from her, cuddling it, and telling the doll and Jana there was no such thing as a "bad baby." She looked surprised. We began a dialogue about how all babies are good babies. Jana asked many questions. I described to her that sometimes parents believe that some babies are bad, but such parents are wrong and don't know better. We had similar chats many times over weeks of treatment. We discussed how she had learned that "babies were bad," and that part of my job was to correct some things she learned that were not right. I allowed her to spank or hit a nondescript cloth "angry doll" that did not look like a real human. I no longer allowed Jana (or others) to hit or treat the baby dolls in a rough manner. Instead, I taught her the tender ways in which to care for a baby, and she seemed fascinated by this play.

After one year of treatment, Jana began using more words in conjunction with her play. Two sessions prior to the Sandtray described below, she chose black sand and made a tray showing household furniture and a "girl who was bad" and a baby in a crib "who is having trouble sleeping." There were ten women in the tray and three were designated as "the moms." She brought out a first-aid kit and set each item carefully in the sand, describing its function. Jana did not want to end this session and did not "feel finished." Careful photographs were taken, as Jana stated she wanted to continue with this play on her next turn.

For the next session I was prepared with the photographs. Jana came in, glanced at the pictures, and emphatically stated, "I don't want to do that anymore!" Then she said, "I'm not coming back (to therapy)." Jana did not admit to feeling angry and she insisted on taking the photographs of the previous Sandtray and placing them in her purse. Jana chose to play a game and made comments including, "I don't love myself," and, "I don't love people." Regarding her therapeutic foster parents, she told me, "Dad doesn't love me. Mom does—all the time, even when I am bad." Jana had much difficulty attaching to a "dad" who clearly refused to be sexual with her. That day, our play evolved into interactive play with our gentle doctoring of the baby dolls.

The very next visit, Jana entered ignoring the Sandtray materials again. She played a game and then played with the baby dolls. With less than half of the session remaining, she rushed over to the black sand. Jana formed the sand world shown. First she placed two Native American dolls and called them "the sisters." She then set the shorter doll in the tray as "the little girl." Next, Jana added the glass bottle, filling it with sand, dumping it, and refilling it, over and over again. She then placed the first-aid kit in the sand. She set a few fairy tale figures in the tray, but immediately removed them. The Witness only reflected her words intermittently as she worked. Jana then picked up "the scary man" and removed a small green slime figure with a noose around its neck that he carries in his hand. She detached and buried the tiny green figure. Of the "scary man" she says, "He is a monster; he bites me," and then she poured sand on his head. The "sisters" and "the little girl" are watching this process. The Witness feels an increased sense of danger and Jana looks tense and alert. She picks up the first-aid kit and sets out all of the tools on top of the sand. Picking up the "scary man," she plays with him and the first-aid kit tools in silence, removing the "monster head" and putting it back on several times. (This figure has a more human face under the removable monster head figure.) She then selects a zoo cage for the world and places the "scary man" in and out of the cage several times, holding him often. The feeling of danger in the room is strong as she says, "I don't know where he goes." Jana places him in the sand; the zoo cage has been set outside the tray. She says, "He's not real," and denies that this guy scares her (see figure 11.2).

We are out of time and I cue Jana to end. We begin to clean up items outside the sand world and Jana becomes obviously distressed and begins to talk about the scary man in a frightened voice. Referring to the "scary man" she insists, "He can't just stay there!" By now her body is shaking and she is squeezing her legs together, and hugging herself tightly. Jana demands that he leave the sand world. The Witness asks, "Where does he need to be for you to feel safe?" We briefly discuss options and she moves him into the zoo cage next to the tray. She is still distressed, so we move the cage to a table farther away from the sand world. This appears to be helping her calm down. Walking to the door to leave, she looks back at the caged figure again, "Look! He can get out the top!" Pressed for time, the *Witness* grabbed a tissue box from the table and set it firmly on the top of the cage asking, "Will this work for you?" Jana smiled, "Yes! Now he can't scare anyone." The *Witness* reiterated that his cage completely surrounded him, that the box was full, heavy, and strong, and that he could not get himself out of the cage (see figure 11.3). Jana left the session calm and much relieved.

Figure 11.2.   Jana's "scary man": View from the east side

Figure 11.3. The "scary man" caged

One reason to share Jana's story is that it shows her gradual self-directed exposure to threatening material. She also readied herself for this exposure by playing with positive and supportive themes first. In a session prior to bringing in "the scary man," she experimented with the first-aid kit, talking about the healing function of some items it contained. She also had multiple "moms," a concept that she was now regularly identifying as supportive, even loving. In this way she was preparing herself, modulating her tolerance, to manage this "scary guy" and the experiences he evoked for her. I had no intellectual knowledge of this process at the time. Since then, I have recognized this function and have seen this pattern of preparation and gradual self-exposure repeatedly.

Also, Jana's denial of her self-created image when she stated, "He's not real," about the "scary man," is an example of a common defensive shift made by traumatized children. It demonstrates how both the intrusive re-experiencing and the avoidance of trauma stimuli may be seen within a single session. Because Jana was unable to shore up her denial, she again became frightened of this figure at session's end. Rather than hold her to the usual clean-up tasks, the *Witness* intervened to address Jana's distress, supporting the transformation of her state of mind prior to leaving the treatment session.

Further, being with Jana's abusive beatings of the baby dolls, I just knew (gnosis) that to allow her to continue that behavior would be harmful. This occurred early enough in my career that my thinking mind (logos) was telling me that I "should" be nondirective. Sometimes not listening to my left brain is the best choice I can make. Rather than allowing Jana to become retraumatized through her abuse of the baby dolls, I redirected her toward mastering the gentle treatment and care of them. I could model the love and affection that this girl did not know from her biological parents. This single act may have been one of the most important events of her therapy.

Jana was in treatment foster care and play therapy for four years. She did return to her relative foster home once her dangerous behaviors subsided. By that time the elder had moved out of the home and Jana's baby sister was older and less vulnerable.

Toxic versus Healing Play

I have referred to patterns of play as positive or negative, using Jana's baby doll beatings as a negative example and her resolution and relief with the caging of the "scary man" as a positive one. Psychotherapist and play specialist Eliana Gil describes these differences as dynamic and toxic. She states that "dynamic posttraumatic play meets its basic intent of achieving a sense of mastery for the client; toxic posttraumatic play is play that becomes stuck, without movement, without relief, devoid of new options, explorations, or release" (Gil, 2010, p. 56). Gil's terms, *toxic play* and *dynamic play*, are very instructive for us. *Witnesses* can observe the circular or stuck nature of toxic play, often feeling the frustration and poisoned nature of it within the intersubjective relationship.

Mastery of traumatic material is achieved only over multiple sessions and usually cannot be determined on a session-by-session basis. The true value of the components of dynamic play is most often revealed over time. A *Witness*'s attention to details and to careful documentation can aid in the accurate assessment of a *Creator*'s play patterns. Jana's story highlights the distinction between recurrent play themes and play that is actually stuck, as she was when beating the baby dolls. For Jana, the above Sandtray did not resolve her fears of the "scary man." Yet her sand world does spotlight a shift that Jana made to initiate dealing with her trauma more directly. Subsequently, Jana dramatized many sand worlds that included the "scary man," repeating this theme without becoming stuck.

The vignette below offers an example of how a *Witness* can continue to support a *Creator's* play even when the play pattern is not intellectually understood. The definite shifts in Luc's play patterns were noted and acknowledged when appropriate, although the likely reasons for these changes were not always apparent to the *Witness* during the session. Working with the sand world directly in front of us, *Witnesses* can apply the Sandtray aspects while attending to the intersubjective communication to both receive and support a *Creator's* budding experiences. This complex case also demonstrates how changes in Luc's environment over time were reflected in his play patterns.

Luc's Story: Waiting for a Home

A dimple-cheeked Luc was brought to play therapy at three and a half years of age at the urging of his county social worker. Although generally meeting his physical developmental milestones, Luc had a two-year speech delay and was not potty trained.

Luc had been just two years and ten months old when he and his two little brothers were removed from his biological parents. Multiple previous attempts by Children's Protective Services to work with his biological parents had proved unsuccessful. As the biological parents were not responsive to efforts to reunify the family, the children were removed permanently and released for adoption.

While living with his birth parents Luc was often dirty, unfed, and locked in a room or closet. The investigators determined that Luc suffered beatings, verbal abuse, cigarette burns, and profound neglect. Luc and his siblings did not receive adequate medical care. Both biological parents had histories of domestic violence and substance abuse. At a later time, Luc's mother admitted to physical abuse and indicated that she suspected her former boyfriend of sexually abusing Luc.

As treatment began, Luc had been living in his second foster home for six months. He demonstrated a positive attachment to his foster mother. However, Luc began to become aggressive, pushing, hitting, or biting to get his needs met. He had a history of depressive episodes during which he became lethargic, fretful, and whiney for several days at a time. These incidents worsened to include throwing things, screaming, and trying to hurt others. A psychiatric consultation yielded a recommendation against medication. The foster parents also cared for Luc's two younger brothers and two other foster children, all under age five. The foster parents' teenage son was helpful with the younger children when he was available.

Due to Luc's delays, PTSD, and attachment difficulties, the treatment plan included individual play therapy twice weekly for three weeks and weekly thereafter. At the beginning of his first session Luc was reserved. He eventually engaged comfortably in play with the *Witness* on the floor. His only expression of delight occurred when he dumped small items on the floor and mixed them up to make a "mess." In the final twenty minutes Luc went to a dry sand tray. He moved sand constantly for fifteen minutes. He pushed, pulled, stirred, grabbed, poked, clawed, formed mounds in the sand, and then smoothed them over. He vigorously repeated these actions in various patterns, again and again, with full bodily engagement. The energy of this play was intense and chaotic, even violent. Lastly, he pushed a whale figure into the sand pile very hard, hitting it repeatedly, and then removed it from the tray. After this Sandtray Luc seemed calm and followed clean-up instructions easily. Considering his history Luc's engagement in therapy began well.

When initially brought into foster care, Luc acted shy and even withdrawn. His affect appeared flat and he possessed no speech, only grunting and pointing when in need. Luc did not know how to play, feared men, and was emotionally distant and rejected affection. After nine months of foster care, Luc had learned to make eye contact, play with toys, give and accept hugs. He demonstrated less fear of men. The speech therapist noted that Luc had learned to speak fifty-five words.

During Luc's second therapy session he came in eagerly and went directly to the sandtray. He moved the sand around. He then began to make a world with characters from *The Lion King* and *Barney the Friendly Dinosaur*. Throughout Luc's play, the *Witness* strove to stay in harmonic resonance with him, reflecting his few words and sounds. He worked primarily in silence, yet looked up at the *Witness* frequently, seemingly to check if she were attentive. Once the objects were in the tray he energetically moved the sand, forming great tides of sand movements. The figures tumbled and flowed, at the mercy of the shifting waves (see figure 11.4). Although Luc was verbally unable to validate his meaning, I nonetheless believed that the experiences that he created accurately depicted his life.

This play pattern continued to be dominant over the next two months. The *Witness* reflected words and actions whenever this seemed useful. Luc would nod his head to affirm comments or shake his head "no," only occasionally trying to clarify his meaning in words. He also asked for "rock-a-bye" play, in which he pretended to be a baby. I asked the foster parents to provide this activity for Luc at home, but they were unable to do so.

After two months of therapy the foster parents reported that Luc was no longer protesting the use of time outs, and he needed 60 percent fewer than before. His bowel and bladder control had improved and his whining and lethargy became less frequent. Luc's aggression had declined as well. In general, Luc was behaving better despite the foster parent's inability to do the recommended "homework," which also included attachment-promoting methods such as

Figure 11.4. Luc's tumbling figures in the waves of sand

child-directed play with one parent at a time. The foster parents found the suggestions to support treatment too demanding, complaining that they had "too many kids" to provide Luc the individual attention he required. They most often provided care to the children in groups of at least two.

In his third month of treatment, Luc made a definite change in his play. He began sorting out items into categories. For example, he lined up some men and some keys, then placed animals and treasures in their own groups. As he returned more often to sorting miniatures, the sweeping tides seen earlier receded. Luc continued to make sand worlds and began to form areas that looked and felt more organized. Sometimes he could tell me a little about what he made.

As she reported Luc's progress, the foster mother also informed me that they had decided to adopt his two younger brothers and his new infant sister, who had recently been placed in their home. They were feeling frustrated by Luc's need for constant supervision and by his negative behaviors, including a sexual touching incident. She stated that they would not adopt Luc but were willing to keep him until a permanent home could be found.

Reviewing the foster parents' adoption request, the county agency subsequently decided that these siblings could be placed for adoption only as a group. The county began to search for a home that would accept the entire sibling group. This response to the foster parents' request came at the end of Luc's third month of treatment. The children were not directly told of these decisions.

Despite the advancement in Luc's interactions at home, after three months of regular treatment, he began to fail to appear for his appointments. This change coincided precisely with the county's decision not to separate these siblings for adoption. By then the county worker also directed the foster parents to follow up with "rock-a-bye" and the other treatment supports. Yet, in the next four months Luc missed 25 percent of his scheduled weekly visits, often without notice. The county worker informed me that Luc was not attending speech therapy consistently either and expressed her concern that the foster parents were sabotaging Luc's care.

Throughout this four-month period, when Luc was able to attend his play sessions, he nearly always asked to play "rock-a-bye" for the first part of his time. It was taking longer than during his initial treatment to encourage him to make eye contact and connect to the *Witness*. His previous behavioral gains at the foster home were slipping and he directly expressed more anger in the playroom. In Luc's sand worlds, the sweeping tides of sand and objects returned, as did the feeling of anger and the sense of chaos. Luc used water more often, creating "floods." He identified a "bad guy," containing or burying him. Some days he appeared overtly sad.

Midway through this period of erratic attendance, Luc pointed at a mask with sharp teeth and said firmly, "He bites." He then picked up two crying baby

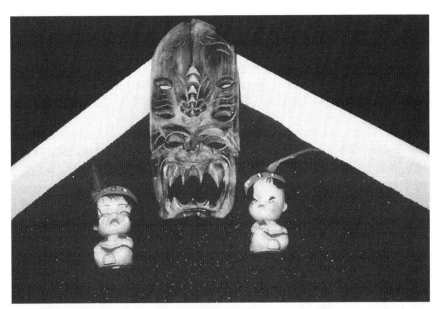

Figure 11.5. "He bites" and the "crying babies"

figures and whispered, "The babies are crying." Luc held these two for a while, and then he placed all three items in the black Sandtray (see figure 11.5). The foster parents reported that Luc expressed "glee in hurting people," and that he was "spacing out" more frequently. They felt at a loss in disciplining him. By the end of the four months the county began supporting the foster parents by providing transportation to therapies and Luc again began attending his sessions more regularly.

A couple of unfortunate events occurred beginning one month after routine treatment was reinstated. The foster parents still wanted to adopt Luc's younger siblings and were in conflict with the county over this issue. The first incident occurred when the foster mother brought Luc to therapy. Prior to the session, with Luc present, she informed me about the events of the week and then stated, "He still needs intensive supervision. We're just not able to do it long term, it's a real strain." During his session, Luc used the Sandtray to act out fighting, biting, and stuffing sand in figures' mouths with greater intensity than had been seen in months. When I returned Luc to the waiting room after the session, his foster mother said to me, "We want to keep the other kids but not," and she made a gesture toward Luc tipping her head. Looking down I saw him staring directly at her. I had no doubt that he completely understood her meaning.

Luc's play continued in the above pattern through the next session as well. Then another clear transformation occurred. Luc came to the playroom

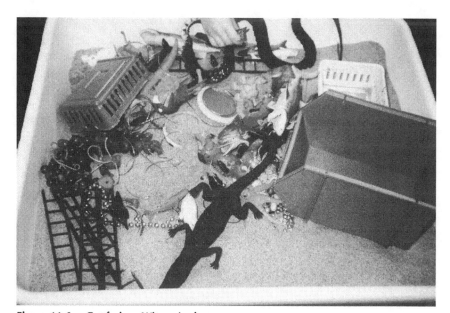

Figure 11.6.   Confusion: *Witness's* view

appearing even more emotionally disorganized, distant, and less able to be interactive with this *Witness* than he was at the beginning of his treatment, although he warmed up and engaged in play eventually. His Sandtrays began depicting increased confusion as he dumped many bins and stirred items. Conflict was present, but was not the focus of his energies or his play content. Confusion appeared as the main feature of Luc's play during this time (see figure 11.6).

Three sessions later, Luc's county worker notified me that he had been visiting his "new friends" for two weeks. A family had been located who wanted to adopt all the children. There had been no preparation of the children for these visits although Luc was now four years of age. He clearly still struggled to speak in sentences, but his receptive language and intellectual capacity appeared normal. During the two-week period of visitation with this new family, Luc regressed in his daytime bowel and bladder control. His whining and temper tantrums increased.

I later discovered that the foster parents had taken legal action to stop these visitations, but the visits continued for over a month. After a five-month legal battle with the county, the foster parents' rights to adopt were upheld by the court if they would keep all the siblings together. Subsequently, Luc's foster parents made a greater effort to work with Luc and appeared more committed to him. The intensity of his chaotic and confused play decreased once the legal conflict was resolved.

By this time, Luc had been in treatment for one year. He had clearly become attached to both of his foster parents. Luc's extreme aggressiveness and his sexual acting out had resolved completely. However, he continued to be hypervigilant and to suffer nightmares, depression, and to display oppositional behaviors. His speech gradually improved with speech therapy and special educational services. Luc continued treatment throughout the next year and a half. PTSD symptoms re-emerged for him only when major changes such as a new classroom occurred. Luc and his siblings were adopted by the foster parents.

In working with disorganized *Creators* like Jana and Luc, *Witnesses* may need to strive to remain engaged throughout long periods of treatment that have little cognitive content. Many of Jana's early Sandtrays appeared and felt both primitive and chaotic. Neither child's play exhibited a sequencing of events. Luc's initial tidal waves felt tumultuous. At times, each *Creator* expressed intense affects of fear, rage, anger, and sorrow, in the midst of total chaos. This form of play feels intently serious and does not invite interaction from the *Witness*. Using Margaret Lowenfeld's framework of play as a cipher language, these *Creators* communicated their utter confusion and terror about life.

As therapy progresses, play patterns evolve. The earliest changes are likely to be pieces of coherent interaction between objects in the midst of many disordered items. This type of modification is easy for a *Witness* to miss when the Sandtray is piled with figures and seemingly purposeless movement. Other signs of growth may be minor affective or energetic shifts, along with improvements in behavior outside the playroom. As portions of Jana's and Luc's play became more organized, depictions of being brutally attacked, being devoured, and being annihilated were common. During this type of play both children exhibited observable bodily tension, and often a diffuse sense of terror was present.

Later in the Sandtray process, *Creators* often learn to name different figures and begin to assign specific qualities to them. Chaos generally decreases, although it may return when the child is distressed as in Luc's case. Initially, Sandtray *Witnesses* rely on the aspects of "Silent Reverie" and "Reflecting" with these traumatized children. The *Witness* stays alert for moments when a *Creator* is more open and verbal. Then the "Directing" portion of that aspect may be attempted. Over time the other aspects may become useful when *Creators'* ability to tolerate engagement with their sand worlds increases.

However, even for older disorganized *Creators*, using the aspects of "Entering into the World" and "Exploring from Inside the World" requires caution. Preferably, these aspects are initiated by the *Creator*. If *Creators* have not differentiated themselves from the play itself, entering chaotic and dangerous sand worlds may elicit increased disorganization and fear and result in greater distress. Until this differentiation occurs, *Witnesses* do not join *Creators* in their play from the internal perspective. When *Witnesses* are able to enter play with a *Creator*, they can promote healing by being alert for opportunities to strengthen experiences which depict safety, hope, nurturing, and self-empowerment. This was my rationale for taking the time to emphasize to Jana that her "scary man" was secure in his cage.

Severely injured *Creators*, like Jana and Luc, come to therapy with a damaged capacity to attach and engage. Opportunities for attachment-promoting play were encouraged when the *Creators* did not choose Sandtray. Luc's rock-a-bye remained one of these activities for him. Both of these children enjoyed wearing animal noses and, face-to-face with the *Witness*, could practice improving their eye contact and facial expressions while becoming various animals. Hand mirrors were also available for the children to see their own expressions and to hide behind. When disorganized *Creators* become highly confused, they may be unable to discriminate between feeling a feeling, naming a feeling, and acting a feeling. They may be so confused as to be unclear about what is inside of them and what is outside. During painful abuse and profound neglect, these maltreated children absorb anger, rage, and hate. Psychotherapist Shoshana Ringel aptly portrays the perspective of these children as developing "a psychic equivalent of being bad, incompetent, and untrustworthy, translated into a view of the world as threatening and unsafe. . . . They create a distortion view of others and the nature of their interactions with others" (Ringel, 2011, p. 62). Often the first part of treatment is to provide safety and woo the child into a relationship, which will serve as the core for further healing.

This initial step of therapy most often looks like we are "just playing" with the child. Not so. The *Witness* is doing the demanding and delicate job of resonating with a *Creator* who has little or no organized internal structure. We provide a secure container and mirror the child, while staying alert to any minute shift of energy or play pattern that will give us an opening to support and validate the *Creator*'s true self. *Witnesses* help these *Creators* increase their tolerance for authentic human connection and expand their capacities for experiencing a greater range of feeling states. This style of play parallels the dyadic systems view of parent-child interaction described by Beebe and Lachmann (2002, pp. 21–24). Yes, in play therapy we may be having fun, but there is nothing simple about developing and maintaining a sincere connection to abused children. Tremendous energy to remain present and grounded in the face of intense negative affects and painful images is required. A solid knowledge base and a clear understanding about the work being done will aid *Witnesses* in their tasks.

Working with disorganized and traumatized *Creators* necessitates trust in the Sandtray process, in the *Creators'* essential capacity for health, and in the *Creators'* ability to set their own pace. Should the *Witness* apply cognitive interventions or techniques early in treatment, their actions may be perceived as authoritarian or commanding to these fragile *Creators*. A *Witness*'s poking and prodding with the Sandtray techniques devalues the play that a *Creator* is engaged in. Such actions will often backfire and may create a serious rupture in the budding therapeutic relationship.

The healing and growth processes of both Jana and Luc included lulls in progress as well as reversals of newly gained skills. Over time, children with chaotic histories, poor attachment, and doubtful futures have a better opportunity to integrate new learning when additional stability is provided. To supply this needed stability over time often requires the *Witness*'s flexibility to accommodate the needs of various caregivers and providers of other therapeutic modalities.

A Cautionary Tale

Many *Creators* are unable to report the traumatic events they have experienced. Some traumas may be unknown to caregivers as well. This is particularly true for foster children who are generally removed from their biological parents due to a singular incident. Despite direct inquiry by the *Witness*, both the *Creator* and the *Witness* may enter treatment with little or no knowledge of the extent of distressing past events. Sometimes, when trauma is suspected, the wiser option may be not to enter those experiences and learn about the details. Just because a *Witness* has the skill to intervene does not mean that exploring trauma serves a *Creator*'s needs. The following vignette is one such example.

Mumi's Story: Staying on the Safe Side

A friendly girl, eleven-year-old Mumi was brought to therapy by her foster/adoptive mother Joy. These two had enjoyed a positive relationship since Mumi was five years of age. They met when Joy was a college acquaintance of Mumi's biological mother, Efua, who later suddenly became unable to care for her child.

By the time Mumi entered treatment she had been living with Joy since age nine. Joy was concerned that Mumi was "overly sensitive" because Mumi could not take even minor criticism or allow Joy to help with homework. Overwhelmed by deep sadness, Mumi sobbed easily, was forty pounds overweight, and frequently sneaked food. She made statements to Joy like "My mom left without saying good-bye" and "Mom was mean to me. I don't know why; I'm a good girl." Joy asked for parenting assistance as well treatment for her daughter. There were no reports of abuse or domestic violence in Mumi's history.

Mumi was the daughter of a West African mother who was born while her mother attended college in the United States. Therefore, Mumi was a U.S. citizen. Her parents were engaged but the pregnancy was unplanned and unwanted. The couple broke their engagement right after Mumi's birth, and she never knew her father. Efua had planned on returning to Africa with Mumi. Due to the scarcity of food in her homeland, Efua allowed Mumi to eat only one small meal a day. This home was also quite restrictive and Efua did not allow her daughter out to play with others. Mumi did not display a tendency to be physically active and Joy reported that she was "physically inactive by nature."

When Mumi was nearly seven, Efua had a mental health crisis requiring hospitalization and was diagnosed with bipolar disorder. That day, Mumi was picked up at school by the sheriff and taken to the children's shelter, never to live with her mother again. Efua did not comply with the Children's Protective

Services reunification plan and eventually was deported to Africa. Contact between Efua and Mumi came primarily through intermittent letters.

Mumi lived in her first foster home for two years and Joy visited her regularly. When Mumi was nine, her foster father died and she moved into Joy's home. The adoption process began. While in her first foster home Mumi was sent to therapy. Joy reported that Mumi would "become hysterical" afterward because the therapist continuously told her that she "would never see her biological mother again." Quite understandably, this girl demonstrated trepidation on entering therapy with me.

Mumi took several sessions to begin to relax with me. She did tell me how much she missed her mom but she denied the depression symptoms that Joy reported. She did describe angry outbursts and irritability, saying, "I have a temper but I don't want to deal with it." On the fourth visit, Mumi tentatively approached the Sandtray and started moving sand. Quietly she formed the world shown, making a few revisions as she worked (see figure 11.7).

Mumi formed the two sides of the sand world simultaneously, not sequentially. With little time left in the session, we did a few brief "Reflecting/Directing" exchanges. I then invited her to look at the world with me to see what we might discover (sitting side-by-side).

Figure 11.7. Mumi's "safe side" and "very scary side"

Mumi: "There is a safe side and a very scary side."

Witness: "Tell me what you know about these two sides."

Mumi: "There is an invisible dome over the safe side."

Witness: "Describe this dome and how it works."

Mumi: "It covers and protects the safe side completely; it's very tight, and no one can ever break it. No sounds can go through it. The dome covers the bridge, which is really a wall."

Witness: "Is there some place in this world where we can go inside the world and still be feel safe?"

Mumi: "With Dorothy and her friends [from *The Wizard of OZ*]. We can only go on the safe side. The war side is awful—there are no good guys there."

Witness: "So, let's look around from in here." (She does not initiate, so I ask her about one of the few items she has named.) "What could we see from that wall-bridge?"

Mumi: "We could see the scary side and still be safe but I want to stay here."

Witness: "Okay. So, you know that the scary stuff is right outside that wall and you do not want to see it."

Mumi: "No, it feels too scary. Oh, it should have a big volcano too." (She does not move or look around for a volcano.)

Witness: "That's okay. Just because we know something is there does not mean we have to go look at it. Maybe some day you will want to know about that place or maybe never. You are the one who gets to make that choice. You certainly don't have to go visit it now."

Mumi: "In the future I am only making the safe side."

In Mumi's session above, she had the experience that the boundaries she set would be respected and that she had a say in what topics we covered. This approach provided enough safety for her treatment to progress rapidly. Forcing difficulties from the past into current awareness does not necessarily facilitate their integration, and doing so may be harmful. *Creators* need the power to set limits, particularly when they feel fearful or overwhelmed. One valuable attribute of the Sandtray process is that *Creators* of any age can delicately explore trauma experiences, increasing their tolerance for the material at their own rate.

Working with play, somatic-emotional techniques, and cognitive methods, Mumi improved her anger management, self-soothing, and assertiveness skills. She also described patterns of hypervigilance and learned to alter them. Throughout our work, Mumi shared images and memories from living with her mother, some of which indicated an overcontrolling and bizarre parenting pattern and the likelihood of parental drug use. A narrative began to unfold that correlated with complex relational trauma. However, no such information had been included in Mumi's child welfare history. I also made a point not to say to Mumi that she would "never" see her mother again. Philosophically, I told Mumi that "never" was a long time and that I had no knowledge of what her future options might be. We even discussed future job possibilities that could lead her to travel to Africa once she was an adult.

Providing her adoptive mother with a more accurate developmental perspective of Mumi's earlier life experiences assisted Joy in understanding Mumi's early physical and emotional starvation. Joy found herself more able to be a compassionate parent. We viewed her daughter's tendency for inactivity not as "her nature," but instead spoke of a tired, poorly fed child, with little energy, who was constantly controlled and contained. As Joy realized that Mumi's behaviors had originally been learned to help her survive, Joy demonstrated increased patience as she found greater hope for Mumi to grow into a wonderful woman.

In this chapter the Sandtray process is applied in work with young *Creators* suffering from complex trauma. When infants and young children are maltreated, their basic framework for human interaction remains unformed or grossly distorted. Evident is the need for a relationally based Sandtray approach with this fragile population. Posttraumatic play, as we have explored in clinical examples, involves both dynamic and toxic play patterns. The review of the tasks and personal characteristics required of a *Witness* and the cautions for the misuse of the Sandtray methods will provide useful guidance for Sandtray practitioners.

Conclusion

A seemingly unremarkable trio of sand, water, and miniatures—Sandtray—can become essential elements for transformation in psychotherapy. To create a three-dimensional "world" in a tray of sand offers a flexible vehicle to access unknown and implicit parts of ourselves, allowing for healing, recovery, and growth. The stories of real people, from toddlers to seniors, have helped illustrate my instruction of Sandtray techniques and have shown how we can apply them. For example, consider this presentation of young Kirsten:

Kirsten's Story

Kirsten is a six-year-old African American girl with a seriously ill mother. On her second therapy visit she comes into the playroom and heads to the Sandtray area. Saying not a word after "Hello," Kirsten begins to form her sand world. Starting with a giant ice cream cone and a cluster of grapes, she then places keys near them. She does not look up, intent upon her work. Seemingly haphazardly, Kirsten adds figures of Scar (from *The Lion King*); Dorothy and Toto (from *The Wizard of OZ*); Marge Simpson (a cartoon TV mom); a male in a blue cap and gown; a Day of the Dead cap-and-gown figure; a Caucasian wedding couple; a Hawaiian totem; and a ghost standing over another person huddled in a tiny boat. She piles coins in the center of the sand tray, and then she places a white cross and a coffin nearby. A soccer ball, gas pump, and plastic Halloween teeth fill out her world.

As Kirsten's Sandtray *Witness*, I closely observe her, resonate with her affect, and take notes of the events in the sand tray itself. Yet, I truly have no idea what her world is about. Items are placed apparently at random, and Kirsten makes no comments during her work. I notice that her energetic focus remains intense and that her body moves with solid purpose.

All of my training and wisdom alerts me that this child has just created an experience of great importance to her. I sense that she is striving to communicate with me using her whole being. Then Kirsten stops forming her world, looks at it carefully, and quietly and expectantly looks to me.

As her psychotherapist, how would you meet Kirsten emotionally, energetically, and intellectually, without distorting the message she brings to you and to herself? How would you aid her when you are unclear about her language of play? By applying the theories and techniques explored in this volume, you now know how to respond effectively to a Sandtray *Creator* such as Kirsten. By learning to implement the ten identifiable occurrences called "aspects of a Sandtray session," you have prepared yourself to facilitate any Sandtray session. Employing the schema of "energetic modes" and "contextual fields" enables you to track and to understand a *Creator*'s work, both in the moment and over time.

Like Kirsten, many people begin the Sandtray process silently. Sandtray allows *Creators* to compose a dialogue between their implicit (right brain) and their explicit (left brain) ways of understanding. With the help of a skilled and attuned *Witness*, *Creators* can learn from the images and actions of their own sand worlds and implement new approaches in their daily lives.

Sandtray, as presented here, is rooted in the theories and techniques of the play-research pioneer Margaret Lowenfeld. Informed further by the contemporary fields of neurobiology and attachment, Sandtray promotes the expression of the unspoken self. The multisensory nature of Sandtray increases our abilities to synthesize and communicate our experiences, promoting a more coherent sense of self.

By definition, constructing a Sandtray requires action. Integrating Sandtray theories and techniques necessitates that *Witnesses* touch, play, and form sand worlds themselves. An intellectual understanding of the Sandtray process is the foundation for developing our skills as *Witnesses*. An initial step toward experiencing the power that the Sandtray method may hold for others is for *Witnesses* to use these tools ourselves, and to grasp what is evoked in us. While in the future the field of interpersonal neurobiology may offer further scientific clarity of the workings of the Sandtray process, for now we can roll up our sleeves and play.

As for Kirsten, by exploring her world with her *Witness*, guided by the Sandtray aspects, she eventually articulated her meaning of the items that she chose and engaged in a dialogue about how they reflected her daily experiences. Creating sand worlds over time, Kirsten learned how to verbalize her needs, wants, and feelings, advancing her healing process.

Appendix A

Materials, Sandtray
Set-ups, and Miniature Basics

Sand

I recommend only real, clean sand. "Manufactured" sands or those that can be molded without water are not optimal for a *primary* Sandtray offering. These products are fine playroom items, but I do not routinely use them for Sandtray. They do not hold the same "feel" of the earth deep in our lives and do not interact with water in the same fashion as true sand. I do not use "play sand" sold in hardware and home-improvement stores. These products are inconsistent in the size of the grains and color, thus forming a different tactile experience. Colored sands may be available with fewer size choices. These are only recommended as additional options, not as the sole Sandtray choice. I have used a sand box with a mixture of tan, black, and red sands. A multiracial child initiated this mix after he let me know he *needed* to combine the sands, and this mixture was later used by many other people.

The sand that I recommend is commonly used for sandblasting. This sand is washed and graded by size—the larger the number the smaller the grains. The consistent size of the grains creates a smoother feel and forms well when wet. I follow Dr. Schubach De Domenico's direction, using size 030 tan sand as my basic equipment. This neutral color is a good place to start. Of course, my designation of *neutral* is a judgment, as seen in chapter 4. Size 0100 is very fine and tactilely attractive to many people. The smaller the grains the greater the amount of dust emerges once the sand is moved. If your office space is small, sand dust may become a problem. Any natural sand can be washed multiple times to reduce the dust. The 030 sandblasting sand is generally available in 100-pound bags at landscaping and sandblasting supply stores. One bag will fill three or four sand trays. As with all recommended materials, please play with these tools yourself to decide what works for you.

Containers for Sandtrays

There are many beautiful wooden sand boxes as well as plastic trays available for world-making. I recommend that you have at least two sand trays. Considering the combined weight of the sand and the container, I use plastic flat-bottom photo developing trays. Make the inside bottom blue with contact paper, which does require changing more frequently with wet sand use. My "regular" sand boxes are 20 × 24 × 3-inches. I use trays with 6-inch sides for those people who desire deep sand. Younger *Creators* often prefer the 16 × 20 × 6-inch rectangular sand tray because they can reach all the areas of their world more easily. With preschool children, extra trays can be made by placing blue contact paper on the flat inside bottom of large rectangular clear plastic storage boxes. An empty box of this size or a dish pan is useful for water play if no sink is available. Sand boxes often slide on their tables when large movements of sand occur. To reduce significantly the chance of the tray sliding onto the floor, use nonskid shelf liner under each tray.

Water

Adding water during the Sandtray process allows *Creators* a greater range of experiences. The properties of wet sand are very different from dry sand. Don't be concerned if you do not have a sink in your playroom. Sinks are convenient but not necessary. Even Sandtray studios with a sink will need to inform *Creators* to use rinse buckets prior to washing, as sand is damaging to plumbing. Water can be kept nearby in lidded containers ready for use. Other containers may be provided as tools to add the water to the sand. Starting with a sand box that someone else has made wet is a different experience from making one wet yourself. Squirt bottles, spray bottles, pump bottles, and watering cans are among the tools for making the sand wet. Additional water and sand items include: scoops and utensils; funnels; turkey basters; beach sand shovels, rakes, and sifters; buckets for rinsing hands and sandy miniatures; Styrofoam containers (such as those mushrooms are sold in); clean plastic containers and lids of all sizes and shapes; tin foil; plastic wrap; bowls; and, of course, towels. This is a basic list. Please let your imaginations play. Be sure to try any objects you may think of in your own sand worlds prior to adding them to your collection for *Creators* to use.

General Sandtray Needs

As noted in the body of this work, *Witnesses* will need paper, a writing utensil, a camera, and a clipboard to hold the note-taking paper, or an electronic device that allows both writing and drawing. I use an old sheet to cover the floor when Sandtray play might become messy. A tarp or oil cloth may work for this purpose as well. A vacuum cleaner, step ladder, and collecting baskets are valuable aids in the Sandtray playroom. Because *Creators* may use candles, a small fire extinguisher at hand is prudent. To aid *Witnesses* and *Creators* in exploring the Archetypal and Universal Contextual Fields, supply academic reference books on topics that include myths and legends, cultures and world religions, and symbol dictionaries.

Miniatures: Collection

No list of Sandtray miniatures could ever be complete. What follows is only a guideline, a basis for ideas. Some special considerations are presented in chapter 5. *Witnesses* need to provide a variety, not just a quantity, of objects. Clearly, multiple trees are required for a forest and a battle may demand many soldiers. Although most items are about six inches or smaller, I do not limit my collection to this scale. Sometimes a *Creator* craves a big experience, and a larger object would express this desire best. Remember that in the beginning it may be necessary to try to spray or hand-paint items to provide various skin tones, colors, or the appearance of gold and silver. Natural and oven-cook clay may be readily used to create your own items. Choose items that are made of various substances, such as resin; bone; plastic; wood; ceramics; metal; glass; and any other substance that will not crumble into the sand. Consider the following collectible items.

Plants: It is important to depict various types, seasons, and sizes of trees, bushes, leaves, and flowers. Provide items that depict different aspects of plant-life cycles, including: seeds; roots; fruit; flowers; leaves; dried twigs; mosses; pine cones and pods; and full-grown plants. Some larger artificial trees may be up to fourteen inches tall.

Animals: Land, air, and sea creatures: domestic and wild; real; extinct; and those of fantasy; alive and dead; mythical and allegorical. Also needed are items that can be used to form animal environments and habitats. Natural or artificial bones; antlers; shells; feathers; eggs; or preserved animals are also useful.

People: Include people alone and together; of different ages; sizes; sexes; engaged in various activities and occupations; of different cultures, races, and time periods; ordinary-appearing people as well as those from fantasy, myth, and religion. Provide people demonstrating emotions, such as suffering, anger, and rejoicing; alive or dead; ancient or modern; miniature human body parts; or tiny broken dolls. Various babies are needed, from tiny to 2-inches high and doll-house people of various races and cultures.

Human Environments: Everything people use or create: miniature household items; food; doll-house furniture; hospital and medical items; books; items of daily life; buildings and habitats of various cultures; communities and historical time periods, including science fiction and fantasy; bridges; roads; walls; fences; road and other signs; transportation in various cultures: land, air, water, outer-space, and emergency vehicles, mass transit, small-scale fire, rescue, police, tow trucks, construction, and other vehicles.

Elements: Natural and artificial: sea shells; coral; sea environments; rocks; precious gems; crystals; geodes; fire or light sources; water; lakes; rivers; waterfalls (Styrofoam containers that mushrooms are sold in; blue container lids; planter saucers); cotton balls; and plastic ice and snow. Find objects that depict or indicate air or wind (tornados, hurricanes, or clouds).

Miscellaneous: Objects that make a noise; have a scent; have various textures/weights; move or indicate movement in any fashion; and those objects that reflect or illuminate. Objects that may be associated with torture and physical and sexual abuse (chains, duct tape, barbed wire, ropes, whips, and sexual body parts); drug culture and substance abuse (weapons, syringes w/o needles; dope pipes; mirrors); healing; communication; the cosmos (marbles and stars); the passage of time (hour glasses, clocks, sundials); religious objects from all religions and cultures over the history of human kind. Provide popsicle sticks; toothpicks; Styrofoam pellets; tape; string; cardboard centers from toilet paper; paper towels; wax paper; tin foil; and plastic wrap as tools for *Creators*.

Miniatures: Preparation

Driftwood/deadfall: Wash and simmer these objects in vinegar water for fifteen minutes. Then rinse and dry completely in the sun.

Pods, mosses, leaves, nuts: Shake off the dust, and spray with a disinfectant spray. Leave items in a sealed plastic bag (I double it) for three days. Air the items out in the sun to remove any fragrance.

Rocks: Rinse off well outside, and put in a dishwasher to clean. This does *not* work and is contraindicated for sandstone and other crumbly stones.

Thrift store/yard-sale items: Wash in warm soapy water and dry thoroughly.

Plastic or glass food containers: All will need thorough cleaning and degreasing. Use various sizes and shapes (for example, butter, yogurt, cottage cheese, baby food, and pudding). These items may be used as scoops, molds, candle holders, pedestals, or anything a *Creator* can dream up.

Appendix B

Frequently Asked Questions

Q. What if a client prefers "talk therapy" but also wants the sand tray near just to touch or to move the sand?
A. Allow this request. Some individuals are soothed by the action or tactile experience of touching the sand. This approach can make some people more comfortable and therefore emotionally available to work. If I sense that the person is at ease, I may ask him or her to share with me his or her experience of the sand and what qualities it provides.

Q. How does the Witness *make time for the other "Sandtray aspects" when the* Creator *is taking all the time to make the world?*
A. The *Witness*'s response depends on how early in the treatment process and how often this situation occurs. In the initial period of treatment I wait to learn the *Creator*'s process. The weight of this decision relies on the intersubjectivity of the moment and my assessment of the *Creator*'s sense of safety. When the *Creator* is an active builder of worlds, applying the Sandtray aspects to a moving sand world is the best option.

Q. How do I avoid the feeling that I am parroting the Creator's *words?*
A. Consider your own process at these times. Mirroring is not parroting. Parroting is repeating verbal content without a life-to-life linking of affect and nonverbal energies. True mirroring includes affective resonance. Consider if you are tired, bored with this *Creator*'s work, or distracted in some way that keeps you from a more connected presence. Also consider the *Creator*'s

attachment capacity and how the two of you function together in terms of attachment.

Q. *What does a* Witness *do when a* Creator *denies permission to come around and sit by him or her to explore further the world after the Reflecting/Directing aspect?*
A. Respect the *Creator's* boundary. Don't move, become distressed, or take the *Creator's* response personally. The therapeutic priority is to stay connected to the *Creator* within a safe environment. Accept that a *Creator* is getting what he or she needs. But invite *Creators* to let you know if they change their mind later. Explore if a *Creator* would benefit from further time in the "Silent Reverie" or the "Reflecting/Directing" aspects. Perhaps he or she feels unfinished with an earlier aspect and may be helped by returning to one of these. Consider if a *Creator* might be feeling pushed, overwhelmed, or rushed. Could a *Creator* be feeling fearful or uncomfortable in some way? Saying "no" may be a cue that a *Creator* needs the *Witness* to slow down the process. It may also be appropriate to ask a *Creator* if he or she needs physically to move back from or completely away from his or her sand tray. It is possible to continue to explore the world while sitting across from a *Creator*. However, the result will be different from exploring the sand world from the same side together.

Q. *What do I do when I invite* Creators *to experience the world and they say, "I don't know," or, "These figures are just statues"?*
A. Try: "Let's just go and be there." Support the *Creator* with "Silent Reverie" from this position prior to attempting any verbalization. You may also choose to be with the experience of "not knowing" about a world that was just created. Consider what it might mean to allow one's self to know about this world. Might there be risks or benefits to such acknowledgment? Regarding statues, the experience of the "statues" could be examined. A *Witness* might say: "Let's be with these statues and learn about them." Discover if the statues have any sense of themselves. A *Witness* may also ask a *Creator* to focus on one statue. Consider if this image could be about a deadened feeling or a sense that nothing in life is real. If working with the sand world does not seem useful, explore the *Creator's* experience of having formed this world and not knowing about it.

Q. *What if a* Creator *is really stuck after we have entered the world?*
A. When a *Witness* has been in harmonic resonance with a *Creator*, he or she might say something like, "I don't know what this figure or experience is

for you, but what is coming to me right now is (add a descriptive statement). Does this make any sense to you?" The *Witness* may also consider exploring the experience of being stuck, particularly if it is identified with a concrete depiction within the tray. Another option would be to return to a previous experience that felt clearer to both parties.

Q. What do I do when I am inside the world with a Creator and I err, either disrupting the Creator's flow or sensing a rupture?
A. Depending upon the relationship, it may be important to apologize for getting off-track. Return together to the last place in the world that you were in resonance. At that point reflect again what the *Creator* shared and experience this together. For example, "Let's go back to where we were together in these experiences." A *Witness* may also attempt, "Take us back into the tray, anywhere you feel comfortable now." If a *Creator* cannot choose, the *Witness* might suggest, "I remember we seemed to be on the same page when we were (name the place in the tray and the experience in the *Creator*'s words)." It is important to take these incidents to consultation, particularly when this occurs repeatedly with the same *Creator*.

Q. When should Sandtray be avoided?
A. My answer begins with the focus on the capacities of *Creators* themselves. First, if the *Creator*'s body does not go to the sand tray or the objects on the shelves, or perhaps his or her gaze avoids the world materials, honor this boundary. I am not referring to avoidance based on the person's intellectual judgment as described in "Owen's Story" in chapter 6. The second major reason to avoid the use of Sandtray is related to developmental or functional capacity. The use of this technique is enriched by the capacity to symbolize. Very young children may be able to accomplish more than we realize. Yet the desire to put the sand and objects in his or her mouth or the lack of enough fine motor coordination to manipulate the materials may be prohibitive. Sandtray may not be useful for clients who require treatment to be focused on containment, grounding, and developing the skills for activities of daily life functioning.

Other areas of consideration relate to the Sandtray environment itself. First, an inadequate collection of objects translates to limiting a *Creator*'s expression. Impoverishment of one form or another is an experience that many people know and as *Witnesses* it is not helpful to recreate this lack. I prefer that the Sandtray studio or playroom hold a variety of opportunities. Second, a chaotic Sandtray room is a disservice to *Creators*. The *Witness* is the "guardian" of the play space. Items need to be organized, clean, and undamaged. This role is often a source of problems in a shared playroom when every person does not take individual responsibility for this task. Creators do best in an environment of stability, predictability, and safety. When *Witnesses* do not keep the playroom safe, this gives a message of caution to *Creators*. Chaos formed in the sand world or in play is acceptable *when it is made by* the *Creator*.

A third consideration regarding the Sandtray environment: countertransference of the *Witness* may become an inhibiting factor in Sandtray use. A *Witness's* distress, anxiety, grief, or inability to be present emotionally may form a paradox for the *Creator*. Our overall direction may be one that says that the Sandtray is a safe place to do anything. Yet our anxiety or distress due to our own personal history or current limitations may communicate "don't make a mess; be too violent; too scary; too sexual; too energetic; or create the same experience over and over." All countertransference matters need to be addressed in consultation as they impact *Creator* and *Witness* intersubjectivity. The fourth reason for not using Sandtray, adult interference and sabotage, is more common while treating children. This problem may include forcing or manipulating a *Creator* to use Sandtray instead of other methods of expression or indicating or telling a *Creator* not to create sand worlds. Parents, spouses, caregivers, and even therapists who are fearful about what will be revealed in the Sandtray process can greatly inhibit a *Creator's* free expression.

Appendix C

Exercises for the Sandtray Witness

Allow yourself the gift of time to play, to reflect on your process, and to take photographs and notes. I recommend ninety minutes to two hours if you are working alone. Another option is to play with another therapist working in a *Creator* and a *Witness* dyad with each person taking a turn at each role. These exercises may also be conducted in a small group. With group members playing in parallel, each person records his or her own observations and, perhaps, shares these with the others. Each participant can bring fifteen items to share with others. The important elements for learning are to allow yourself to play freely, to observe, and to record your process. Experiment with these exercises by repeating them at intervals and observing your reactions over time. The following ideas are designed to get you started.

- Play in dry sand alone. Notice the sand's qualities, including the sound, smell, feel, and energy that it takes you to move it. Try this with your hands and with tools.
- Play in wet sand with your hands and a variety of tools. Notice its qualities as above. Discover how wet the sand needs to be to make good shapes and molds; observe what occurs when the sand is too dry, and when it is too wet. Finish by flooding the tray and playing in it for a while. Discover the properties of "soupy" sand.
- Choose one object to play with for at least thirty minutes. Then add any other items and see what happens. You can do this exercise repeatedly, beginning with a figure from a different category of miniatures each time.

- Play with any single category of items, not allowing objects from other groups. You may choose your category or make this activity random. A random experience may be provided by preparing a list of options on paper, cutting them apart, and then choosing one from a container.
- Play as above with three to five categories.
- Create a Sandtray using only objects from nature.
- Form a sand world solely using plastic items.
- As with the angel image exercise in chapter 4, choose at least six objects with the same "name." These may be vehicles, goddesses, fish, anything. Place them in the tray and view them together. Ask yourself, "What qualities does this particular (vehicle, goddess, or fish) have?" Handle each item, look at it carefully, and consider it with all of your senses. Move the object around in the tray. Imagine how it would function and what it could offer you if it were real. Let your imagination play with each miniature in this manner. Then look at these items as a group again. Notice what characteristics each object in this group has in common and the individual attributes of each. Note any differences in your perception of them now that you have played with them both as individual objects and as a group of objects.
- Expand the tree exercise in chapter 2 by using trees from your Sandtray collection or trees you observe in real life. Note where each image takes you. The same may be done with anything: houses, animals, images, or figures of people. The list is as long as you would want to make it.
- Start with a single miniature of your choosing. After ten minutes of Sandtray play with it alone, choose another. Allow an additional ten minutes to play with these two figures. At intervals, add one other item at a time, observing how each new object comes into the world and relates to the sand and other miniatures present. How does each item change as it enters and relates to what is already present? How is each new object perceived by those miniatures preceding it? Remember always to take notes of your observations.

References

Beebe, B., and Lachmann, F. M. (2002). *Infant research and adult attachment: Co-constructing nteractions.* Hillsdale, NJ: Analytic Press.

Begley, S. (2007). *Train your mind, change your brain.* New York: Ballantine Books.

Bolen, J. S. (2003). *Crones don't whine.* Boston: Conari Press.

Bowlby, J. (1969). *Attachment and loss.* Volume I: *Attachment.* New York: Basic Books.

Brown, S. (2010). *Play: How it shapes the brain, opens imagination, and invigorates the soul.* New York: Avery.

Carroll, R. (2006). A new era for psychotherapy. In J. Corrigall, H. Payne, and H. Wilkinson (Eds.), *About a body: Working with the embodied mind in psychotherapy* (pp. 50–62). New York: Routledge.

Cliburn, V. (2008). Video interview. Southern Oregon Public Television, November 11.

Daishonin, N. (1999). *The writings of Nichiren Daishonin.* Tokyo: Soka Gakkai.

De Saint-Exupéry, A. (1943). *The little prince.* New York: Harcourt, Brace and World.

Dillard, J. M. (1996). *Star trek: First contact.* New York: Pocket Books.

Ford, J. D., and Courtois, C. (2009). Defining and understanding complex trauma and complex trauma distress disorders. In C. Courtois and J. D. Ford (Eds.), *Treating complex traumatic stress disorders: An evidenced based guide* (pp. 13–30). New York: Guilford Press.

Frankl, V. (1959). *Man's search for meaning.* New York: Washington Square Press.

Gibran, K. (1970). *The prophet.* New York: Knopf.

Gil, E. (2010). Children's self-initiated gradual exposure: The wonders of posttraumatic play and behavioral reenactments. In E. Gil (Ed.), *Working with children to heal interpersonal trauma: The power of play* (pp. 44–63). New York: Guilford Press.

Gray, P. (2011). The decline of play and the rise of psychopathology in children and adolescents. *American Journal of Play, 3,* 443–63.

Hall, C. S., and Nordby, V. J. (1973). *A primer of Jungian psychology*. New York: Penguin/Mentor.

Hannah, B. (2001). *Encounters with the soul: Active imagination as developed by C. G. Jung*. Wilmette, IL: Chiron.

Holmes, J. (2001). *The search for the secure base: Attachment theory and psychotherapy*. New York: Brunner Routledge.

Ikeda, D. (2010). Capturing the moment. *Living Buddhism, 14* (4), 1.

Ikeda, D. (2010). Learning from the writings: The teachings for victory: Letter to the brothers— part 2 of 3. *Living Buddhism, 14* (2), 48–63.

Ikeda, D. (2012). The flowering of creative life force. *SGI Quarterly, 67*, 7.

Kalff, D. (1980). *Sandplay: A psychotherapeutic approach to the psyche*. Boston: Sigo Press.

Keleman, S. (1985). *Emotional anatomy*. Berkeley: Center Press.

Lowenfeld, M. (1991). *Play in Childhood*. London: Mac Keith Press.

Lowenfeld, M. (1993). *Understanding children's sandplay: Lowenfeld's world technique*. Cambridge, UK: Margaret Lowenfeld Trust.

Panksepp, J. (1998). *Affective neuroscience: The foundation of human and animal emotions*. New York: Oxford University Press.

Panksepp, J. (2010). Science of the brain as a gateway to understanding play: An interview with Jaak Panksepp. *American Journal of Play, 2* (3), 245–77.

Porges, S. (2007, March). *Application of polyvagal theory to clinical treatment*. Presentation at the UCLA and Lifespan Learning Institute conference: Being present in body and mind: An integration of clinical treatment and neuroscience research, Los Angeles, CA.

Ringel, S. (2011). Developing the capacity for reflective functioning through an intersubjective process. *Clinical Social Work Journal, 2* (3), 61–67.

Rowling, J. K. (2007). *Harry Potter and the deathly hallows*. New York: Arthur A. Levine Books.

Schore, A. N. (2003). *Affect regulation and repair of the self*. New York: Norton.

Schore, A. N. (2003, March). *The right hemisphere is dominant in clinical work: Implications of recent neuroscience for psychotherapists*. Presentation at the UCLA Extension and Lifespan Learning Institute conference: New developments in attachment theory: Application to clinical practice, Los Angeles, CA.

Schore, A. N. (2008, March). *Regulation theory and the paradigm shift: From conscious cognition to unconscious affect*. Presentation at the UCLA and Lifespan Learning Institute conference: From attachment to regulation theory, Los Angeles, CA.

Sendak, M. (2006). Audio interview. National Public Radio, September 26.

Siegel, D. (1999). *The developing mind*. New York: Guilford Press.

Siegel, D. (2010). *Mindsight: The new science of personal transformation*. New York: Bantam.

Siegel, D., and Hartzell, M. (2003). *Parenting from the inside out: How a deeper self-understanding can help you raise children who thrive*. New York: Tarcher/Putnam.

Stern, D. (2004). *The present moment in psychotherapy and everyday life*. New York: Norton.

Taylor, J. B. (2008). *My stroke of insight.* New York: Viking.

Thomkins, J. (2007). Healing the innocent. In Z. Gaudioso and G. Martin (Eds.), *The Buddha next door: Ordinary people, extraordinary stories* (pp. 22–27). Santa Monica, CA: Middleway Press.

Tolkien, J. R. R. (1987). *The lord of the rings.* Boston: Houghton Mifflin.

Urwin, C., and Hood-Williams, J. (Eds.) (1988). *Child psychotherapy, war, and the normal child: Selected papers of Margaret Lowenfeld.* London: Free Association Books.

Winnicott, D. W. (1982). *Playing and reality.* New York: Routledge.

Woodman, M. (1994). *The stillness shall be the dancing: Feminine and masculine in emerging balance.* Audio recording. Boulder, CO: Sounds True.

Index

initiated by, 127–29; explicit and implicit life components explored by, 45; harmonious resonance influence of, 89, 98; honoring type of play by, 144; image-thinking right brain activated by, 97; information requested by, 119–21; intersubjective fields attended to by, 46–47; intrusions minimized by, 78; judgments made by, 67–68; language and meaning agreement of, 51; linear cognition of, 167–68; Lowenfeld's approach of, 63–64; neutral language used by, 101–2; not-being-pushy suggestions for, 96; note taking of, 87; openness provided by, 84; physical and energetic environment and, 63; playing in sand with *Creators*, 89–90; questions examining work of, 90; "Reflecting/Directing" techniques used by, 86, 92; reflective techniques used by, 150; Sandtray process coherently framed by *Creators* and, 129; Sandtray process exercises for, 201–2; Sandtray process not interpreted by, 63–68; Sandtray value assessment assistance from, 125; self-care of, 69–70; trauma and, 181; treatment plan dialogue introduced by, 132–34

Woodman, Marion, 107

"World Formation," 4–5, 82–87

"World Technique," 4, 12–13